187.3

THE MOSHER SURVEY

Clelia Duel Mosher

Clelia Duel Mosher

THE MOSHER SURVEY

sexual attitudes of 45 victorian women

edited by
James MaHood & Kristine Wenburg

---

introduction by
Carl N. Degler

ARNO PRESS
A New York Times Company
New York – 1980

First edition 1980 by Arno Press Inc.
Copyright © 1980 by the Board of Trustees of the
Leland Stanford Junior University

Manufactured in the United States of America

Library of Congress Cataloging in Publication Data

Mosher, Clelia Duel, 1863-1940
    The Mosher survey.

    1. Women—United States—Sexual behavior—History.
2. Sex customs—United States—History. I. MaHood,
James. II. Wenburg, Kristine. III. Title.
HQ29.M67   1980   306.7'088042   79-48014
ISBN 0-405-13090-2

PREFACE

We edited the Mosher Survey with the excitement of archaeologists at a new excavation. Here was a primary historical document of premodern sex and marriage in America that had never been published — but it was in dizzying disarray. We undertook to make it readable and accessible, and to clarify its structure and unity. We did not want to intrude upon its meaning or flavor. We did not want to interpret or abridge it. We wanted to clear the way for 45 married Victorian women to speak for themselves — for the first time in history.

We began with 650 pages of spidery handwritten questionnaires, which sometimes omitted the questions for which we had answers. They were bound neatly into Volume X of *Hygiene and Physiology of Women,* the unpublished research papers of Dr. Clelia Duel Mosher (1863-1940), a trove of women's history kept alive by Stanford University Archives. Much later, we emerged with almost 500 pages of typescript, published here in their entirety thanks to Leslie Parr and the late Harry M. McConnell of Arno Press. The editors shared responsibilities as follows: Kristine Wenburg made the difficult initial "translation" and reconstruction, and I served as senior editor and literary agent.

We imagined that many people would be interested in the complete survey, for it contains statements of great rarity directly from Victorian women, whose lips previously have been sealed on the intimate questions of their private lives and cravings. Although one day it may come to light, we know of no other sex survey of Victorian women, in fact no earlier sex survey of women, perhaps no earlier American sex survey of any kind, and certainly no earlier survey conducted by a woman sex researcher. The list of "firsts" apparently captured by the Mosher Survey is indeed impressive. The document should fascinate students of women's history, the family, medicine, sexual attitudes and behavior, and others ready to explore their sexual roots.

The Victorian women interviewed by Mosher relished sex, claimed higher rates of orgasm than women reported on a survey conducted in 1972, and practiced effective birth-control techniques beyond merely abstinence or withdrawal. Most were in their late 30s at the time of interview; they were mature, married, experienced American women. Fear of unwanted pregnancy deeply colored their attitudes toward sex, but there is little evidence here of Victorian prudery.

The Mosher Survey contains other fascinations. It probes not only the sexual lives of 45 Victorian women, but also their families, education, occupations, and other personal areas. Mosher received a doctorate in medicine from Johns Hopkins University in 1900, and the survey reflects her lifelong interest in medical research. It pays particular heed to gynecological, obstetrical, and pediatric details, including menstruation, contraception, labor, delivery, and children's histories.

The Mosher Survey offers clues to psychohistory. Many women report that "nervous disorders" — "chronic headache," "melancholia," "insanity" — plagued their families. Anxiety was apparently so rampant that one woman (Blank No. 24) found it necessary to specifically note its *absence* in her husband. Pre-Freudian, fin de siècle America may have been as much an age of anxiety as the later twentieth century, if these women's families were representative.

Food must have been atrocious, especially when anxiously stomached. Almost every woman reported "dyspepsia," or more severe gastrointestinal distress in her family.

Infant mortality was another appalling reality of late nineteenth-century America, and the survey offers moving testimony of mothers who survived their babies, together with bitter firsthand evidence of the crudities of Victorian medicine.

The Mosher Survey can be read as human drama. The women's staccato answers to questions about the lives and deaths of loved ones sometimes reflect peace and happiness, but more often understate pathetic tragedy.

We would have liked merely to transcribe the original handwritten Mosher Survey, but that was not possible. We had to edit it, and in many places reconstruct it, if it were to be read and studied with any ease. In other words, we attempted unobtrusively to move the survey a few notches closer to internal consistency, logical order, and comprehensibility. But all of the women's responses that do not appear here within brackets may be read, with difficulty, in the original. What we added to make the work more comprehensible appears now within brackets, or is clearly signified some other way.

The survey is not uniform, nor is it complete, and we found no significant analyses or conclusions of the information collected. Mosher's questionnaires — she called them blanks — evidently evolved over the entire 28-year span (1892–1920) of the survey; she apparently had no survey models to follow. What she labelled "Form A" and "Form B" are the earliest questionnaires; the majority she labelled "Series II, Form B"; toward the end of the survey are "Series II, Form C" and "Series III, Form C." We retained her evolving designations.

How many different women did Mosher interview? It is difficult to know for sure. The blanks are consecutively numbered, and the last is No. 51. But Blanks No. 7, 37, 39, and 48 are missing in the original, and practically no information appears on Blanks 16A and 49. (We included incomplete blanks.) It appears that Mosher reinterviewed some women over the years, and Stanford Historian Carl Degler identified Blanks 30 and 33 as from the same woman. Despite the fact that Mosher's original title for the work was *Statistical Study of the Marriage of Forty-Seven Women*, our best estimate is that significant information for a total of only 45 different women has come down to us and appears here. (As for the word *Statistical* in Mosher's title, she apparently never got around to that, or perhaps she understood something quite different by the word than we do today.)

In addition to the loss of entire blanks, portions of some surviving blanks also did not come down to us, or perhaps never existed. An additional subtraction is that some women chose not to answer certain questions. We found that interesting, so we retained the unanswered questions for the convenience of future researchers.

Sometimes the women themselves wrote their answers directly on the questionnaires. Other times, their answers appear in Mosher's handwriting. Readers will notice the resulting shifts of voice from first person singular to third. Sometimes Mosher used quotation marks when she wrote the women's answers, sometimes not. We do not know whether she interviewed the women face-to-face and simultaneously recorded their answers like present-day sex researchers; we suspect a much more informal procedure. We reconstructed what we found.

Thirteen blanks, most of them located toward the end, do not record the questions Mosher asked, only the women's responses in Mosher's hand. Based on previous, more complete blanks, we attempted to match appropriate questions to the answers we found. At the beginning of each, we noted these reconstructed blanks.

Neither Mosher nor the women she interviewed hesitated to write vertically up and down the pages, as well as horizontally. Sometimes they wrote the answers to one question under another that they chose not to answer. Some women added information not requested (see for instance the long supplement at the end of Blank No. 2). Mosher often scribbled additional comments about the women or their families in the margins or at the ends of questionnaires. We attempted to decipher and logically position all supplementary information, even when some of it was not immediately intelligible. When some women answered merely by underlining words in the question, we wrote out and bracketed their answers.

We gave the Mosher Survey a consistent format and style in such matters as the placement of questions, answers, comments, and notes. We attempted to make punctuation and other elements consistent, but we left each woman's idiom intact. We did not choose to strew the manuscript with (sic) so we corrected obvious spelling errors. But we did not modernize spelling; we retained spelling identified as correct or unestablished in Mosher's time.

Perhaps the most serious problem was deciphering the code of Mosher's handwriting. When we ran into difficulty, we enclosed our best reading in brackets. We indicated a lesser degree of certainty by enclosing a question mark with a bracketed interpretation. Where we could not decipher the meaning, we inserted the word *illegible* or *unintelligible* in brackets.

In that effort, we wish to thank Professor Degler and his wife Catherine. They undertook to check the entire edited manuscript and Degler's special knowledge of the period and subject helped clear up many illegibilities. We wish to state, however, that the editors alone are responsible if errors are identified or additional writing fathomed.

The editors also owe a special debt of thanks to the staffs and administrations of Stanford University Archives and Special Collections. Because we were not employees of Stanford University, but rather freelance writer/editors in the community at large, we wish to thank Florian J. Shasky, Chief of the Department of Special Collections, who first brought the survey to my attention in October, 1977.

We especially wish to thank the following individuals connected with Stanford University Archives where the original handwritten Mosher Survey is carefully preserved: Ralph W. Hansen, Archivist and Chief of the Acquisition Department, was our official Stanford contact throughout the project. Roxanne-Louise Nilan, Assistant University Archivist, and Margaret Coesfeld, Manuscripts Specialist, both greatly facilitated our work on the survey itself in the charming Hopkins Room. Without the help, consideration, and encouragement of these and other Stanford employees, the Mosher Survey might never have seen print.

Finally, we wish to thank Dr. Clelia Duel Mosher who courageously interviewed 45 women who courageously answered what were then questions of exceptional delicacy. The pioneering document they left us may help dispel persistent myths of Victorian women's sexuality.

Los Altos, California   *James MaHood*

INTRODUCTION

Most Americans today are quite accustomed to learning about the private sexual habits of their contemporaries; even newspapers report intimate details of sexual activities. But such public discussions of the hitherto unmentionable are very recent. The books on the sexual behavior of males and females by Alfred C. Kinsey are probably the best known of such studies, yet both of the Kinsey volumes were published only after World War II. Kinsey's studies, it is true, were not the first scientific or scholarly inquiries into women's sexual behavior. Katharine B. Davis, a social worker and penologist, published *Factors in the Sex Lives of Twenty-Two Hundred Women* in 1929, and two years later Robert Latou Dickinson, the well-known gynecologist and proponent of birth control, and Lura Beam issued their *A Thousand Marriages: a Medical Study of Sex.* Nonetheless, the great majority of the women studied in even these two pre-Kinsey studies, like those in Kinsey's *Sexual Behavior in the Human Female,* were born in the 1890s and early twentieth century.

It is the absence of systematic evidence on the sexual habits of women living in the nineteenth century that makes the survey compiled by Dr. Clelia D. Mosher of such great historical interest and value. It is simply the earliest examination of the subject we have: 70 percent of the women in the Mosher Survey were born before 1870. In fact, 17 of the 45 women who answered the questionnaires were born before the Civil War. (Mosher refers to 47 women, but cases 30 and 33 are from the same woman twenty-three years apart and case 49 is so incomplete as not to provide much information.) In short, most of the women in this survey spent their formative and early adult years in the nineteenth century. And just because they did, their answers to the questions in the survey throw a flood of light on a very shadowy aspect of the nineteenth century as well as call into question some widely accepted views about the sexuality of Victorian women. To appreciate quickly the novelty of the information one needs only to learn that one question is: "do you always have a venereal orgasm?" The question, please note, was not "do you *ever* have an orgasm," as might be thought would be the query, given the conventional view of nineteenth century matrons. Or take the answer that one woman in 1892 gave to the question of how she felt about sexual intercourse: "usually very delightful."

Startlingly intimate questions and answers are only a part of the wide range of information about the private lives of women in the nineteenth century that may be garnered from the completed questionnaires of these forty-five women. Since Mosher was a medical doctor, she asked a number of questions about the health not only of the woman filling out the questionnaire, but also about each respondent's parents, grandparents, husband, and children. Habits of sexual intercourse, ideal sexual practices, attitudes toward sex, number of conceptions, means of contraception used, experiences with menstruation, sleeping arrangements, and even condition of the bowels were among the questions posed. And because the questions were systematically asked they can be systematically analyzed, as random comments from private correspondence or personal diaries — even if such intimacies could be found in the writings of highly diffident nineteenth century women — could not. Here one has 45 answers, each one dated in response to the same questions.

Where did this unique source come from and who are the women who answered the questionnaires? The forms were all completed between 1892 and 1920. No clues are provided as to how the respondents were selected. Presumabbly they were self-selected as is still the case with respondents to modern questionnaires on sex. The existence of the survey was not known until I happened to stumble upon it in 1973 while going through the papers of Clelia Mosher in the Stanford University Archives. Mosher never published any conclusions from the questionnaires, nor did she leave among her papers anything more than a few rudimentary conclusions concerning peripheral aspects of the survey. (Perhaps the explanation is contained in the remark of a friend: "She has been, all her life, a procrastinator.") Mosher merely left the bound completed questionnaires among her papers, which were deposited in the Stanford Library after her death in 1940. Soon after I found the questionnaires I published an article in the *American Historical Review* in 1974, drawing upon the evidence, and describing the survey. Since then other scholars have used the data, including Professors Paul A. David and Warren Sanderson of the Stanford Economics Department. They have pointed out that the Mosher information on fertility can be linked to that of wives of urban professionals in the United States, as published in the Census of 1910. This suggests that the attitudes expressed in the survey may well be representative of the larger group. (Many of the Mosher women seem to be faculty wives.) David and Sanderson go on to call the survey data "a veritable Rosetta Stone for the study of the demographic and social history of an important segment of the American population. It allows us to give quantitative form to dimensions of household behavior about which historians hitherto have been able only to offer vague conjectures or to hazard only unfoundedly concrete assertions."[1]

The questionnaires themselves contain sufficient evidence to allow us to corroborate the correlation suggested by David and Sanderson. Thirty-four of the 45 women attended college or normal school; the education of three is unknown. Since very few women or men attended college in the nineteenth century, these women were clearly not typical of the general population. From the information given about their areas of birth and from the colleges attended, it seems that the respondents are primarily from the North and the West; none of them seems to have come from the South; all are probably white, and born in the United States. The colleges attended also bear out the view that they are upper middle-class women: Cornell University, Smith College, Vassar College, Iowa State University, Indiana University, Stanford University, and the University of California. Nonetheless, these are not women of the leisure class. Thirty of the women reported that they had worked prior to marriage, usually as school teachers. Seven women did not answer the question about work experience and eight said they married immediately after schooling.

Despite their high level of education, most of the women seem to have been poorly informed about sexual matters or even, as several phrased it, "the meaning of marriage." Only eleven said they knew much about sex before marriage and another thirteen said that they had some knowledge. In short, almost half had no knowledge at all, one even going so far as to say that she did not know what was happening to her during pregnancy until "the waters broke."! On the other hand, when asked about sexual experiences during marriage, 34 of the women said that they had experienced an orgasm, with over a third saying they achieved one "always" or "usually." This is a rate of orgasmic response that compares favorably with that reported by Kinsey for women born between 1910 and 1919.

Perhaps the most intriguing aspect of the survey is its initiator, Dr. Clelia Duel Mosher. Although during her lifetime Mosher devoted herself to studying many aspects of women's physical life — she wrote

---

1. Paul A. David and Warren C. Sanderson, "Comparative Technology and Fertility Control in Victorian America: From Facts to Theories," Memorandum 202, Center for Research in Economic Growth, Stanford University, June, 1976, p. 15.

articles and books on women's health and was a strong advocate of exercise and physical activity for women — she never made public her long interest in the sexual habits of women. As she explains at the beginning of her survey, she undertook to collect the information as part of her preparation for a talk to the Mothers' Club while she was a biology student at the University of Wisconsin in 1892. At the time, Mosher was older than most undergraduates — 28 — a fact, which, when coupled with her knowledge of biology and with her sex probably explains why a group of mothers would ask this unmarried woman to speak on such an intimate subject. In any event, Mosher reports, over the subsequent 18 years she added information gathered from other women. The only use she seems to have made of the information obtained from the questionnaires was in her teaching and in advising women students at Stanford University.

Who was Clelia Mosher? She was born in Albany, New York on December 16, 1863 into the home of a physician; four of her uncles were also physicians. (Eliza Mosher, a pioneer woman physician in New York and Michigan, was a distant cousin.) Clelia's parents encouraged her intellectual efforts, sending her to Albany Female Academy (later Albany Girls Academy), from which she graduated in 1881. By that time, however, her only sister had died and she had been weakened by a bout with tuberculosis, all of which caused her father, Cornelius, to deny her ambition to enter college. To make up for frustrating her plans, Cornelius engaged a local gardener to instruct her in horticulture and turned over to her space in the family greenhouse, from which she soon conducted a thriving business as a professional florist. (This early training in horticulture was to provide a life-long interest for Clelia Mosher. She left a magnificent garden of exotic and semitropical trees and flowers at her home on the Stanford campus.) Horticulture caused another side of Clelia to emerge, even at that early age: independence. After a few years as a florist, Clelia surprised her father by revealing that she had saved $2,000, a sum sufficient to pay her way to college. Despite Cornelius Mosher's continued objection, she entered Wellesley College as a freshman at the advanced age of 25. Clelia bore no animosity against her father. Rather, she celebrated in 1931 his support and that of her mother in the dedication of her unpublished autobiography: "to my father who believed in women when most men classified them with children and imbeciles and to my mother who unselfishly gave her daughter freedom to make her own career, saying she had had her own life." (Her mother had lent her the money to enter medical school.)

Her father's concern about her health was not unfounded, however; within two years she was out of college with nervous exhaustion. When she picked up her education again she enrolled at the University of Wisconsin. It was there that she began her invaluable survey. But she did not stay at Wisconsin, for the next year, after convincing the newly opened Stanford University to accept most of her credits, she enrolled for her senior year at that California institution. At the age of 29 she obtained her A.B. and a job as an assistant in the girls' gymnasium at Stanford.

It was her work in that job that fostered an interest in women's health, particularly the effects on women of restrictive clothing and inadequate exercise. She encouraged young women to engage in a variety of sports and soon gathered data on women's breathing habits, her analysis of which overthrew the standard view that it was natural for women to breath from the upper part of their chests as contrasted with the fuller, diaphragmatic breathing alleged to be natural to males. The evidence Mosher collected showed that the so-called costal breathing of women was the result of convention and poor habits, not nature, a conclusion subsequently corroborated by another researcher. In 1894 she was granted a Master of Arts degree for this work. She then turned to study the debilitating effects of menstruation on women. Her goal had now become that of exploring, and if possible, exploding the clichés that limited women's lives.

Mosher quickly recognized that if she were to challenge successfully the entrenched view of women as weak beings, she needed more than a master's degree in physiology. Therefore in 1896 she wrote the authorities at the Johns Hopkins Medical School, in her characteristically independent and direct way, that she would soon be arriving to enroll for training in medicine. In the light of her experience at Stanford, she added, she expected that they would also award her advanced standing! Dr. William Welch, one of the distinguished founders of the medical school, was not willing to admit her immediately, nor to give her advanced standing. But when Mosher completed over the summer the training in physics and chemistry that he stipulated, she was admitted.

Though not a brilliant student at the Hopkins and still impeded by her unreliable health, Mosher nonetheless completed her medical training in the normal time. She was sufficiently well thought of to be taken on as an intern upon graduation in 1900, and in the following year to be offered a permanent job with one of her professors. She did not accept the offer, however, even though it would have provided a guaranteed income of $3,000 a year, a level of salary she was not to achieve until twenty years later. One of the reasons she turned down the offer was that her professor told her that even if she were trained as a gynecological surgeon, as she wished to be, no man would serve under her.

With her widowed mother, Mosher returned to California to open a private practive in the university town of Palo Alto. Life was not easy there, though, for the town was small and the established physicians at first turned over to her only neurasthenic women, and patients who had failed to pay their bills. Gradually Mosher built up a practice among women and children, for she was always fond of children, though destined never to have any of her own. When Stanford University offered her a post as assistant professor of personal hygiene and medical advisor to women students, she leaped at the chance to abandon a rather unstimulating practice and resume her research activities, which had always been her prime interest in medicine. She soon published articles on women's physique, notably a study on the effects of menstruation on women's activities — an interest that is reflected in several of the inquiries in the questionnaires — and a comparison of the muscular strength of men and women. In a subsequent publication she showed that the average height of Stanford women over a period of twenty years increased more than 1.5 inches, a finding later substantiated by a study of many more cases at Vassar College. The purpose behind her work was succinctly expressed in a comment she wrote in her journal after the publication in 1917 of her and Ernst Martin's article on women's and men's muscular strength: "Another tradition destroyed, and new freedom for women."

Mosher's interest in serving others extended beyond her own gender. During the typhoid epidemic in Palo Alto in 1903 she worked with the local department of health, and when war with Germany was declared in April, 1917 she was eager to play a part. Even though women physicians had been around a long time by then, it was still difficult for a woman to serve in the armed services, especially if she wanted to go abroad, as Mosher did. "I am tired of filling out blanks for various mobilizations of research workers, college workers, etc.," she wrote in her journal in June, 1917. "My application for a chance to go to France as a Surgeon's assistant comes to nothing." She had called upon her old medical school teachers, Drs. Welch and Simon Flexner, but they had ignored her appeal. "Everyone says no woman physician stands any chance of serving. Yet they take nurses," she pointedly observed. Nevertheless, later that year, after face-to-face importuning, Flexner did obtain a post for her. By November, 1917 she was on her way to France, where she helped relocate refugees, particularly children. As usual, however, she exerted herself beyond the call of duty. On her leave time she worked as a postal clerk because she felt sorry for the soldiers when their mail was delayed.

When the war was over, Mosher returned to Stanford, where she was promoted to associate professor in 1922. The following year she published a small book, *Women's Physical Freedom,* which was a revision and expansion of an even briefer book entitled *Health and the Woman Movement,* which she had first issued in 1915. The subject was apparently of sufficient public interest and the advice practical enough for the book to be slightly expanded and republished in 1927 as *Personal Hygiene for Women.* In all versions of the work the message was the recognition of the physical capabilities of women which were to be achieved through simple and nutritious diet, sensible clothes, and regular exercise. Just as she played down the debilitating effects of menstruation, so she encouraged women to confront menopause without fear, pointing out that it was a married woman's change in circumstances as her children left the home that was the primary source of depression, not the change in a woman's body.

Mosher's career had started late, and she was, by now, an old woman herself. In 1928 she was made full professor, just a year before she retired at the mandatory age of 65. From then until her death in 1940 she devoted herself to her garden. She lived alone, her mother having died years before.

For all her activities and apparent energy, Clelia Mosher's life was neither easy nor altogether satisfying. Behind her vigorous exterior contemporaries remember her purposeful stride, her sensible, somewhat mannish, but undistinguished attire, the style of which was not altered over thirty years, her shapeless tweed hat, and her relentless commitment to her research. But her papers reveal a less severe and less monolithic person. Among them is the plan for a novel which she never completed, but which reveals the strong romantic spirit buried within her. The sketch depicted a career woman who fell passionately in love with a man after she had resolved never to marry. They did marry and have a son, but they soon separated so that the woman might continue her career. The couple did not see each other again until they meet over the grave of their son who had been killed at the battle of the Marne! When one reflects on Mosher's career, and her love of children, it does not require much imagination to see autobiography in the projected story.

Her personal struggle is evident in a more obvious if somewhat different way in her journal. Over the years she wrote letters full of expressions of love of beauty, her flowers, and her work. Not until March, 1919, however, does it become clear that the beloved friend to whom the letters are addressed is imaginary. For at that date the letter begins: "To you, my friend who does not exist."

Later that same year she wrote that she was "finding out gradually why I am so lonely. The only things I care about are things which use my brain. The women I meet are not much interested and I do not meet many men, so there is an intellectual solitude which is like the solitude of the desert — dangerous to one's sanity." However pressing the personal problems may have seemed in the early 1920s, by the 1930s she had apparently surmounted them, for when she began to write the story of her life in 1931, she entitled it "The Autobiography of a Happy Old Woman."

During her lifetime Clelia Mosher helped to dispel a number of myths about women, beginning with her research into the way women breathed. A third of a century after her death, her pioneering survey on the sexual habits of women is furthering that purpose. For it is difficult to read through the answers to the questions she asked without casting heavy doubt upon many of the clichés about the sexual habits and attitudes of Victorian matrons. From what little we know of Clelia Mosher's own attitudes, however, some of the answers may well have seemed shocking. To her, displays of physical affection in public were disgusting, and as early as 1915 she was complaining that American women were becoming too sex conscious! During her sojourn in France she was rather shocked by the emphasis she thought the French placed upon sex. Even in the 1920s her notes make clear that she was at best ambivalent about sexuality, and women's in particular. "These lectures in Personal Hygiene are exhausting me more than they should," she wrote in June, 1926. "Where should I draw the line? My Victorian sense of decent reticence is constantly shocked although my secretary says I have given no sign." There was no doubt that intellectually she agreed "that these girls should have any question they asked answered honestly and sanely." But she was frankly amazed "that they should be able to ask without hesitation in class. Is it," she wondered, "that these things of sex go over their heads, are purely academic questions?" She rather doubted it, given what she had heard about the young, for "when there is so much smoke there must be some fire." Sexual behavior, for her, could not be divorced from morals. For though she conceded that "it is a new age, new thinking, new ideals," she also asked "does it mean no ideals?"

Surely it is pertinent that of all feminists, George Sand was believed by

Mosher to be the greatest. By the end of her life she had collected ninety volumes of Sand's works. It may well have been that from Sand, Mosher learned to add women's sexual freedom to the other freedoms of women she worked to advance. Mosher herself was clearly ambivalent about sex, as she was about marriage; Sand would have made acceptable to Mosher what her own background could not, yet which her nature probably pressed upon her. In the end, her willingness to confront systematically the role of sexuality in women marked her as a pioneer in the struggle for women's freedom. That had been her goal from the beginning, when she first defied her father by earning her own money to go to college.

Stanford, California   *Carl N. Degler*

THE MOSHER SURVEY

STUDY OF THE PHYSIOLOGY AND HYGIENE

OF MARRIAGE

WITH SOME CONSIDERATION

OF THE BIRTH RATE

CLELIA DUEL MOSHER

BEGUN IN 1892

Introduction

In 1892, while a student in Biology at the University of Wisconsin, I was asked to discuss the marital relation in a Mothers' Club composed largely of college women. The discussion was based on the replies given by the members to a questionnaire. Since that time additional information has been added as it has come to me in the course of ten years experience in the practice of medicine. To this data have been added certain observations made on athletic college women. This material, which represents the experience of 47 women, has given the investigator a priceless knowledge for a practicing physician and teacher; a background sufficiently broad to avoid prejudice in her work with women.

About twenty years after this study was undertaken, the writer received from Dr. David Starr Jordan a letter stating that he had given testimony before the Physiologic Committee of the Royal Birthrate Commission in England. He also stated that he had given the commission my name, and that I would probably hear from them. Later, one or more letters were received from Mr. Walter Heape, M.A., F.R.S., the chairman, and from Dr. Salebe, requesting my publications on menstruation. These were sent. These letters, which have been mislaid, will be included in this volume if possible.

Some thought of arranging this work for publication at that time was prevented by pressure of other routine work.

Clelia Duel Mosher

DATA COMPILED ABOUT 1912

Marriage: 40 complete blanks
         Incomplete data 1 **and** 2
         Dyspareunia cases 3
         Second hand information 2

College women   30
Not stated   5
High Normal or
  Public School   9

Colleges: Penn. State   1
         Cornell   6
         Seminary   1
         Pub. School   1
         Ripon Col.   1
         Smith   2
         Syracuse   1
         Cambridge, Eng.   1
         Canadian Weslyn   1
         Oxford, Ohio   1
         High School   2
         Univ. Pac.   1
         So. Bend Acad.   1
         Radcliffe   1
         Indiana Univ.   1
         Normal Sch'l   2
         Wellesley   1
         Not Stated   3
         Walker Col.   1
         Vassar   2
         Stanford   5
         California   1
         Iowa State Univ. 1
                              40

EFFECT OF MENOPAUSE ON DESIRE

a - **Sex instinct still persists** in women but is less insistent.

b - **Absence of or increased** frequency of absence of orgasm following menopause.

No difference (no 45) no 43

THE FALLING OFF OF BIRTHRATE IS DUE

1 - Voluntary restriction of birthrate by contraceptive methods for economic reasons.

2 - a) To increasing selfishness of (I) <u>men</u>:

    man wishes companionship of wife
        unhampered by children   3 cases

    (II) women:

    dangers of childbirth to women   1 case

    women who desire a life of ease
        and social freedom   1 case

3 - Physical maladjustments due [to]

    a) lack of consideration of the woman by too frequent coitus destroys psychologic sex impulse

    b) lack of understanding of slower time reaction in women making marital relation for the woman without the normal physical response. This leaves organs of woman over congested.

4 - Physical maladjustments

    A. Dyspareunia due to

        1) Physical terror though mutual
            consent   1 case

        2) Unusual angle of long axis of
            vagina causing undue suffering
            to woman   2 cases

        3) Physical disproportion.

<u>Note</u>: The maladjustments in marriage occasionally occur at the first consummation of the marital relation. The woman comes to this new experience of life often with no knowledge. The woman while she may give mental consent often shrinks physically. Her slower time reaction deprives her of all physical response, or (2) too often her training has instilled the idea that any physical response is coarse, common and immodest which inhibits proper part in this relation.

BLANK NO. 1					FORM A.

1. Name in full:

2. Address:

3. Date of birth:

   February 8th, 1867.

4. Place of birth:

   New Gloucester, Maine.

5. Where educated; give degrees if any. Occupations before marriage, giving length of time spent in each:

   Pa. State College. Taught music more or less for five years. During that time taught two terms of country school. Practiced piano a great deal for two or three years, during the aforesaid four years.

6. Nationality of mother:

   American.

7. Nationality of father:

   American.

8. Age of mother when married:

   About twenty-five.

9. Age of father when married:

   About twenty-seven.

10. General health of parents:

    Well & robust.

BLANK NO. 1   FORM A.

11. Nationality of husband:

    American.

12. Date of birth of husband:

    1869.

Notes: Perfectly well baby until 6 months old. Took cold. Sudden change of food impaired digestion, **catarral trouble, sleeplessness, nervousness.**

BLANK NO. 1   FORM B.

Date: April 11th, /92.

   1. Age when married?

      Twenty-two.

   2. General health a) before marriage? b) since marriage?

      (a) Fairly well, but no strength or endurance. At time of
          marriage, in very poor health.

      (b) Health improved rapidly, but conception soon occurred.
          Poor health during period of pregnancy & slow recovery
          after birth of child, with uterine trouble. At present,
          fairly good health, about the same as before marriage.
          Better in some ways.

   3. What knowledge of Sexual Physiology had you before marriage?

      Knew process of ovulation & menstruation in fairly well-defined
      way. [Hence] knew when conception was likely to take place
      & why. Very little about male sexual physiology. Knew, in
      regard to intercourse, condition of man at time [hence]
      necessity also need of self-control; danger of its occurring
      too often; time when woman was supposed to desire intercourse,
      if ever; best time for conception, as regards health of
      mother & child; several means of preventing conception.
      Realized little how important it is to a man and how much
      self-control it may entail. Did not suppose   it was
      often desired by women. Considered that it sh'd be
      regulated largely by the woman.

   4. Number of times married? If more than once, additional blanks
      will be furnished you to answer the following questions
      separately in regard to each marriage.

      Once.

   5. Number of years married?

      2 1/2 years.

BLANK NO. 1   FORM B.

6. Do you habitually sleep with your husband?

   Yes.

7. Number of conceptions?

   One.

8. Number of children? State in connection with each, date of birth, sex, whether healthy or not, note any characteristic and the cause if you know it.

   One: born Nov. 16, 1891: girl. First six months, extremely delicate, poor digestion, and very nervous. At present, well and quite strong, good digestion but extremely nervous and timid. Subject to fits of nervous crying, showing tendency to lack of self-control: at time of conception, mother had not regained usual strength, and the father was much overworked, causing dyspepsia, attended by great nervousness, inability to sleep or think: might be called brain exhaustion as the work was mental. During pregnancy, mother was morbidly sensitive, with tendency to weep, & not sufficient self-control. Mother's digestion **always been poor--always been nervous and sensitive.**

9. Did conception occur by choice or by accident?

   Accident.

10. Habit of intercourse? Average number of times per week?

    per month?

    Two or three times. Before conception, once or at most twice per month.

    per year?

11. Was intercourse held during pregnancy? **No. If so,** a) how often? b) did you desire it at this period?

    Occasionally during first months. Not at all, during last half--or more.

10

BLANK NO. 1   FORM B.

12. At other times have you any desire for intercourse?

    Yes.

    (a) How often?

        Once or twice a month.

    (b) At what time in relation to your menses?

        Immediately after. Occasionally just before--and rarely at some other time. Except in 1st case, it is scarcely ever except when there is some outside exciting cause.

13. Is intercourse agreeable to you or not?

    Usually.

    Do you always have a venereal orgasm?

    No.

    1. - When you do,

    (a) Effect immediately afterward

    (b) Effect next day

    2. - When you do not, effect immediately after?

    (b) Effect next day?

14. What do you believe to be the purpose of intercourse?

    (a) Necessity to the man?

        Yes.

        to the woman?

        No.

    (b) Pleasure?

    (c) Reproduction?

        Yes. Primarily.

BLANK NO. 1   FORM B.

15. Have you ever used any means to prevent conception? If so,
    a) What? b) what was the effect on your health?

    (a) Thin rubber covering for man. Depended on so-called
        "safety **week**" at first.

    (b) I have not perceived any effect on my health.

        [An intriguing note follows:] "Condrum" [sic] 1.50 - 2.00
    per doz.

16. What to you would be an ideal habit?

BLANK NO. 2   SERIES II, FORM B.

Date: January, 1892

Your Father:

1. Nationality; if American, of what descent?

    Welsh descent

2. Home in city or country before marriage?

    Country - farm

3. Home in city or country after marriage?

    Country - farm

4. Age when married?

    24

5. Occupations before your birth?

    Carpentering and schoolteaching

    (b) After your birth?

    Schoolteaching and farming; after the age of 34, College Professor.

6. Health previous to your birth?

    Excellent

    (b) After your birth?

    Excellent

7. Number of children living:

    (a) Boys: 2

BLANK NO. 2   SERIES II, FORM B.

   (b) Girls: 1

8. Number of children dead; give age at time of death and cause.

   (a) Boys: None

   (b) Girls: [None]

9. If your father is living, give his age and present health;
   if dead, age at death and cause?

   58; health not very good, largely [the] result of continuous
   overwork for 30 years; trouble chiefly nervous.

10. Name any diseases in his family.

    Melancholia; his mother and two brothers subject to this;
    one brother died insane and one committed suicide. General
    inability to stand up against misfortunes, resulting in
    melancholia, a tendency in family.

Your Paternal Grandfather: home in city or country?

Country

   1. Age when married?

      Probably quite young.

   2. Occupations?

      Farming

   3. Health?

      Good

   4. Number of children?

      Eleven

BLANK NO. 2   SERIES II, FORM B.

    Number reaching maturity?

    Eight

Your Paternal Grandmother: home in city or country?
Country

    1. Age when married?

    2. Occupations?

       Housekeeping

    3. Health?

       Excellent. Great vigor and endurance.

    4. Age and cause of death?

       79, cause [was either] Rheumatism or dropsy?

Your Mother:

    1. Nationality; if American, of what descent?

       American. 1/2 Scotch, 1/2 Penn. Dutch descent

    2. Home in city or country before marriage?

       Country - farm

      (b) Home in city or country after marriage?

         Country - farm

    3. Occupations before her marriage?

       Housekeeping

BLANK NO. 2   SERIES II, FORM B.

   (b) After her marriage?

   Housekeeping

4. Note any prenatal influences before your birth.

5. Her health previous to your birth?

   Rather delicate, without any definite disease.

   (b) After your birth?

   Same though gradually growing better in following years.

6. Number of miscarriages?

   None.

7. Her age if living and present health? if not, age at time of death and cause?

   53; health not very good; Rheumatism, nervous disorders, result of too easy a life, too little exercise, and unhygienic conditions of her own making in the last ten years: at 40, she was an unusually well woman, though not strong or robust.

8. How was your mother's health affected by the climacteric (change of life)?

   She had a tumor of a cancerous nature on her neck at that time, but otherwise was reasonably well, though irritable.

9. Name any diseases in her family.

Your Maternal Grandfather: home in city or country?

Country

   1. Age when married?

BLANK NO. 2   SERIES II, FORM B.

   2. Occupations?
      Farming

   3. Health?

   4. Number of children?
      10 or 11.
      (b) Number reaching maturity?
         7

Your Maternal Grandmother: home in city or country?
Country
   1. Age when married?

   2. Occupations?
      Housekeeping

   3. Health?
      Excellent

   4. Age and cause of death?
      70 -- took cold and died of old age.

Your Husband: nationality; if American, of what descent?
   1. Date of birth?
      Aug. 30th, 1856

BLANK NO. 2   SERIES II, FORM B.

2. Early life in city or country?
   Country village

3. Height?
   6 ft.

4. Weight?

5. Muscular or weak?
   Muscular

6. Where educated? degrees if any?
   Cornell, '78, [M?].M.E.

7. If a college man, has he been athletic?
   Yes: boating

8. Complexion?
   Very fair

9. Temperament?

10. Does he use tobacco?
    No

11. Occupations?
    Practical Machinist '78-'85; College Professor '86-

12. Health?
    Good, but not of vigorous make; lacks physical **exuberance.**

BLANK NO. 2   SERIES II, FORM B.

13. Diseases in his family: Nervous Disorders? Rheumatism? Consumption? Dyspepsia? Varicose Veins? Heart Disease? Hernia? Habitual Constipation? Catarrh?

    Tendency to derangement of the heart.

Yourself:

1. Date of birth?

    Oct. 28th, 1860

2. Early life in city or country?

    Country

3. Height?

    5 ft. 3 3/4 in.

4. Weight?

    110 lbs.

3. Complexion?

    Gray eyes, dark hair and brown complexion.

6. Temperament?

    Nervous, sensitive, impulsive

7. Where educated, give degrees if any?

    Cornell, '80 + '82, Ph.B., M.S.?

8. Occupations before marriage? a) in city or country? b) time spent in each?

    Newspaper office, '81-'82, N. York City.

BLANK NO. 2   SERIES II, FORM B.

Teaching high school, '82-'84, Washington, D.C.
Teaching private school, '84-'86, Cincinnati, Ohio
Teaching and clerical work, '86-'90, Wellesley College,
Wellesley, Mass.

9. Diseases in your family? from father or mother's side?
Nervous Disorders? Rheumatism? Consumption? **Dyspepsia?**
Varicose Veins? Heart Disease? Hernia? Habitual
Constipation? Catarrh?

[Nervous disorders.] Myopia and Astigmatism (Father);
defective hearing probably result of catarrh, or small-pox
in childhood, or may have been inherited from Mother who
is now at age of 53 growing deaf.

10. General health before marriage? b) since marriage?
Paralysis? Brain Fever? Chronic Headache? Nervous
Prostration? Catarrh? Hernia? Dyspepsia? Habitual
Constipation? Inflammation of Bowels? Pleurisy? **Bronchitis?**
Shortness of Breath? Spitting Blood? Consumption? **Laryngitis?**
Tonsillitis? Insomnia? Rheumatism? Pneumonia? Jaundice?
Varicose Veins?

   (a) [Illegible] Paralysis, Catarrh, Tonsillitis, Pneumonia.
   Contagious diseases before marriage: measles, small-pox,
   whooping-cough, Diptheria (malignant) with resulting
   paralysis.

   (b) **Bronchitis, Tonsillitis. Grippe severely resulting in
   bronchial cough which lasted four months.**

11. Menstruation:

   First menstruation at what age? and when thoroughly
   established?

   At 13 yrs, 4 months; regular from beginning.

   Present condition as regards menstruation:

   (a) How frequent?

      Every 27th or 28th day

   (b) Is it regular or not?

      Regular

BLANK NO. 2   SERIES II, FORM B.

   (c) Amount? how many napkins?

       8 napkins

   (d) Duration?

       Five days

   (e) Pain or not? at what time as to the flow?

       From 13-32 always more [or] less painful, increasingly
       so as I grew older. While in College, very bad the
       first day. Pain always on first day, but lassitude and
       excessive languor on second.

   (f) Is there any leucorrhoea (whites)? character? amount?
       constant or occasional?

       None

   (g) Have you pain either frequently or habitually in the
       head, small of the back? abdomen or limbs?

       None

   (h) Disease or trouble in Uterus (womb) or other pelvic
       organs?

       No disease; flexion of the neck of uterus.

   (i) Habit of bowels; how often?

       Once a day, morning, absolutely regular.

12. What knowledge of sexual physiology had you before marriage?
    b) how did you obtain it?

    A great deal; obtained first from talk with other children;
    later (after 16 yrs old) from books chiefly scientific, such
    as Dr. Trall's, Dr. Wilder's <u>Tokology</u>.

13. Number of times married. If more than once, additional
    blanks will be furnished you to answer the following questions
    separately in regard to each marriage?

    Once.

BLANK NO. 2   SERIES II, FORM B.

14. Number of years married?

    1 1/2

15. Do you habitually sleep with your husband?

    During first year of marriage, not regularly afterward.

    (b) What reasons for so doing or not?

        Because sleeping on my guard made me nervous and irritable. It made the necessary control on my husband's part, too hard.

16. Number of conceptions?

    None.

17. Number of children? State in connection with each a) date of birth? b) sex? c) whether healthy or not? d) note any characteristic and the cause. e) note either immediate or after effect on your health of the birth of each of your children. f) give time of first menstruation after birth of each child.

    None.

18. Did conception occur by choice or accident?

19. Habit of intercourse, average number of times per week?

    Once.

    Per month?

    3

    Per year?

20. Was intercourse held during pregnancy? If so, how often? b) had you any desire for it during this period?

21. At other times have you any desire for intercourse? a) how often? b) at what time in relation to your menses?

   More desire immediately after cessation of menses.

22. Is intercourse agreeable to you or not?

   Yes

   Do you always have a venereal orgasm?

   Generally, not always.

   1. - When you do?

   (a) Effect immediately afterwards?

   Great lassitude and sleepiness.

   (b) Effect next day?

   Almost always backache slightly, and general weariness, often great nervousness.

   2. - When you do not?

   (a) Effect immediately afterwards?

   Same as above (1)

   (b) Effect next day?

   More so than under (1) (b)

23. What do you believe to be the true purpose of intercourse?

   (a) Necessity to man?

   Yes

   To woman?

   Yes, if she be normal.

   (b) Pleasure?

   Yes.

(c) Reproduction?

   Primary object

(d) What other reasons beside reproduction are sufficient to warrant intercourse?

   Physical union possibly is necessary to complete harmony between two people.

24. Have you ever used any means to prevent conception? a) if so, what?

   Rubber sheath for man.

   (b) Effect on your health?

   None whatever, so far as I know.

25. What, to you, would be an ideal habit?

   Perhaps twice a month immediately after cessation of menses; once a week too often for health in my case.

BLANK NO. 2 (a)   SUPPLEMENT   Dec. 18, 1913

    In June, 1903, I separated from my husband and was subsequently divorced. During 1903 and 1904 my general health was very poor; I was in a Sanitarium for some time with "nerves" -- no specific ailment -- and had grown very thin. Rested one year and then began work on certain sociological researches, still having to be careful about overdoing. In 1906 I went through the experience of earthquake and fire in San Francisco and worked very hard during the relief period. In 1906 I married a second time and have been exceptionally happy and steadily improving in health ever since. My husband is an unusually considerate man; during the earlier months of marriage, intercourse was frequent -- two or three times a week and as much desired by me as by him. After that, we formed the habit of about once a week; but if either is too tired or working very hard, it may occur only once or twice a month. My husband is a literary man and when he is doing hard brain work has very little desire for intercourse. Whenever he stops work he at once becomes as passionate as before.

    About 1909   . . .   my menses began to decline and in the course of a year ceased altogether, without any nervous disturbance whatever. During this time I was doing heavy intellectual labor -- published a statistical and sociological book in 1906, another in 1908 and another in 1912; gained some weight (from average of 110 to 120) and did my own housework beside lecturing frequently in public. My health has steadily improved during the last seven years and I am (at 53) much stronger and

BLANK NO 2. (b)

capable of doing both more physical and mental work every day than any woman of my acquaintance and more than most women of forty. I can walk 15 miles without feeling it and lift my own weight.

Although my <u>passionate</u> feeling has declined somewhat and the orgasm does not always occur, intercourse is still agreeable to me.

BLANK NO. 3   FORM A.

   1. Name in full.

   2. Address.

   3. Date of birth:

      Jan. 23, 1863.

   4. Place of birth:

      Auburn, N.Y.

   5. Where educated; give degrees if any. Occupations before
      marriage. Give length of time spent in each:

      Cornell Univ. B.L.

      Taught two years in Grammar School. Two years in Normal
      School.

   6. Nationality of mother:

      American

   7. Nationality of father:

      American

   8. Age of mother when married?

      Twenty five.

   9. Age of father when married:

  10. General health of parents:

      Father asthmatic; health otherwise good. Mother died of
      consumption.

BLANK NO. 3   FORM A.

11. Nationality of husband:

    American.

12. Date of birth of husband:

    Jan. 18, 1864.

BLANK NO. 3   FORM B.

Date: April 9, 1892.

   1. Age when married:

      25

   2. General health:

      (a) Before marriage:

         Excellent. Did not lose a day [through] illness in college course.

      (b) Since marriage:

         First and second year afterward was in poor health, largely caused by miscarriage four mos. after marriage.

   3. What knowledge of sexual physiology had you before marriage?

      Very slight; had read parts of <u>Tokology</u> but had never discussed or heard discussed functions of reproductive system.

   4. Number of times married? If more than once, additional blanks will be furnished you to answer the following questions separately in regard to each marriage.

   5. Number of years married?

      3 1/2.

   6. Do you habitually sleep with your husband?

      No.

   7. Number of conceptions?

      Two

BLANK NO. 3								FORM B.

8. Number of children?

   One.

   State in connection with each, date of birth, sex, whether healthy or not; note any characteristic and the cause if you know it.

   Feb. 28, 1891; male; healthy.

9. Did conception occur by choice or by accident?

   Both; after miscarriage, feared I would not conceive again, and did not feel that the matter of choice was left me, so did not consciously choose.

10. Habit of intercourse? average number of times per week?

    per month?

    Six

    per year?

11. Was intercourse held during pregnancy?

    Yes.

    If so, a) how often?

    After 5 mos. once a month approximately.

    (b) Did you desire it during this period?

      No, - but was not averse to it.

12. At other times have you any desire for intercourse?

    To a very slight degree.

    (a) How often?

      When it may give pleasure.

    (b) At what time in relation to your menses?

      I could not answer that. Have never observed any relation.

BLANK NO. 3   FORM B.

13. Is intercourse agreeable to you or not?

    Sometimes

    Do you always have a venereal orgasm?

    Not that I am aware of.

    1. - When you do,

    (a) Effect immediately afterward?

    (b) Effect next day?

    2. - When you do not,

    (a) Effect immediately afterwards?

    (b) Effect next day?

       No apparent effect, if in good health. If not, weakness
       and numb feeling.

14. What do you believe to be the purpose of intercourse?

    Reproduction, and a physical communion, which is an outward
    token of the spiritual and intellectual marriage.

    (a) Necessity to the man?

       Not a necessity, but next door to it.

       to the woman?

       Not at all.

    (b) Pleasure?

       Yes, aside from the physical aspect.

    (c) Reproduction?

       Yes.

15. Have you ever used any means to prevent conception? If so,
    a) what? b) What was the effect on your health?

    Several times during first months of marriage, took a soap

BLANK NO. 3								FORM B.

and water injection, but with no effect on health that I am aware of. Since then [I have?] used nothing.

16. What would be to [you] an ideal habit?

About twice a month.

BLANK NO. 3   SERIES II, FORM B.

Date: Feb. 15, 1893.

Your Father:

1. Nationality, if American, of what descent?
    American. English descent.

2. Home in city or country before marriage?
    Country.

3. Home in city or country after marriage?
    City.

4. Age when married?
    24.

5. Occupations before your birth?
    Teaching.
    (b) After your birth?
        Real estate.

6. Health previous to your birth?
    Excellent.
    (b) After your birth?
        Good, aside from chronic asthma.

7. Number of children living:
    (a) Boys?
    (b) Girls: Two.

BLANK NO. 3   SERIES II, FORM B.

   8. Number of children dead; give age at time of death and cause.

      (a) Boys: One son. Aged 26, Consumption.

      (b) Girls.

   9. If your father is living, give his age and present health, if dead, age at death and cause?

      [Living.] 68. Fairly good [health], aside from asthma.

 10. Name any diseases in his family

      Asthma, rheumatism.

Your Paternal Grandfather: home in city or country?

Country

   1. Age when married?

   2. Occupations?

   3. Health?

   4. Number of children?

      8

     Number reaching maturity?

      7

Your Paternal Grandmother: home in city or country?

Country

   1. Age when married?

      18

BLANK NO. 3   SERIES II, FORM B.

2. Occupations?
   Care of home.

3. Health?
   Good.

4. Age and cause of death?
   80. Weakness of old age. Paralysis.

Your Mother:
1. Nationality, if American, of what descent?
   American. English [descent].

2. Home in city or country before marriage?
   Country.
   (b) Home in city or country after marriage?
   City.

3. Occupations before her marriage?
   Teaching.
   (b) After her marriage?
   Housekeeping. Family cares.

4. Note any prenatal influences before your birth.

5. Her health previous to your birth?
   Fairly good.

BLANK NO. 3   SERIES II, FORM B.

   (b) After your birth?

       As good as could be expected when constantly overworked.

6. Number of miscarriages?

   One.

7. Her age if living and present health? if not, age at time of
   death and cause?

                    [Died at] 56 [of] consumption.

8. How was your mother's health affected by the climacteric
   (change of life)

9. Name any diseases in her family

   Consumption.

Your Maternal Grandfather: home in city or country?
Country.

   1. Age when married?

      28

   2. Occupations?

      Drayman.   Farmer.

   3. Health?

      Good.

   4. Number of children?

      10

BLANK NO. 3   SERIES II, FORM B.

    (b) Number reaching maturity?

        6

Your Maternal Grandmother: home in city or country?
Country.

    1. Age when married?

    2. Occupations?

    Care of family.

    3. Health?

    Good.

    4. Age and cause of death?

        48. Immediate cause measles with cold which caused quick consumption.

Your Husband: nationality, if American, of what **descent**?

        American. English [descent].

    1. Date of birth?

    1864

    2. Early life in city or country?

    Country

    3. Height?

    5 feet, 10 3/4 inches.

BLANK NO. 3   SERIES II, FORM B.

 4. Weight?

    160

 5. Muscular or weak?

    Muscular.

 6. Where educated? degrees if any?

    Cornell, C.E.

 7. If a college man, has he been athletic?

    Not especially

 8. Complexion?

    Dark.

 9. Temperament?

10. Does he use tobacco?

    Not habitually

11. Occupations?

    Teaching.

12. Health?

    Excellent.

13. Diseases in his family: Nervous Disorders? Rheumatism?
    Consumption? Dyspepsia? Varicose Veins? Heart Disease?
    Hernia? Habitual Constipation? Catarrh?

    Rheumatism. Consumption.

BLANK NO. 3   SERIES II, FORM B.

Yourself:

1. Date of birth?

   1863

2. Early life in city or country?

   City.

3. Height?

   5 feet 7 3/4 inches.

4. Weight?

   130

5. Complexion?

   Medium.

6. Temperament?

7. Where educated, give degrees if any?

   Cornell B. L.

8. Occupations before marriage? a) in city or country? b) time spent in each?

   Teaching in Normal School in Town.

   (b) Four years.

9. Diseases in your family? from father or mother's side? Nervous Disorders? Rheumatism? Consumption? Dyspepsia? Varicose Veins? Heart Disease? Hernia? Habitual Constipation? Catarrh?

   Consumption on mother's side, also scrofula. Asthma on father's side.

BLANK NO. 3   SERIES II, FORM B.

10. General health before marriage? b) since marriage? Paralysis? Brain Fever? Chronic Headache? Nervous Prostration? Catarrh? Hernia? Dyspepsia? Habitual Constipation? Inflammation of Bowels? Pleurisy? Bronchitis? Shortness of Breath? Spitting Blood? Consumption? Laryngitis? Tonsillitis ? Insomnia? Rheumatism? Pneumonia? Jaundice? Varicose Veins?

   Catarrh.

   (a) <u>Excellent</u>.

   (b) First two years not good, since then fair.

11. Menstruation:

   First menstruation at what age?

   17.

   and when thoroughly established?

   At that time.

   Present condition as regards menstruation:

   (a) How frequent?

   Once in five weeks.

   (b) Is it regular or not?

   Varies within a week.

   (c) Amount? how many napkins?

   10.

   (d) Duration?

   5 days.

   (e) Pain or not? at what time as to the flow?

   Some pain, but great weakness, first two days.

   (f) Is there any leucorrhoea (whites)? character?

   Yes. Thick, viscid.

BLANK NO. 3   SERIES II, FORM B.

   Amount?

   Variable.

   Constant or occasional?

   Occasional

   (g) Have you pain either frequently or habitually in the head, small of the back? abdomen or limbs?

   No.

   (h) Disease or trouble in Uterus (womb) or other pelvic organs?

   None.

   (i) Habit of bowels; how often?

   Always once, frequently more than once in 24 hours.

12. What knowledge of sexual physiology had you before marriage? b) how did you obtain it?

   (a) Very slight and indefinite.

   (b) From reading parts of Tokology.

13. Number of times married. If more than once additional blanks will be furnished you to answer the following questions separately in regard to each marriage?

14. Number of years married?

   4

15. Do you habitually sleep with your husband? b) what reasons for so doing or not?

   Yes.

   (b) Convenience.

BLANK NO. 3   SERIES II, FORM B.

16. Number of conceptions?

    3.

17. Number of children? State in connection with each: a) date of birth? b) sex? c) whether healthy or not? d) note any characteristic and the cause. e) note either immediate or after effect on your health of the birth of each of your children. f) give time of first menstruation after birth of each child.

    [One child. (a)] Feb. 28, 1891.

    (b) Male.

    (c) Healthy.

    (d) A tendency to enlarged tonsils, showing, I suppose, inherited scrofulous tendencies.

18. Did conception occur by choice or accident?

    First time, accident.
    Second time, choice with accident.
    Third time, choice with accident.

19. Habit of intercourse, average number of times per week?

    Per month?

    Six or more.

    Per year?

20. Was intercourse held during pregnancy? If so, how often?

    Yes. Two or three times per month.

    (b) Had you any desire for it during this period?

    Yes, in one case.

BLANK NO. 3   SERIES II, FORM B.

21. At other times have you any desire for intercourse?

    (a) How often?

        Infrequent intervals.

    (b) At what time in relation to your menses?

        Can not see any relation.

22. Is intercourse agreeable to you or not?

    Usually indifferent.

    Do you always have a venereal orgasm?

    I don't know.

    1. - When you do?

    (a) Effect immediately afterwards?

    (b) Effect next day?

    2. - When you do not?

    (a) Effect immediately afterwards?

    (b) Effect next day?

23. What do you believe to be the true purpose of intercourse?

    (a) Necessity to man? to woman?

        Necessity to neither.

    (b) Pleasure?

        Yes, to the man, and to the normal woman.

    (c) Reproduction?

        [Yes]

    (d) What other reasons beside reproduction are sufficient to warrant intercourse?

        It seems to me to be a natural and physical sign of a

BLANK NO. 3   SERIES II, FORM B.

spiritual union, a renewal of the marriage vows.

24. Have you ever used any means to prevent conception? a) if so, what?

Once used a syringe after intercourse.

(b) Effect on your health?

Nothing perceptible.

25. What, to you, would be an ideal habit?

Once, or possibly twice per month.

[Later, Dr. Mosher appended this note:]

Dec. 1894. In sixth month of pregnancy. Has been running down since last summer. Examination by Dr. Keith of San Jose who said she had prolapsis and that the uterus was very low, as low **as at 7 mo.** Was given book to read, "Health by Exercise." Took 1 wk. for rest away from home. Dr. recommended the using of hot injections followed by cold injections with some astringent. Leucorrhoea very bad, more than usual. Health worse after going away, time **correspond[s] with the use of injections. Also thought the fact that she had time to think about herself might be cause.** Thoroughly alarmed about her health.

Is not strong since   birth of last child. Illness during the last summer of her oldest child was a **serious strain. Has been** having intercourse on an average of once a week until the last month. Very painful to her. Now occupies a single bed.

Her digestion is bad although appetite is good. Is very constipated and has trouble with flatulence.

Did breathing exercises vigorously (while away from,) using book as a guide. Finds it necessary to lie down most of the time.

Has gained 1 lb. since last summer. Expects confinement in March.

BLANK NO. 4   FORM A.

1. Name in full:

2. Address:

3. Date of birth:

   October 13, 1857.

4. Place of birth:

   [Windham?], Connecticut

5. Where educated; give degrees if any. Occupation before
   marriage. Give length of time spent in each

   In public & private schools of [Conn.?]. Typewriting--one
   year--Accountant in [St.?] R.R. office about one year.
   (Baltimore)

6. Nationality of mother:

   American. (English)

7. Nationality of father:

   American. (Dutch-Irish-English)

8. Age of mother when married?

   Twenty-three

9. Age of father when married?

   Twenty-two

10. General health of parents?

    Fair

BLANK NO. 4   FORM A.

11. Nationality of husband:

    American (New England)

12. Date of birth of husband:

    Jan. 26, 1859

BLANK NO. 4   FORM B.

Date: May 12, 1892

   1. Age when you married?

      Twenty-nine

   2. General health:

      (a) Before marriage:

          Fair

      (b) After marriage:

          Fair

   3. What knowledge of sexual physiology had you before marriage?

      Not any.

   4. Number of times married? If more than once additional
      blanks will be furnished you to answer the following ques-
      tions separately in regard to each marriage.

   5. Number of years married?

      Six.

   6. Do you habitually sleep with your husband?

      Yes.

   7. Number of conceptions?

   8. Number of children? State in connection with each, date of
      birth, sex, whether healthy or not; Note any characteristic
      and the cause if you can give it.

   9. Did conception occur by choice or accident?

BLANK NO. 4   FORM B.

10. Habit of intercourse? average number of times per week?

    Per month?

    Per year?

    Possibly 6 or 8

11. Was intercourse held during pregnancy? If so, a) how often?
    b) did you desire it during this period?

12. At other times have you any desire for intercourse?

    Yes.

    (a) How often?

    (b) At what time in relation to your menses?

        The menses do not seem to make much difference.

13. Is intercourse agreeable to you or not?

    Sometimes agreeable but oftener disagreeable.

    Do you always have a venereal orgasm?

    No.

    1. - When you do,

    (a) Effect immediately afterward?

        Usually beneficial.

    (b) Effect next day?

        Sometimes increased vitality -- not always

    2. - When you do not,

    (a) Effect immediately afterward?

        Nervousness.

(b) Effect next day?

   Sometimes exhaustion--not always.

14. What do you believe to be the purpose of intercourse?

    (a) Necessity to the man? to the woman?

      [Both sexes:] Think it depends upon previous training in self control. Do not think it is an absolute necessity.

    (b) Pleasure?

      The pleasure is the smallest part.

    (c) Reproduction?

      I believe this to be the main purpose.

15. Have you ever used any means to prevent conception? If so, a) What? b) What was the effect on your health?

    Yes, a cover for the male organ. Not injurious to my health.

16. What to you would be an ideal habit?

    One governed by self control & the desire for offspring.

BLANK NO. 5   FORM A.

[This questionnaire was started in 1892 and supplemented in 1915.]

1. Name in full.

2. Address.

3. Date of birth.
   Aug. 10, 1864.

4. Place of birth.
   Phoenix, N.Y.

5. [a.] Where educated? [b.] give degrees if any. [c.] Occupations before marriage. [d.] length of time spent in each:
   [a.] Phoenix Acad. Cornell Univ. [b.] B.S. [c.] School teaching. [d.] Four years.

6. Nationality of mother.
   American (from N.Y. Dutch)

7. Nationality of father.
   American (from English)

8. Age when father was married.
   Thirty one

9. Age of mother when married.
   Twenty five

10. General health of parents.
    Good.

BLANK NO. 5   FORM A.

11. Nationality of husband.

    American (Dutch)

12. Date of birth of husband.

    Oct. 26, 1855

BLANK NO. 5   FORM B.

Date: April 1892

1. Age when married?

   Twenty five

2. General health:

   (a) Before marriage:

       Excellent

   (b) After marriage:

       Excellent

3. What knowledge of sexual physiology had you before marriage?

   Knowledge of plant reproduction and casual observation of animals.

4. Number of times married? If more than once additional blanks will be furnished you to answer the following questions in regard to each marriage.

   Once.

5. Number of years married?

   Nearly two.   [Married]   June '90)

6. Do you habitually sleep with your husband?

   No.

7. Number of conceptions?

   One

BLANK NO. 5   FORM B.

8. Number of children? State in connection with each, date of birth, sex, whether healthy or not; Note any characteristic and the cause if you can give it.

   Daughter born June 25, 1891. Very strong perhaps due to good care in pre-natal condition.

9. Did conception occur by choice or by accident?

   Indifferent - though not deliberate choice.

10. Habit of intercourse? Average number of times per week?

    About once or twice

    Per month?

    Per year?

    Note - First occurrence nearly a month after marriage. Continence a few days before menstrual period and at least eleven days after.

11. Was intercourse held during pregnancy? If so, a) how often?

    Occasionally.

    (b) Did you desire it during this period?

12. At other times have you any desire for intercourse?

    Not initiative. [Presumably, what this woman does not take.]

    (a) How often?

    (b) At what times in relation to your menses?

        Earlier more prominent.

13. Is intercourse agreeable to you or not?

    Yes - not necessary.

BLANK NO. 5   FORM B.

   Do you have a venereal orgasm?

   Yes

   1. - When you do?

   (a) Effect immediately afterwards?

   (b) Effect the next day?

       Note - Early morning - [Response incomplete]

   2. - When you do not?

   (a) Effect immediate afterward?

   (b) Effect the next day?

14. What do you believe to be the purpose of intercourse?

    Reproduction

    (a) Necessity to the man?

        Perhaps.

        to the woman?

        No.

    (b) Pleasure?

        Secondary - though to be recognized from mental & physical point of view.

    (c) Reproduction?

15. Have you ever used any means to prevent conception? If so, a) what?

    Syringe, tepid water.

    (b) What was the effect on your health?

        No apparent effect.

BLANK NO. 5   FORM B.

16. What to you would be an ideal habit?

   Never formulated. Satisfied with present circumstances.

BLANK NO. 5   SERIES II, FORM B.

Your Father:

1. Nationality, if American, of what descent?

   Am[erican] from [England or English]

2. Home in city or country before marriage?

   New country [which] grew into village.

3. Home in city or country after marriage?

   New country [which] grew into village.

4. Age when married?

   31

5. Occupations before your birth?

   Most everything except manual labor.

   (b) After your birth?

   Banking.

6. Health previous to your birth?

   Comparatively good, but always delicate. Small fair man with small hands & feet, very small neck.

   (b) After your birth?

   Same.

7. Number of children living:

   (a) Boys: One

   (b) Girls: One

   Second child, 4 1/2 [years] younger than brother.

BLANK NO. 5   SERIES II, FORM B.

8. Number of children dead; give age at time of death and cause.

   (a) Boys: 0

   (b) Girls: 0

9. If your father is living, give his age and present health, if dead, age at death and cause?

   About 69, feeble, but does business still.

10. Name any diseases in his family:

    Grandfather had Asthma. Catarrh trouble.

Your Paternal Grandfather: home in city or country?

1. Age when married?

2. Occupations?

   Small farm as remembered.

3. Health?

   Feeble but lived over 80 [years]. Consumptive.

4. Number of children?

   8

   Number reaching maturity?

Your Paternal Grandmother: home in city or country?

1. Age when married?

2. Occupations?

BLANK NO. 5   SERIES II, FORM B.

   3. Health?
      Very good

   4. Age and cause of death?
      87. Age, one stroke of paralysis

Your Mother:
   1. Nationality, if American of what descent?
      American   Dutch descent.

   2. Home in city or country before marriage?
      City, then moved into town [of] 2 or 3,000 people.
      (b) Home in city or country after marriage?
         City, then moved into town [of] 2 or 3,000 people.

   3. Occupations before her marriage?
      Taught school for a year.
      (b) After her marriage?
         Housewife.

   4. Note any prenatal influences before your birth:
      Mother much annoyed by bands of music. [I was] born after a hot summer.

   5. Her health previous to your birth?
      Very good.
      (b) After your birth?
         Very good.

BLANK NO. 5   SERIES II, FORM B.

    6. Number of miscarriages?

    7. Her age if living and present health? if not, age at time of death and cause?

       62 nervous trouble, eyes droop. At 50 very well.

    8. How was your mother's health affected by the climacteric (change of life)?

       Present condition may be due to it but was not sick as many women are.

    9. Name any diseases in her family:

       One member had cancer taken from his lip.

Your Maternal Grandfather: home in city or country?

    1. Age when married?

    2. Occupations?

       Farmer & teacher.

    3. Health?

       Died suddenly at [64?].

    4. Number of children?

       11.

      (b) Number reaching maturity?

         11.

Your Maternal Grandmother: home in city or country?

    1. Age when married?

BLANK NO. 5   SERIES II, FORM B.

   2. Occupations?

   3. Health?
      Good.

   4. Age and cause of death?
      Died suddenly [at] 81.

Your Husband: nationality, if American, of what descent?
American   French descent.
   1. Date of birth:
      26 Oct. 1855.

   2. Early life in city or country?
      [Country?]

   3. Height?
      6 - 3 1/2

   4. Weight?
      250.

   5. Muscular or weak?

   6. Where educated? degrees if any?

   7. If a college man, has he been athletic?

   8. Complexion?

   9. Temperament?

BLANK NO. 5   SERIES II, FORM B.

   10. Does he use tobacco?

   11. Occupations?

   12. Health?

       Good, but has catarrh.

   13. Diseases in his family: Nervous Disorders? Rheumatism?
       Consumption? Dyspepsia? Varicose Veins? Heart Disease?
       Hernia? Habitual Constipation? Catarrh?

       Rheumatism. Catarrh.

Yourself:

   1. Date of birth?

      Aug. 10, [18]64.

   2. Early life in city or country?

   3. Height?

   4. Weight?

   5. Complexion?

   6. Temperament?

   7. Where educated, give degrees if any?

   8. Occupations before marriage? a) in city or country? b) time
      spent in each?

   9. Diseases in your family? from father or mother's side?
      Nervous Disorders? Rheumatism? Consumption? Dyspepsia?

BLANK NO. 5   SERIES II, FORM B.

Varicose Veins? Heart Disease? Hernia? Habitual Constipation? Catarrh?

[Mother had Varicose Veins.] Catarrh.

10. General health before marriage? b) since marriage? Paralysis? Brain Fever? Chronic Headache? Nervous Prostration? Catarrh? Hernia? Dyspepsia? Habitual Constipation? Inflammation of Bowels? Pleurisy? Bronchitis? Shortness of Breath? Spitting Blood? Consumption? Laryngitis? Tonsillitis? Insomnia? Rheumatism? Pneumonia? Jaundice? Varicose Veins?

Before: Typhoid, scarlet fever, measles, etc.

11. Menstruation:

First menstruation at what age?

14.

and when thoroughly established?

14.

Present condition as regards menstruation:

At 51--reg[ular] still.

(a) How frequent?

2 or 3 days **over 4 wks.**

(b) Is it regular or not?

Fairly.

(c) Amount? how many napkins?

One per day.

(d) Duration?

Five.

(e) Pain or not? at what time as to the flow?

First day.

BLANK NO. 5   SERIES II, FORM B.

   [Mosher's note is unintelligible.]

   (f) Is there any leucorrhoea (whites)? character?

   Before marriage.

   Amount?

   Very little.

   Constant or occasional?

   Constant

   (g) Have you pain either frequently or habitually in the head,
       small of the back? abdomen or limbs?

   No.

   (h) Disease or trouble in Uterus (womb) or other pelvic organs?

   (i) Habit of bowels; how often?

   Once a day, varies two or 3 hours.

12. What knowledge of sexual physiology had you before marriage?
    b) how did you obtain it?

13. Number of times married. If more than once additional blanks
    will be furnished you to answer the following questions
    separately in regard to each marriage?

14. Number of years married?

    3.

15. Do you habitually sleep with your husband? b) what reasons
    for so doing or not?

    No.

    (b) Pleasanter, and more comfortable, more healthful. Habit
        of both to sleep alone before marriage.

16. Number of conceptions?

BLANK NO. 5   SERIES II, FORM B.

[A Mosher note indicates there were two conceptions when this
questionnaire was originally filled out, and four by 1915.]

17. Number of children? State in connection with each, a) date
of birth? b) sex? c) whether healthy or not? d) note any
characteristic and the cause. e) note either immediate or
after effect on your health of the birth of each of your
children. f) give time of first menstruation after birth of
each child.

[First child]

    (a) 25 June [18]91.

    (b) girl

    (c) yes

    (d)

    (e)

    (f) Once 6 months after but not established. 2nd time
about 8 months. Not established in next summer.

[Second child]

    (a) June 14, [18]93

    (b) girl

    (c) healthy

    (d)

    (e)

[Third child]

    (a) Jan. 28, [18]97

    (b) girl

    (c) healthy

    (d) develop back? trouble? if any [of children?] not
tubercular, no symptoms.

    (e) no trouble

(f) dev[eloped] enlarged legs [10?] days after.

[Fourth child]

(a) Jan. 15, 1900

(c) perfectly healthy

Mother has same trouble with legs after birth of this child.

2 weeks after birth of 2nd baby the first little girl fell out of 2nd story window. Great fright but labor did not come on. No harm to either & no apparent effect. Great financial worry [on account?] of father's financial condition. News came day before birth & lonesome because husband had to be away too much.

18. Did conception occur by choice or accident?

Accident. 12 days after menstrual period. No reason why it should not occur but not a deliberate choice. [Third conception by choice?]

19. Habit of intercourse, average number of times per week? per month? per year?

(1915) Gradual decrease in frequency. Now 1 per month or less.

20. Was intercourse held during pregnancy? If so, how often?

(1915?) None for 2 months before baby's birth. Perhaps once or twice a week. [Small?] limit. May have been longer.

[A Mosher note seems to indicate that after 1915 she "almost never" had intercourse.]

(b) Had you any desire for it during this period?

Can regulate it by thinking. 1915: With later children - gradual [decrease?].

21. At other times have you any desire for intercourse? a) how often? b) at what time in relation to your menses?

BLANK NO. 5   SERIES II, FORM B.

More interest at time [of menses].

(1915) Never objectionable--seldom would think. More desire just before [menses].

22. Is intercourse agreeable to you or not?

　　Fairly.

　　Do you always have a venereal orgasm?

　　No, generally.

　　1915 yes. Probably orgasm even frequently with [coitus?].

　　1. - When you do?

　　(a) Effect immediately afterwards?

　　(b) Effect next day?

　　2. - When you do not?

　　(a) Effect immediately afterwards?

　　(b) Effect next day?

　　　　Usually morning rather than night. No effect in [general].

　　　　Usually sleep better after it.

23. What do you believe to be the true purpose of intercourse?

　　(a) Necessity to the man?

　　　　Yes - relieves what would be a discomfort. Husband temperate.

　　　　to the woman?

　　　　Perhaps - would have hated to have omitted the experience.

　　(b) Pleasure?

　　　　Yes - does not know why not.

　　(c) Reproduction?

BLANK NO. 5   SERIES II, FORM B.

Yes - does not think she has had too many children.

(d) What other reasons besides reproduction are sufficient to warrant intercourse?

A close bond making marriage more stable. Can not imagine a new relation established with new people.

1915 - Binds people together and holds family together - is a bond. Not only reason but a strong family.

24. Have you ever used any means to prevent conception?

No.

(a) If so, what?

Withdrawal.

(b) Effect on your health?

25. What, to you, would be an ideal habit?

Anything which was conducive to general [comfortable] living. Not for reproduction only. To vary with age, less desire in later years.   For yrs. [have] not slept together, connecting rooms--always has access to room. Once a month before period.

BLANK NO. 6   FORM A.

   1. Name in full:

   2. Address:

   3. Date of birth:
      Jan. 16th, 185[5?]

   4. Place of birth:
      Wesel, Germany?

   5. Where educated; give degrees if any. Occupations before marriage. Give length of time spent in each.
      My whole life was one of mental & physical strain. I studied three years in Ripon College and taught five years.

   6. Nationality of mother:
      German. (Grandmother French)

   7. Nationality of father:
      German.

   8. Age of mother when married:
      Nineteen.

   9. Age of father when married:
      Thirty-seven.

   10. General health of parents:
       Good.

BLANK NO. 6   FORM A.

11. Nationality of husband:

    American. (Father [was] Spanish, Mother [was] French Huguenot)

12. Date of birth of husband:

    Oct. 16th, 1859.

BLANK NO. 6   FORM B.

Date: Aug. 1892

   1. Age when married:

      Thirty-one.

   2. General health:

      (a) Before marriage:

          Poor.

      (b) Since marriage:

          Better.

   3. What knowledge of sexual physiology had you before marriage?

      None.

   4. Number of times married? If more than once additional blanks
      will be furnished you to answer the following questions
      separately in regard to each marriage.

   5. Number of years married?

      Four.

   6. Do you habitually sleep with your husband?

      Have tried both.

   7. Number of conceptions?

   8. Number of children? Note in connection with each, date of
      birth, sex, whether healthy or not; note any characteristic
      and the cause if you know it.

   9. Did conception take place by choice or by accident?

BLANK NO. 6   FORM B.

10. Habit of intercourse? average number of times per week?

    per month?

    One to four times.

    per year?

11. Was intercourse held during pregnancy? If so, a) how often?
    b) did you desire it during this period?

12. At other times have you any desire for intercourse?

    Seldom.

    (a) How often?

        About once a month.

    (b) At what time in relation to your menses?

        Soon after.

13. Is intercourse agreeable to you or not?

    Generally agreeable.

    Do you always have a venereal orgasm?

    Yes.

    1. - When you do,

    (a) Effect immediately after?

        None. (Sleep)

    (b) Effect next day?

        None.

    2. - When you do not,

    (a) Effect immediately after?

    (b) Effect the next day?

BLANK NO. 6   FORM B.

14. What do you believe to be the purpose of intercourse?
    Reproduction.
    (a) Necessity to the man?
        No.
        to the woman?
        No.
    (b) Pleasure?
        No.
    (c) Reproduction?
        Yes.

15. Have you ever used any means to prevent conception?
    No.
    If so, what?
    (b) What was the effect on your health?

16. What to you would be an ideal habit?
    Intercourse at desired intervals until pregnancy occurs, then abstinence until end of lactation.

BLANK NO. 6   SERIES II, FORM B.

Date: April 3rd, 1893.

Your Father:

1. Nationality, if American, of what descent?
   German.

2. Home in city or country before marriage?
   City.

3. Home in city or country after marriage?
   City.

4. Age when married?
   37.

5. Occupations before your birth?
   Officer in the army.
   (b) After your birth?
       None.

6. Health previous to your birth?
   Good.
   (b) After your birth?
       Excellent.

7. Number of children living:
   (a) Boys: One
   (b) Girls: Three

BLANK NO. 6   SERIES II, FORM B.

   8. Number of children dead; give age at time of death and cause.

      (a) Boys:

      (b) Girls: One girl died by accident at the age of three.
          The other died from meningitis when over twenty.

   9. If your father is living, give his age and present health,
      if dead, age at death and cause?

      He died at the age of 92 from old age.

   10. Name any diseases in his family:

       Asthma.

Your Paternal Grandfather: home in city or country?
City.

   1. Age when married?

   2. Occupations?

      Government official.

   3. Health?

      Good.

   4. Number of children?

      Three.

      Number reaching maturity?

      All.

BLANK NO. 6   SERIES II, FORM B.

Your Paternal Grandmother: home in city or country?
Village.
   1. Age when married?

   2. Occupations?

   3. Health?
      She was an invalid for many years.

   4. Age and cause of death?

Your Mother:
   1. Nationality, if American of what descent?
      German.

   2. Home in city or country before marriage?
      Village.
      (b) Home in city or country after marriage?
          City.

   3. Occupations before her marriage?
      Student.
      (b) After her marriage?
          Teacher and student.

BLANK NO. 6   SERIES II, FORM B.

4. Note any prenatal influences before your birth:

5. Her health previous to your birth?
   Good.
   (b) After your birth?
       Later in life heart disease **developed, and she was not** very strong.

6. Number of miscarriages?

7. Her age if living, and present health? if not, age at time of death and cause?
   75. Health good.

8. How was your mother's health affected by the climacteric (change of life)?
   Not at all, as far as I know.

9. Name any diseases in her family:
   Her mother had chronic head-ache.

Your Maternal Grandfather: home in city or country?
Country(?)

1. Age when married?

2. Occupations?
   Student

BLANK NO. 6   SERIES II, FORM B.

   3. Health?

      Delicate

   4. Number of children?

      One.

      (b) Number reaching maturity?

         One.

Your Maternal Grandmother: home in city or country?
Country or village.

   1. Age when married?

   2. Occupations?

   3. Health?

      Fairly good.

   4. Age and cause of death?

Your Husband: nationality, if American, of what descent?
American

   1. Date of birth?

      1859, Oct. 16.

   2. Early life in city or country?

      Country.

   3. Height?

BLANK NO. 6   SERIES II, FORM B.

   5 ft. 9 in.

4. Weight?

   15[6] lb.

5. Muscular or weak?

   Muscular.

6. Where educated? degrees if any?

   A.B. Ripon College, Ph.D., [J.?]H.U. [Johns Hopkins University, probably]

7. If a college man, has he been athletic?

   No.

8. Complexion?

   Dark.

9. Temperament?

   Sang[u]ine.

10. Does he use tobacco?

    No, not habitually.

11. Occupations?

    Teacher.

12. Health?

    Excellent.

BLANK NO. 6   SERIES II, FORM B.

13. Diseases in his family: Nervous Disorders? Rheumatism? Consumption? Dyspepsia? Varicose Veins? Heart Disease? Hernia? Habitual Constipation? Catarrh?

    [Nervous disorders and **sporadic** case of consumption].

Yourself:

1. Date of birth?

   1858, Jan. 16.

2. Early life in city or country?

   Country.

3. Height?

   5 ft, 4 1/2 in.

4. Weight?

   135 lb.

5. Complexion?

   Rather light.

6. Temperament?

7. Where educated, give degrees if any?

   Studied three years in Ripon College.

8. Occupations before marriage? a) in city or country? b) time spent in each?

   Taught five years in the City.

BLANK NO. 6   SERIES II, FORM B.

9. Diseases in your family? from father or mother's side? Nervous Disorders? Rheumatism? Consumption? Dyspepsia? Varicose Veins? Heart Disease? Hernia? Habitual Constipation? Catarrh?

   [Dyspepsia, Heart Disease, and Habitual Constipation on mother's side. Asthma on father's side.]

   (b) [Age of your father and mother at your birth?]

   Father was 57 years old, mother 39.

   How many children older than yourself?

   There were five children older than myself, the youngest 10 years older.

10. General health before marriage? b) since marriage? Paralysis? Brain Fever? Chronic Headache? Nervous Prostration? Catarrh? Hernia? Dyspepsia? Habitual Constipation? Inflammation of Bowels? Pleurisy? Bronchitis? Shortness of Breath? Spitting Blood? Consumption? Laryngitis? Tonsillitis? Insomnia? Rheumatism? Pneumonia? Jaundice? Varicose Veins?

    Chronic Headache, Dyspepsia, Habitual Constipation, and Insomnia.

    General health better since marriage.

11. Menstruation:

    First menstruation at what age? and when thoroughly established?

    Began at thirteen and was regular thereafter, as far as I remember.

    Present condition as regards menstruation:

    (a) How frequent?

        Once in 21--26 days. Is improving.

BLANK NO. 6   SERIES II, FORM B.

    (b) Is it regular or not?

        No, but is growing more regular.

    (c) Amount? how many napkins?

        Amount very small, two or three napkins would suffice if I chose to be economical.

    (d) Duration?

        About four or five days.

    (e) Pain or not? at what time as to the flow?

        There is pain in the small of the back either before or during the first part of the flow.

    (f) Is there any leucorrhoea (whites)? character?

        No.

        Amount?

        Constant or occasional?

    (g) Have you pain either frequently or habitually in the head, small of the back? abdomen or limbs?

        There is chronic head-ache generally all over the head.

    (h) Disease or trouble in Uterus (womb) or other pelvic organs?

        No.

    (i) Habit of bowels; how often?

        Daily, but most of the time only with aid of a syringe.

12. What knowledge of sexual physiology had you before marriage?

None.

BLANK NO. 6   SERIES II, FORM B.

   (b) How did you obtain it?

13. Number of times married. If more than once additional blanks will be furnished you to answer the following questions separately in regard to each marriage?

   Once.

14. Number of years married?

   Almost five.

15. Do you habitually sleep with your husband? b) what reasons for so doing or not?

   Together in winter, apart in summer is what we found most comfortable. The matter is left entirely at my preference.

16. Number of conceptions?

   None.

17. Number of children? State in connection with each, a) date of birth? b) sex? c) whether healthy or not? d) note any characteristic and the cause. e) note either immediate or after effect on your health of the birth of each of your children. f) give time of first menstruation after birth of each child.

18. Did conception occur by choice or accident?

19. Habit of intercourse, average number of times per week?

   per month?

   Two or three times.

   per year?

20. Was intercourse held during pregnancy? If so, how often? b) had you any desire for it during this period?

BLANK NO. 6   SERIES II, FORM B.

21. At other times have you any desire for intercourse? a) how often? b) at what time in relation to your menses?

   About two or three times a month, after menstruation and sometimes before it.

22. Is intercourse agreeable to you or not?

   Yes, at times.

   Do you always have a venereal orgasm?

   Yes.

   1. - When you do,

   (a) Effect immediately afterwards?

      Sleep[i]ness.

   (b) Effect next day?

      None.

   2. - When you do not,

   (a) Effect immediately afterwards?

   (b) Effect next day?

23. What do you believe to be the true purpose of intercourse?

   (a) Necessity to man?

      No.

      to woman?

      No.

   (b) Pleasure?

      No. Pleasure only incidental.

   (c) Reproduction?

      Yes.

BLANK NO. 6   SERIES II, FORM B.

   (d) What other reasons beside reproduction are sufficient to
       warrant intercourse?

       None.

25. Have you ever used any means to prevent conception?

    No.

    (a) If so, what?

    (b) Effect on your health?

25. What, to you, would be an ideal habit?

    Intercourse when desirable to wife and agreeable to husband
    until conception takes place. No intercourse during gestation
    and lactation.

BLANK NO. 8   SERIES II, FORM B.

[No Blank No. 7 appears in the original. Dr. Mosher noted the
loss of the first three pages of this questionnaire.]

Date: Dec. 16, 1912[?] **or** 1917[?]

Yourself:

1. Date of birth?

    Feb. 23, 1867.

2. Early life in city or country?

    Country until 18.

3. Height?

    5 [ft.], 4 [in.].

4. Weight?

    156 [lbs.].

5. Complexion?

    Dark.

6. Temperament?

    Nervous.

7. Where educated, give degrees if any?

    Smith Col[lege] 3 yrs.

8. Occupations before marriage? a) in city or country? b) time spent in each?

    [Taught for more than a year and tutored for a year.]

BLANK NO. 8   SERIES II, FORM B.

9. Diseases in your family? from father or mother's side? Nervous Disorders? Rheumatism? Consumption? Dyspepsia? Varicose Veins? Heart Disease? Hernia? Habitual Constipation? Catarrh?

10. General health before marriage? b) since marriage? Paralysis? Brain Fever? Chronic Headache? Nervous Prostration? Catarrh? Hernia? Dyspepsia? Habitual Constipation? Inflammation of Bowels? Pleurisy? Bronchitis? Shortness of Breath? Spitting Blood? Consumption? Laryngitis? Tonsillitis? Insomnia? Rheumatism? Pneumonia? Jaundice? Varicose Veins? Any other diseases?

    Not robust. Better after going to college.

    (b) Worse.

11. Menstruation:

    First menstruation at what age? and when thoroughly established?

    About 14.

    Present condition as regards menstruation:

    Menopause

    (a) How frequent?

        Very [regular.]   4 wks.

    (b) Is it regular or not?

        Reg[ular].

    (c) Amount? how many napkins?

        Profuse.

    (d) Duration?

        7 (3). [Maximum and minimum days duration?]

    (e) Pain or not? at what time as to the flow, before, during, or after?

        Not since marriage. Terrible pain [during the year that] she taught.

BLANK NO. 8   SERIES II, FORM B.

   (f) Is there any leucorrhoea (whites)? character?

      No.

      Amount?

      Constant or occasional?

   (g) Have you pain either frequently or habitually in the head,
       small of the back? abdomen or limbs?

   (h) Disease or trouble in Uterus (womb) or other pelvic organs?

   (i) Habit of bowels; how often?

      Reg[ular].

12. What knowledge of sexual physiology had you before marriage?
    b) how did you obtain it?

   Not one thing no knowledge of [illegible] few weeks before
   [remainder of response   unintelligible].

13. Number of times married. If more than once additional blanks
    will be furnished you to answer the following questions
    separately in regard to each marriage?

14. Number of years married?

15. Do you habitually sleep with your husband? b) what reasons
    for so doing or not?

16. Number of conceptions?

   5.

   [First conception was a] miscarriage [illegible]. **About 2 mo.
   result of overwork.**

   [Second conception was a] miscarriage following year--great
   strain--**riding wheel.**

17. Number of children? State in connection with each, a) date
    of birth? b) sex? c) whether healthy or not? d) note any

BLANK NO. 8   SERIES II, FORM B.

characteristic and the cause. e) note either immediate or
after effect on your health of the birth of each of your
children. f) give time of first menstruation after birth
of each child.

[First child]

    (a) Oct. 9, 1895

    (b) Boy

    (c) Healthy

    (e) Mother was perfectly miserable for [a year]. No anesthesia at labor. Very long hard labor. Shock and kidney trouble before. Nursed 3 months.

    (f) Menstruated at end of [illegible].

[Second child]

    (a) Dec. 30, 1899.

    (b) Boy.

    (c) Very healthy.

    (e) Nursed 3 mo.

    (f) **Menstruation [illegible]**

[Third child]

    (a) Feb. 3, 1901.

    (b) Girl.

    (c) Very healthy.

    (e) Nursed 9 [months] with pleasure [and] profit. **Finest child.**

18. Did conception occur by choice or accident?

    [accident]

19. Habit of intercourse, average number of times per week?

BLANK NO. 8   SERIES II, FORM B.

   per month?

   3 to 4.

   per year?

20. Was intercourse held during pregnancy? If so, how often?
    b) had you any desire for it during pregnancy?

   [Mosher notes that the woman had intercourse during the
   first two months of pregnancy with about the same frequency
   as before pregnancy, but that she was "very unstable--
   sometimes yes, sometimes no."]

21. At other times have you any desire for intercourse?

   Yes.

   (a) How often?

   (b) At what time in relation to your menses?

      Just before or after.

      Since 1st baby was born & lasseration caused it to be painful.

22. Is intercourse agreeable to you or not?

   Yes until lasseration.

   Do you always have a venereal orgasm?

   Always at first.

   1. - When you do,

   (a) Effect immediately afterwards?

      [No difference?]

   (b) Effect next day?

   2. - When you do not,

   (a) Effect immediately afterwards?

BLANK NO. 8   SERIES II, FORM B.

   (b) Effect next day?

23. What do you believe to be the true purpose of intercourse?

   (a) Necessity to man?

      Yes

      to woman?

      Yes [reasonable?]

   (b) Pleasure?

      Yes.

   (c) Reproduction?

      Yes.

   (d) What other reasons beside reproduction are sufficient to warrant intercourse?

      Ideal marriage - spiritual. Being at one with only person you can [illegible] - nearness.

24. Have you ever used any means to prevent conception? a) if so, what?

   Cundrum [condom] now--must not conceive again after miscarriages. Earlier nothing.

   (b) Effect on your health?

25. What, to you, would be an ideal habit?

   Has had it always. Has always chosen about 2 [times per week?].

26. Additional notes:

BLANK NO. 9   SERIES II, FORM B.

Date: Feb. 9, 1895

Your Father:
   1. Nationality, if American, of what descent?
      American (Welsh)

   2. Home in city or country before marriage?
      Country

   3. Home in city or country after marriage?
      Country.

   4. Age when married?
      About 26

   5. Occupations before your birth?
      Farmer
      (b) After your birth?
          Farmer, and had a saw mill.

   6. Health previous to your birth?
      Always delicate. Said to have weak lungs.
      (b) After your birth?
          Delicate. Grew stronger as he grew older.

   7. Number of children living?
      (a) Boys: 2
      (b) Girls: 3

BLANK NO. 9   SERIES II, FORM B.

   8. Number of children dead; give age at time of death and cause.

      (a) Boys:

      (b) Girls:

      (2d child of father)

   9. If your father is living, give his age and present health, if dead, age at death and cause?

      79 (bilious attack. Did not know.) Had hemorrhage of lungs when he was [young?] and coughed until he was 50 yrs. old, one lung had grown fast to his side.

   10. Name any diseases in his family:

      Dyspepsia (all of them)

Your Paternal Grandfather: home in city or country?
   Country.

   1. Age when married?

      Probably 26- 7, nearer 30.

   2. Occupations?

      Music teacher and later a farmer.

   3. Health?

      Never good. Not strong.

   4. Number of children?

      10

      Number reaching maturity?

      2

BLANK NO. 9   SERIES II, FORM B.

Your Paternal Grandmother: home in city or country?
[Born in the country.]
   1. Age when married?
      About 18.

   2. Occupations?
      Housewife & farm work

   3. Health?
      Always good

   4. Age and cause of death?
      74 or [7]5

Your Mother:
   1. Nationality, if American, of what descent?
      Am[erican]. New England [illegible].

   2. Home in city or country before marriage?
      Country.
      (b) Home in city or country after marriage?
         Country.

   3. Occupations before her marriage?
      Housework.
      (b) After her marriage?
         Housework.

BLANK NO. 9   SERIES II, FORM B.

4. Note any prenatal influences before your birth:

5. Her health previous to your birth?

   Good as far as known.

   (b) After your birth?

       Good until she was 50. Had heart trouble and rheumatism;
       helpless for [9?] years. When children were small had
       [illegible] sore mouth, then had acne in face.

6. Number of miscarriages?

7. Her age if living and present health? if not, age at time of
   death and cause?

   64. Rheumatic pleurisy.

8. How was your mother's health affected by the climacteric
   (change of life)?

   Heart & rheumatism at change of life.

9. Name any diseases in her family:

   Mother had rheumatism, father died of gout. One sister
   dropped dead of heart disease. Sister had rheumatism.

Your Maternal Grandfather: home in city or country?

Country.

   1. Age when married?

      17

   2. Occupations?

      Farmer. [Unintelligible] **in his country salary of $2000.**

BLANK NO. 9   SERIES II, FORM B.

    3. Health?

       Good.

    4. Number of children?

       5

       (b) Number reaching maturity?

           All

Your Maternal Grandmother: home in city or country?
Country.

    1. Age when married?

       16

    2. Occupations?

       Housework

    3. Health?

       Good until change of life. Rheumatism, heart disease [left
       her] helpless for 20 years.

    4. Age and cause of death?

       About 70, opium eater in old age.

Your Husband: nationality, if American, of what descent?
Am[erican]. (French - English)

    1. Date of birth?

       Feb. 21, 1829 (3rd child)

BLANK NO. 9   SERIES II, FORM B.

2. Early life in city or country?

   Country

3. Height?

   6 ft. or 6 ft. 1 in.

4. Weight?

   When married 140 lbs. About 140 or 150

5. Muscular or weak?

   Weak.

6. Where educated? degrees if any?

   Poultney,   Vt., New Brunswick, N.J. Prep school. Albany Med. Col., M.D.

7. If a college man, has he been athletic?

   No

8. Complexion?

   Fair with dark hair & eyes

9. Temperament?

   Nervous

10. Does he use tobacco?

    As a young man smoked incessantly, until 40 [years old when he] stopped entirely.

11. Occupations?

    Teacher and physician

BLANK NO. 9   SERIES II, FORM B.

12. Health?

   Very delicate, always **dyspeptic**, and was threatened with
   consumption as a young man but overcame tendency. Insane
   from use of morphine at 39 or 40 for 2 yrs. **Took morphine
   from 1861 to 1870. Relapsed into habit once about 7 or 8
   years later, but overcame it without going to asylum.**

13. Diseases in his family: Nervous Disorders? Rheumatism?
    Consumption? Dyspepsia? Varicose Veins? Heart Disease?
    Hernia? Habitual Constipation?

   [Mosher notes that his grandmother, after birth of child, had
   a nervous disorder, his mother had rheumatism, his
   brother and mother's father had consumption, and that the
   family history also included dyspepsia, hernia, habitual
   consumption, and "consumption of bowels."]

Yourself:

   1. Date of birth?

      15 Aug., 1834

   2. Early life in city or country?

      Country

   3. Height?

      5 ft. 7 in.

   4. Weight?

      150 [lbs.]

   5. Complexion?

      Florid when young

   6. Temperament?

BLANK NO. 9   SERIES II, FORM B.

7. Where educated, give degrees if any?

   [Illegible]

8. Occupations before marriage?   a) in city or country?

   Country.

   (b) time spent in each?

       In school from 6 to 20 yrs. Taught in country school 2 yrs.

9. Diseases in your family? from father or mother's side?
   Nervous Disorders? Rheumatism? Consumption? Dyspepsia?
   Varicose Veins? Heart Disease? Hernia? Habitual Constipation?
   Catarrh?

   [Mosher indicates that the woman's mother had rheumatism and
   heart disease, and her father had consumption and dyspepsia.]

10. General health before marriage? b) since marriage? Paralysis?
    Brain Fever? Chronic Headache? Nervous Prostration? Catarrh?
    Hernia? Dyspepsia? Habitual Constipation? Inflammation of
    Bowels? Pleurisy? Bronchitis? Shortness of Breath? Spitting
    Blood? Consumption? Laryngitis? Tonsillitis? Insomnia?
    Rheumatism? Pneumonia? Jaundice? Varicose Veins? Any
    other diseases?

    (a) Good.

    (b) Good.

    ["Sick" appears above Chronic Headache, "slight" next to
    Catarrh, and "tendency" above Habitual Constipation.]

       Gout   in toe.

11. Menstruation:

    First menstruation at what age?

    Almost 16.

    and when thoroughly established?

BLANK NO. 9   SERIES II, FORM B.

20 before it was well established.

Condition as regards menstruation:

(a) How frequent?

(b) Is it regular or not?

   Reg[ular] after 20 [years old].

(c) Amount? how many napkins?

(d) Duration?

   6

(e) Pain or not? at what time as to the flow?

   [Pain] first 3 days in morning leaving off later.

(f) Is there any leucorrhoea (whites)? character?

   [Illegible]

(g) Have you pain either frequently or habitually in the head, small of the back? abdomen or limbs?

(h) Disease or trouble in Uterus (womb) or other pelvic organs?

   Once for about six months prolapsis. Husband attended her. [Illegible] from too much walking during menstrual period. 1 1/2 years after 1st child was born.

(i) Habit of bowels; how often?

   Tendency to constipation.

12. What knowledge of sexual physiology had you before marriage? b) how did you obtain it?

   Knew what sexual intercourse was, told by others.

13. Number of times married?

   Once.

14. Number of years married?

BLANK NO. 9   SERIES II, FORM B.

15. Do you habitually sleep with your husband? b) what reasons for so doing or not?

   Always until children were born; then apart for fear husband (doctor) might bring contagious diseases to children. Did not habitually sleep together after **2d child was born**.

16. No. of conceptions?

   3

17. No. of children?

   3

   1. girl, born 3 yrs. & 8 mo. after marriage. Healthy until mother had typhoid fever. Child was nursed during this time; baby never well after. [Baby died?] of scarlet fever & Diptheria at 1 yr. old.

   2. girl, born 3 yrs. after first child. Crying baby had colic for 3 mo. Grew constantly at this time (mother did washing day before this baby's birth) was annoyed by a servant constantly before this baby was born. Menstruated 9 mos. after this baby's birth. Father had taken morphine for 2 yrs. before this baby's birth. Not a confirmed habit. No effect.

   3. girl (born 2 yrs. & 8 mos. after 2nd child's birth) Healthy but did not walk until [19] mo. old. Had large ankles & wrist joints. Grew well & seemed strong. Had a slight fall on her knee, which began to swell. Protrusion on one side of ribs. Had measles which did not come out well (Rickets). Constantly doctored more or less because lame & walked with a crutch. At 16 had running sores on knee for 1 yr., in 19th yr. died of tubercular meningitis.

18. Did conception occur by choice or accident?

   1. - Choice
   2. - Choice
   3. - Choice

BLANK NO. 9   SERIES II, FORM B.

19. Habit of intercourse, average no. times per wk?
    2 or more; at times every night (abnormal condition).

20. Was intercourse held during pregnancy? how often?
    As usual
    (b) Had you any desire for it then?
        As usual

21. At other times have you any desire for it?
    Usually a nuisance. Never cared much for it.
    (b) At what times in relation to your menses?
        Does not remember

22. Is intercourse agreeable to you or not?
    As a rule not
    Do you always have a venereal orgasm?
    No.
    1. - When you do?
    (a) Effect immediately afterwards?
        Fatigued
    (b) Effect next day?
        Felt worse the next day. (Thinks her husband did also.)
    2. - When you do not?
    (a) Effect immediately afterwards?
    (b) Effect next day?

BLANK NO. 9   SERIES II, FORM B.

23. What do you believe to be the true purpose of intercourse?

   (a) Necessity to man?

   Don't know.

   to woman?

   No.

   (b) Pleasure?

   To men.

   (c) Reproduction?

   Yes

   (d) What other reasons beside reproduction are sufficient to warrant intercourse?

24. Have you ever used any means to prevent conception? a) if so, what?

   Withdrawal. (Man worn out next day. Troubled with impotence toward end of the period when he was taking morphine.)

   (b) Effect on your health?

   At times when intercourse was too frequent when he was taking morphine, kept her all tired out. Sometimes intercourse happened more than once in a night not usually, only a few times.

25. What, to you, would be an ideal habit?

26. Additional notes:

   Husband said she was cold blooded.

BLANK NO. 10   SERIES II, FORM B.

Date: April 1894

Your Father:

1. Nationality, if American, of what descent?

    American.

2. Home in city or country before marriage?

    Small city.

3. Home in city or country after marriage?

    Small city.

4. Age when married?

    21 or 22

5. Occupations before your birth?

    Tradesman -- was in the Civil War.

    (b) After your birth?

       Tradesman and inventor.

6. Health previous to your birth?

    Good.

    (b) After your birth?

       Good.

7. Number of children living?

    (a) Boys:

    (b) Girls: 1

BLANK NO. 10   SERIES II, FORM B.

8. Number of children dead; give age at time of death and cause.

   (a) Boys:

   (b) Girls: 2

   Oldest daughter died of acute mania [at age] 24. Youngest daughter of cholera infantum or some similar trouble, aged 1 year.

9. If your father is living, give his age and present health, if dead, age at death and cause?

   Age 51 years 6 mos. Present health very good.

10. Name any diseases in his family:

Your Paternal Grandfather: home in city or country?
City.

1. Age when married?

   Do not know. He was 60 years old when my father was born. (Married twice)

2. Occupations?

   Merchant, I think. Was inventive.

3. Health?

   Good, I think.

4. Number of children?

   6(?)

   (b) Number reaching maturity?

   3(?)

BLANK NO. 10   SERIES II, FORM B.

Your Paternal Grandmother: home in city or country?
City.
   1. Age when married?

   2. Occupations?
      Household

   3. Health?

   4. Age and cause of death?
      Don't know. She died when my father was a child.

Your Mother:
   1. Nationality, if American of what descent?
      American.

   2. Home in city or country before marriage?
      Small city.
      (b) Home in city or country after marriage?
          Small city.

   3. Occupations before her marriage?
      Married at 19.
      (b) After her marriage?
          Household

   4. Note any prenatal influences before your birth:

BLANK NO. 10   SERIES II, FORM B.

5. Her health previous to your birth?

   Good.

   (b) After your birth?

      Good.

6. Number of miscarriages?

7. Her age if living and present health? if not, age at time of death and cause?

   Age 50 in June. Health good.

8. How was your mother's health affected by the climacteric (change of life)?

   Not yet passed. More nervous but not seriously affected.

9. Name any diseases in her family:

Your Maternal Grandfather: home in city or country?
City.

1. Age when married?

2. Occupations?

   Ship Captain.

3. Health?

   Good, I think.

4. Number of children?

   3

BLANK NO. 10   SERIES II, FORM B.

   (b) Number reaching maturity?

       2

Your Maternal Grandmother: home in city or country?
City.
   1. Age when married?

   2. Occupations?
      Household.

   3. Health?
      Poor.

   4. Age and cause of death?
      Age   70(?)   Cancer of breast.

Your husband: nationality, if American, of what descent?
American
   1. Date of birth?
      Oct. 29th 1866.

   2. Early life in city or country?
      Country.

   3. Height?
      6 ft.

BLANK NO. 10   SERIES II, FORM B.

4. Weight?

   160 [lbs.].

5. Muscular or weak?

   Muscular.

6. Where educated? degrees if any?

   Haverford A.B., Johns Hopkins Ph.D. Germany

7. If a college man, has he been athletic?

   Somewhat.

8. Complexion?

   Fair.

9. Temperament?

   Even.

10. Does he use tobacco?

    No.

11. Occupations?

    Teacher.

12. Health?

    Good.

13. Diseases in his family: Nervous Disorders? Rheumatism?
    Consumption? Dyspepsia? Varicose Veins? Heart Disease?
    Hernia? Habitual Constipation? Catarrh?

       Rheumatism

BLANK NO. 10   SERIES II, FORM B.

Yourself:

1. Date of birth:

   July 5th, 1868.

2. Early life in city or country?

   City.

3. Height?

4. Weight?

   About 135 [lbs.].

5. Complexion?

   Fair.

6. Temperament?

   Nervous.

7. Where educated, give degrees if any?

   Private schools.

8. Occupations before marriage? a) in city or country? b) time spent in each?

   (a) In city. Assistant in a Kindergarten

   (b) for 1 1/2 yrs.

9. Diseases in your family? from father or mother's side? Nervous Disorders? Rheumatism? Consumption? Dyspepsia? Varicose Veins? Heart Disease? Hernia? Habitual Constipation? Catarrh?

   Rheumatism

BLANK NO. 10   SERIES II, FORM B.

10. General health before marriage? b) since marriage?

    Good.

    Paralysis? Brain Fever? Chronic Headache? Nervous
    Prostration? Catarrh? Hernia? Dyspepsia? Habitual
    Constipation? Inflammation of Bowels? Pleurisy? Bronchitis?
    Shortness of Breath? Spitting Blood? Consumption? Laryngitis?
    Tonsillitis? Insomnia? Rheumatism? Pneumonia? Jaundice?
    Varicose Veins? Any other diseases?

    ["Slightly" appears after Varicose Veins.]

11. Menstruation:

    First menstruation at what age? and when thoroughly established?

    13 1/2 yrs. Always regular.

    Present condition as regards menstruation:

    (a) How frequent?

    (b) Is it regular or not?

    (c) Amount? how many napkins?

    (d) Duration?

    (e) Pain or not? at what time as to the flow, before, during,
        or after?

    (f) Is there any leucorrhoea (whites)? character?

        Slight.

        Amount?

        Constant or occasional?

        Occasional.

    (g) Have you pain either frequently or habitually in the head,
        small of the back? abdomen or limbs?

    (h) Disease or trouble in Uterus (womb) or other pelvic organs?

BLANK NO. 10   SERIES II, FORM B.

   (i) Habit of bowels; how often?

       Regular, once sometimes twice a day.

12. What knowledge of sexual physiology had you before marriage?

    Very slight.

    (b) How did you obtain it?

        Mostly from Tokology.

13. Number of times married. If more than once additional
    blanks will be furnished you to answer the following ques-
    tions separately in regard to each marriage?

14. Number of years married?

    2 1/2 years.

15. Do you habitually sleep with you husband?

    Yes.

    (b) What reason for so doing or not?

        Preference

16. Number of conceptions?

    2.

17. Number of children? State in connection with each, a) date
    of birth? b) sex? c) whether healthy or not? d) note any
    characteristic and the cause. e) note either immediate or
    after effect on your health of the birth of each of your
    children. f) give time of first menstruation after birth of
    each child.

    (a) Nov. 3rd, 1892. First child.

    (b) First child son.

BLANK NO. 10									SERIES II, FORM B.

    (c) Perfectly healthy.

    (d)

    (e) Very ill at birth of first child; in poor health for 6 months. Then health excellent.

    (f) Either 4 or 6 weeks.

18. Did conception occur by choice or accident?

    First conception by choice. Second by accident.

19. Habit of intercourse, average number of times per week? per month? per year?

    1st time 5 months after marriage. Then not until 7 mos. after our first child was born. After that twice a week usually.

20. Was intercourse held during pregnancy? If so, how often?

    Not during first pregnancy. Yes during second pregnancy. Once or twice a week until 6th or 7th month. Not after that.

    (b) Had you any desire for it during this period?

        Yes, at times.

21. At other times have you any desire for intercourse?

    Yes.

    (a) How often?

    (b) At what time in relation to your menses?

        Immediately after menstruation.

22. Is intercourse agreeable to you or not?

    Yes.

BLANK NO. 10   SERIES II, FORM B.

Do you always have a venereal orgasm?

No, but usually.

1. - When you do,

(a) Effect immediately afterwards?

   I think there is more exhaustion.

(b) Effect next day?

2. - When you do not,

(a) Effect immediately afterwards?

(b) Effect next day?

23. What do you believe to be the true purpose of intercourse?

(a) Necessity to man? to woman?

   No. [The woman's single negative response applied to both sexes.]

(b) Pleasure?

   Not solely.

(c) Reproduction?

(d) What other reasons beside reproduction are sufficient to warrant intercourse?

   I think to the man and woman married from love, it may be used <u>temperately</u>, as one of the highest manifestations of love, granted us by our Creator.

24. Have you ever used any means to prevent conception?

Yes.

(a) If so, what?

   Sulphate of zinc. It is not infallible.

BLANK NO. 10   SERIES II, FORM B.

   (b) Effect on your health?

   None.

25. What, to you, would be an ideal habit?

   Occasional intercourse, with control over conception (?), everything to be absolutely mutual.

BLANK NO. 11   SERIES II, FORM B.
[Date: July 1894?]

Your Father:

1. Nationality; if American, of what descent?

    American of English descent; from New England colonists.

2. Home in city or country before marriage?

    Country and college town.

3. Home in city or country after marriage?

    City.

4. Age when married?

    25 yrs. 7 mos.

5. Occupations before your birth?

    Teacher and school Supt.

    (b) After your birth?

        Teacher and school Supt.

6. Health previous to your birth?

    Good.

    (b) After your birth?

        Good, except from brain overwork for 2 [years].

7. Number of children living?

    (a) Boys: 1

    (b) Girls: 4

BLANK NO. 11   SERIES II, FORM B.

8. Number of children dead; give age at time of death and cause.

   (a) Boys: All living.

   (b) Girls: All living.

9. If your father is living, give his age and present health; if dead, age at death and cause?

   Living, aged 69 yrs. 4 mos.

10. Name any diseases in his family:

    No special diseases, unless a bilious tendency, with occasionally an [apparent] heart complication.

Your Paternal Grandfather: home in city or country?
Country.

1. Age when married?

   27 yrs.

2. Occupations?

   Farmer-pioneer in west New York.

3. Health?

   Better than average. Iron constitution.

4. Number of children?

   3

   Number reaching maturity?

   All.

BLANK NO. 11   SERIES II, FORM B.

Your Paternal Grandmother: home in city or country?
Country.
   1. Age when married?
      31 yrs.

   2. Occupations?
      Farmer's daughter, I believe, and teacher.

   3. Health?
      Hysterical in early life. Good since.

   4. Age and cause of death?
      96 yrs. Died of old age.

Your Mother:
   1. Nationality; if American, of what descent?
      American-English. From New Eng. colonists.

   2. Home in city or country before marriage?
      Small towns and city.
      (b) Home in city or country after marriage?
          City.

   3. Occupations before her marriage?
      Teacher
      (b) After her marriage?
          Domestic.

BLANK NO. 11   SERIES II, FORM B.

    4. Note any prenatal influences before your birth.

    5. Her health previous to your birth?

       Good.

      (b) After your birth?

       Good.

    6. Number of miscarriages?

       None, so far as she knows. Possibly one early abortion.

    7. Her age if living, and present health? if not, age at time of death and cause:

       Living, aged 67 yrs. In ordinarily good health. Lungs a little sensitive, perhaps, not diseased.

    8. How was your mother's health affected by the climacteric (change of life)?

       Never felt it enough to consult physician. Grew fleshy then.

    9. Name any diseases in her family.

Your Maternal Grandfather: home in city or country?

Small towns. Later in city.

    1. Age when married?

       24 yrs.

    2. Occupations?

       Teaching. Later engaged in business.

BLANK NO. 11   SERIES II, FORM B.

   3. Health?

      Fair health, but subject to attacks of pleurisy, or taking cold.

   4. Number of children?

      2

      (b) Number reaching maturity?

         Only one.

Your Maternal Grandmother: home in city or country?
Small towns. Later in city.

   1. Age when married?

      26.

   2. Occupations?

      Taught before marriage.

   3. Health?

      Not very good. **Dyspeptic** tonsils, principally.

   4. Age and cause of death?

      Died when nearly ninety-two. Cause, old age and exhaustion of digestive powers.

Your Husband: Nationality; if American, of what descent?
American-English. (Descended from Pilgrim Fathers & Salem witches.)

   1. Date of birth?

      June 29, 1864.

BLANK NO. 11   SERIES II, FORM B.

2. Early life in city or country?
   City.

3. Height?
   5 ft. 10 1/2 in.

4. Weight?
   208 lbs.

5. Muscular or weak?
   Unusually muscular. Interested in athletics.

6. Where educated? degrees if any?
   Public schools & High School of Syracuse, N.Y.

7. If a college man, has he been athletic?
   Not a college man.

8. Complexion?
   Light-complexioned, tho' not extreme.

9. Temperament?
   Sanguine.

10. Does he use tobacco?
    Never has

11. Occupations?
    Manager of manufacturing business.

BLANK NO. 11   SERIES II, FORM B.

12. Health?

   Very robust, with magnificent frame and constitution, as are all the men of his family. Early diptheria left him with enlarged tonsils, which are very susceptible to colds.

13. Diseases in his family? Nervous Disorders? Rheumatism? Consumption? Dyspepsia? Varicose Veins? Heart Disease? Hernia? Habitual Constipation? Catarrh?

   No special disease, unless possibly a little bronchial trouble. No inherited disease.

Yourself:

1. Date of birth.

   May 18, 1861.

2. Early life in city or country?

   City, with country influences.

3. Height?

   5 ft. 4 in.

4. Weight?
   120 lbs.   Normal weight before marriage, 128 lbs.

5. Complexion?

   Medium light.

6. Temperament?

7. Where educated, give degrees if any?

   Public Schools & Normal, Oswego, N.Y. Degree of Bachelor of Music, Syracuse Univ.

BLANK NO. 11   SERIES II, FORM B.

8. Occupations before marriage? a) in city or country? b) time spent in each?

   a) & b) - 1 yr. teaching in Primary School, Boston, Mass.
            1   "   "   Young Ladies' Sem, Clinton, N.Y.

9. Diseases in your family? from father or mother's side? Nervous Disorders? Rheumatism? Consumption? Dyspepsia? Varicose Veins? Heart Disease? Hernia? Habitual Constipation? Catarrh?

   No special diseases from either side.

10. General health before marriage? b) since marriage? Paralysis? Brain Fever? Chronic Headache? Nervous Prostration? Catarrh? Hernia? Dyspepsia? Habitual Constipation? Inflammation of Bowels? Pleurisy? Bronchitis? Shortness of Breath? Spitting Blood? Consumption? Laryngitis? Tonsillitis, Insomnia, Rheumatism, Pneumonia, Jaundice? Varicose Veins? Any other diseases

   (a) Do not remember having a physician called to see me before marriage. Believe, however, had attacks of fever & ague when a child.

   (b) A slight trouble for a year or so from constipation, now disappeared. Was down with malarial fever for several weeks after birth of second baby. Unusually well aside from this.

11. Menstruation:

   First menstruation at what age? and when thoroughly established?

   14 yrs., I believe. Cannot answer last question.

   Present condition as regards menstruation:

   (a) How frequent?

      Once in 4 weeks.

   (b) Is it regular or not?

      Regular to a day, unless set back by a cold.

BLANK NO. 11   SERIES II, FORM B.

    (c) Amount? how many napkins?

        Very profuse flowing for two days, then lessening for three or four more. Perhaps seven napkins at a time.

    (d) Duration?

    (e) Pain or not? at what time as to the flow, before it is established, When? After?

        No pain. Quite lanquid for one day, tire more easily that day.

    (f) Is there any leucorrhoea (whites)? character?

        Occasionally - thick white.

        Amount?

        Very little, hardly enough for me to notice ever.

        Constant or occasional?

        Occasional, after unusually hard work.

    (g) Have you pain either frequently or habitually in the head, small of the back? abdomen or limbs?

        None - slight sick headache five or six times a year.

    (h) Disease or trouble in Uterus (womb) or other pelvic organs?

        None.

    (i) Habit of bowels; how often?

        Ordinarily regular, once a day. Occasional trouble with constipation.

12. What knowledge of sexual physiology had you before marriage? b) how did you obtain it?

    (a) None to speak of. Nothing at all definite in my mind.

    (b) Miss Shepard's "Talks with Girls." So innocent of the matter that until I was eighteen I did not know the origin of babies.

BLANK NO. 11   SERIES II, FORM B.

13. Number of times married. If more than once additional blanks will be furnished you to answer the following questions separately in regard to each marriage?

    Once.

14. Number of years married?

    7 yrs. (Present date, July '94.)

15. Do you habitually sleep with your husband? b) what reason for so doing or not?

    Yes, as I know no reason for not doing so, and preferred company at night.

16. Number of conceptions?

    Three.

17. Number of children? State in connection with each a) date of birth? b) sex? c) whether healthy or not. d) note any characteristic and the cause. e) note either immediate or after effect on your health of the birth of each of your children. f) give time of first menstruation after birth of each child.

    1. - Frances

    (a) Feb. 12, 1888.

    (b) Girl.

    (c) Yes, though she takes cold readily, and has had two short attacks of pneumonia.

    (d) Very sensitive; feelings easily hurt. Have always laid it to prenatal influence, as I was unnaturally and morbidly sensitive during the 9 mos. preceding her birth.

    (e) No apparent effect on me except in loss of flesh.

    (f) 1st menstruation at 2 mos. This has been the case each time and was the same with my mother and grandmother.

BLANK NO. 11   SERIES II, FORM B.

2. - Hazel

(a) July 21, 1889.

(b) Girl.

(c) Unusual health.

(d) Very happy, but [fiery] Original and will make tools if she cannot find them. Her father's father is an unusual inventive genius.

(e) Have been stronger physically since I recovered from the malarial fever which followed her birth. She was necessarily a "bottle baby."

(f) See 1. - (f).

3. - Benjamin

(a) July 4, 1893.

(b) Boy.

(c) Excellent health.

(d) Everyone remarks his extreme good nature. He is like his father in this and I was very happy beforehand.

(e) Stronger and adding flesh.

(f) See 1. - (f). Menstruation at long, irregular intervals now.

18. Did conception occur by choice or accident?

1st child, by choice, and born just 9 mos. from date of conception. 2nd child, by accident, but not regretted. 3rd child, by choice. He had been wanted for some time before conceived.

19. Habit of intercourse, average number of times per week?

Per month?

Three or four.

BLANK NO. 11   SERIES II, FORM B.

20. Was intercourse held during pregnancy? If so, how often?
    b) Had you any desire for it during this period?

    Yes; as usual at first, not so often later. I had not so
    frequent desire for it as when in normal condition.

21. At other times have you any desire for intercourse? a) how
    often? b) at what time in relation to your menses?

    Yes; usually about once a week, but more intensely directly
    before or during menses.

22. Is intercourse agreeable to you or not?

    Very seldom disagreeable. Usually very delightful.

    Do you always have a venereal orgasm?

    Usually, not so often as my husband.

    1. When you do?

    (a) Effect immediately afterwards?

        Very sleepy and comfortable. No disgust, as I have
        often heard it described.

    (b) Effect next day?

        Sometimes a little stupid. Occasionally I have laid a
        headache to it.

    2. When you do not?

    (a) Effect immediately afterwards?

    (b) Effect next day?

23. What do you believe to be the true purpose of intercourse?

    (a) Necessity to man? to woman?

        To both to some degree.

    (b) Pleasure?

        Partially.

BLANK NO. 11   SERIES II, FORM B.

    (c) Reproduction?

        Primarily.

    (d) What other reasons beside reproduction are sufficient to warrant intercourse?

        I have taken it as a sedative, and have known of its relieving immediately a fallen or displaced womb.

24. Have you ever used any means to prevent conception?

    (a) If so, what?

        Either desisting entirely, or, if apparently necessary, my husband withdraws, that is, during the two weeks following menstruation.

    (b) Effect on your health?

        Can see no effect.

25. What, to you, would be an ideal habit?

    Once a month, when both are well, and during the menstrual period, unless best to avoid conception, and in the daylight.

26. Additional notes:

BLANK NO. 12   SERIES II, FORM B.

Your Father:
1. Nationality, if American, of what descent?
   English and Scotch-Irish.

2. Home in city or country before marriage?
   Country.

3. Home in city or country after marriage?
   Small city; house in country.

4. Age when married?
   25 yrs. 7 mos.

5. Occupations before your birth?
   Teaching and studying.
   (b) After your birth?
   Teaching and school **superintendence.**

6. Health previous to your birth?
   Excellent.
   (b) After your birth?
   Excellent.

7. Number of children living?
   (a) Boys: One
   (b) Girls: Four

8. Number of children dead; give age at time of death and cause.
   (a) Boys: None.
   (b) Girls: None.

BLANK NO. 12					SERIES II, FORM B.

9. If your father is living, give his age and present health, if dead, age at death and cause?

   My father is living, at 68, hale and hearty.

10. Name any diseases in his family:

    Disposition to biliousness; and heart-weakness?   No diseases.

Your Paternal Grandfather: home in city or country?
Country.

1. Age when married?

   26 yrs. 11 mos.

2. Occupations?

   Farming

3. Health?

   Sound; died of pneumonia at 87 yrs. 8 1/2 mos.

4. Number of children?

   3

   (b) Number reaching maturity?

   3

Your Paternal Grandmother: home in city or country?
Country

1. Age when married?

   31 yrs.

BLANK NO. 12   SERIES II, FORM B.

   2. Occupations?

      Teaching and housekeeping; **spinning, weaving,** &c., &c.

   3. Health?

      Always delicate

   4. Age and cause of death?

      96 yrs. less 19 days. "Died of old age."

Your Mother:

   1. Nationality, if American, of what descent?

      English

   2. Home in city or country before marriage?

      Small city

      (b) Home in city or country after marriage?

      Small city; country.

   3. Occupations before her marriage?

      Teaching and housekeeping.

      (b) After her marriage?

         Housekeeping and rearing of children.

         Age when married - 23 yrs. 1 month.

   4. Note any prenatal influences before your birth:

      "Life moved on in a quiet and systematic way, but brought
      me into contact with delightfully agreeable and congenial
      people outside my home-circle, and you do not need to be
      told that my home life has been from the first bright and

BLANK NO. 12   SERIES II, FORM B.

cheery as a dear husband's unswerving and tenderest love could make it."

5. Her health previous to your birth?

   Excellent. "Never a sick or unhappy hour during the period of gestation."

   (b) After your birth?

   Excellent.

6. Number of miscarriages?

   None, to her knowledge; a possible one when I was about five.

7. Her age if living and present health? if not, age at time of death and cause?

   66, and very well indeed.

8. How was your mother's health affected by the climacteric (change of life).

   She does not think it was affected at all. "As I felt perfectly well, I never consulted a physician."

9. Name any diseases in her family

   None.

Your Maternal Grandfather: home in city or country?

Village and small cities.

1. Age when married?

   24

BLANK NO. 12   SERIES II, FORM B.

   2. Occupations?

      Teaching

   3. Health?

      Fair, but delicate lungs

   4. Number of children?

      2

      (b) Number reaching maturity?

          1

Your Maternal Grandmother: home in city or country?
Country, before marriage

   1. Age when married?

      26

   2. Occupations?

      Teaching and housekeeping

   3. Health?

      Delicate

   4. Age and cause of death?

      Nearly 92; exhaustion of digestive [powers?] and old age.

Your Husband: nationality, if American, of what descent?
Dutch and German

BLANK NO. 12   SERIES II, FORM B.

1. Date of birth?
   1860, July

2. Early life in city or country?
   Country.

3. Height?
   5 ft. 10 1/2 inches.

4. Weight?
   180 lbs.

5. Muscular or weak?
   Muscular.

6. Where educated? degrees if any?
   Oswego Normal School, Cornell, Indiana - A.B., M.S.

7. If a college man, has he been athletic?
   No.

8. Complexion?
   Blond

9. Temperament?
   Sanguine

10. Does he use tobacco?
    Occasionally.

BLANK NO. 12   SERIES II, FORM B.

11. Occupations?

   Teaching and studying.

12. Health?

   Seems perfect.

13. Diseases in his family: Nervous Disorders? Rheumatism? Consumption? Dyspepsia? Varicose Veins? Heart Disease? Hernia? Habitual Constipation? Catarrh?

   Hernia and scrofulous tendencies.

Yourself:

1. Date of birth?

   1850, Sept.

2. Early life in city or country?

   Small city and country.

3. Height?

   5 ft. 2 1/2 inches.

4. Weight?

   118 lbs.

5. Complexion?

   Sallow

6. Temperament?

   Sanguine and nervous

BLANK NO. 12   SERIES II, FORM B.

7. Where educated, give degrees if any?

   Oswego Normal School, Ann Arbor, Cambridge England. A.B.

8. Occupations before marriage? a) in city or country? b) time spent in each?

   Teaching, studying and book-making; mostly lived in the country, with occasional seasons in cities.

9. Diseases in your family? from father or mother's side? Nervous Disorders? Rheumatism? Consumption? Dyspepsia? Varicose Veins? Heart Disease? Hernia? Habitual Constipation? Catarrh?

   None.

10. General health before marriage? b) since marriage? Paralysis? Brain Fever? Chronic Headache? Nervous Prostration? Catarrh? Hernia? Dyspepsis? Habitual Constipation? Inflammation of Bowels? Pleurisy? Bronchitis? Shortness of Breath? Spitting Blood? Consumption? Laryngitis? Tonsillitis? Insomnia? Rheumatism? Pneumonia? Jaundice? Varicose Veins?

    (a) Generally delicate - Malaria, weak heart, tendency to hysteria.

    (b) Generally delicate - Malaria, weak heart, tendency to hysteria. On the whole, much quieter and better since marriage. Much improved except the heart.

11. Menstruation:

    First menstruation at what age? and when thoroughly established?

    14; 14.

    Present condition as regards menstruation:

    (a) How frequent?

        Once in 3 or four weeks.

BLANK NO. 12   SERIES II, FORM B.

   (b) Is it regular or not?

       Regular

   (c) Amount? how many napkins?

       From 6 to 12.

   (d) Duration?

       From 3 to 7 days.

   (e) Pain or not? at what time as to the flow?

       No pain now; subject to terrible menstrual colic before marriage, which has totally disappeared since. Heaviest flow the second day.

   (f) Is there any leucorrhoea (whites)? character?

       No.

       Amount?

       Constant or occasional?

   (g) Have you pain either frequently or habitually in the head, small of the back? abdomen or limbs?

       No.

   (h) Disease or trouble in Uterus (womb) or other pelvic organs?

       No.

   (i) Habit of bowels; how often?

       Once a day in [the] evening.

12. What knowledge of sexual physiology had you before marriage? b) how did you obtain it?

    I had a very complete knowledge obtained from lady physicians who were my friends.

BLANK NO. 12   SERIES II, FORM B.

13. Number of times married. If more than once additional blanks will be furnished you to answer the following questions separately in regard to each marriage?

    Once.

14. Number of years married?

    Eight years.

15. Do you habitually sleep with your husband? b) what reasons for so doing or not?

    Yes, when he is at home. I sleep much better and feel altogether more comfortable. The first year in [**our marriage?**], I had a separate bed, believing that was the right thing; but I abandoned it entirely before the end of the year.

16. Number of conceptions?

    One.

17. Number of children? State in connection with each, a) date of birth? b) sex? c) whether healthy or not? d) note any characteristic and the cause. e) note either immediate or after effect on your health of the birth of each of your children. f) give time of first menstruation after birth of each child.

    One child, a perfectly formed boy of twelve pounds weight, and unusual size; head especially large. Child died during labor on account of its length and **severity, the doctor** said. I think I have never had quite the <u>strength</u> since. My illness was unusually long and **severe.** <u>I began to</u> menstruate in the seventh month after my confinement.

18. Did conception occur by choice or accident?

    By accident, but with the thought of its possibility.

19. Habit of intercourse, average number of times per week?

    per month?

    Once or twice.

137

BLANK NO. 12   SERIES II, FORM B.

per year?

20. Was intercourse held during pregnancy? If so, how often?
    b) had you any desire for it during this period?

    Possibly once; I don't remember; I did not notice any apprec-
    iable effect upon myself as to desire.

21. At other times have you any desire for intercourse?

    Yes.

    (a) How often?

    (b) At what time in relation to your menses?

        I think rather more before and after menstruation.

22. Is intercourse agreeable to you or not?

    Yes.

    Do you always have a venereal orgasm?

    Almost invariably.

    1. - When you do?

    (a) Effect immediately afterwards?

        Absolute physical harmony.

    (b) Effect next day?

        Hard to say; often a greater feeling of strength and
        composure; sometimes, physical weariness.

    2. - When you do not?

    (a) Effect immediately afterwards? (b) Effect next day?

        Depressing and revolting.

BLANK NO. 12   SERIES II, FORM B.

23. What do you believe to be the true purpose of intercourse?

   (a) Necessity to man? to woman?

   Not <u>necessary</u> to either.

   (b) Pleasure?

   Not sensual pleasure, but the pleasure of love.

   (c) Reproduction?

   Material purpose.

   (d) What other reasons beside reproduction are sufficient to warrant intercourse?

   I do not think this reason alone warrants it at all; I think it is only warranted as an expression of true and passionate love. That is the prime condition for a happy conception, I fancy.

24. Have you ever used any means to prevent conception? a) if so, what?

   Selection of time for intercourse.

   (b) Effect on your health?

   I cannot say that there has been any.

25. What, to you, would be an ideal habit?

   No <u>habit</u> at all, but the most sensitive regard of each member of the couple for the personal feeling and desires and health of the other. In fact, pure and tender <u>love</u>, wide awake to the whole of life, should dictate marriage relations.

BLANK NO. 13   SERIES II, FORM B.

Date: [1892?]

Your Father:

1. Nationality, if American, of what descent?
   American. English(?)

2. Home in city or country before marriage?
   Early in country later in [city].

3. Home in city or country after marriage?
   Country

4. Age when married?
   30 about.

5. Occupations before your birth?
   Brought up on a farm, merchant **country** [**store?**].
   (b) after your birth?
      Manufacturing business

6. Health previous to your birth?
   Good
   (b) after your birth?
      Good. At 70 looks to be about 55.

7. Number of children living:
   (a) Boys: 1
   (b) Girls: 2

BLANK NO. 13   SERIES II, FORM B.

   8. Number of children dead; give age at time of death and cause.

      (a) Boys:

      (b) Girls:

   9. If your father is living, give his age and present health,
      if dead, age at death and cause?

      69 good

   10. Name any diseases in his family:

Your Paternal Grandfather: home in city or country?
Country

   1. Age when married?

   2. Occupations?

      Farmer

   3. Health?

      Good

   4. Number of children?

      13

      number reaching maturity?

      Probably 12

Your Paternal Grandmother: home in city or country?
[Probably country]

   1. Age when married?

      16

BLANK NO. 13   SERIES II, FORM B.

   2. Occupations?

   3. Health?

     Good

   4. Age and cause of death?

Your Mother:

   1. Nationality, if American of what descent?

     American. English

   2. Home in city or country before marriage?

     Country except for 2 or 3 yrs. before marriage.

    (b) Home in city or country after marriage?

       Country

   3. Occupations before her marriage?

    (b) after her marriage?

       Housewife

   4. Note any prenatal influences before your birth:

   5. Her health previous to your birth?

     Never very strong

    (b) after your birth?

       Very delicate, never very strong. Always had a very hard time at birth of her children.

   6. Number of miscarriages?

     Thinks none

BLANK NO. 13   SERIES II, FORM B.

   7. Her age if living and present health? If not, age at time of
      death and cause?
      64, feeble

   8. How was your mother's health affected by the climacteric
      (change of life)?

      Better since. Very miserable, thin, flowed dreadfully.
      "Seemed as if she would lose her mind. Wandered
      back to her old home nearby in the night because she was
      sleepless."

   9. Name any diseases in her family:

      Father died of Dropsy.

Your Maternal Grandfather: home in city or country?

Country

   1. Age when married?

   2. Occupations?

   3. Health?

   4. Number of children?

      8

      (b) Number reaching maturity?

         7

Your Maternal Grandmother: home in city or country?

Country

   1. Age when married?

   2. Occupations?

BLANK NO. 13   SERIES II, FORM B.

   3. Health?

   4. Age and cause of death?

Your Husband: nationality, if American, of what descent?
American
   1. Date of birth?
      24 Dec. 18[5?]9--33 [years old now?]

   2. Early life in city or country?
      Country

   3. Height?
      5 [ft.,] 10 [in.]

   4. Weight?
      165 [lbs.]

   5. Muscular or weak?
      Muscular

   6. Where educated? degrees if any?
      Colorado University, A.B. & A.M.

   7. If a college man, has he been athletic?
      No, because he is lame

   8. Complexion?
      Dark

BLANK NO. 13   SERIES II, FORM B.

9. Temperament?

   Cool, calm & collected

10. Does he use tobacco?

    Never

11. Occupations?

    Teaching at present. Brought up on a ranch until 14 years old. Thrown from his horse & hip injured.

12. Health?

    Good. Had Typhoid fever before marriage.

13. Diseases in his family: Nervous Disorders? Rheumatism? Consumption? Dyspepsia? Varicose Veins? Heart Disease? Hernia? Habitual Consumption? Catarrh?

    [His mother had rheumatism, consumption, and habitual constipation. Twenty-five years ago, she almost died of consumption. She must live in Colorado. His father had lung trouble, but did not die of it.]

Yourself:

1. Date of birth?

   1863

2. Early life in city or country?

   Country

3. Height?

   5 [ft.,] 1 1/2 [in.]

BLANK NO. 13   SERIES II, FORM B.

4. Weight?

   125 [lbs.]--2 years ago.

5. Complexion?

   [Not?] blond, brown eyes and brown hair.

6. Temperament?

   Fly in 40,000 pieces in a minute.

7. Where educated, give degrees if any?

   In Canada Wesleyan Methodist College. Music.

8. Occupations before marriage? a) in city or country? b) time spent in each?

   Taught music (Washington, D.C.) [for] 4 years.

9. Diseases in your family? from father or mother's side? Nervous Disorders? Rheumatism? Consumption? Dyspepsia? Varicose Veins? Heart Disease? Hernia? Habitual Constipation? Catarrh?

   [When No. 13 was small, her mother had dyspepsia and varicose veins.]

10. General health before marriage? b) since marriage? Paralysis? Brain Fever? Chronic Headache? Nervous Prostration? Catarrh? Hernia? Dyspepsia? Habitual Constipation? Inflammation of Bowels? Pleurisy? Bronchitis? Shortness of Breath? Spitting Blood? Consumption? Laryngitis? Tonsillitis? Insomnia? Rheumatism? Pneumonia? Jaundice? Varicose Veins?

    (a) Good [except for] congestion of liver.

    (b)

11. Menstruation:

    First menstruation at what age?

    12

BLANK NO. 13   SERIES II, FORM B.

and when thoroughly established?

12

Present condition as regards menstruation:

(a) How frequent?

   Few days over 4 weeks.

(b) Is it regular or not?

   Regular

(c) Amount? how many napkins?

   Every other time flows dreadfully.   (Perfectly regular & normal amount before marriage.)

(d) Duration?

   5 or 6 days sometimes more.

(e) Pain or not? at what time as to the flow?

   Very little [pain the] day before the flow.

(f) Is there any leucorrhoea (whites)? character?

   Very little.

   amount?

   Very little.

   constant or occasional?

   [Constant] just before period.

(g) Have you pain either frequently or habitually in the head, small of the back? abdomen or limbs?

   Pain in back almost constantly from bladder trouble.

(h) Disease or trouble in Uterus (womb) or other pelvic organs?

(i) Habit of bowels; how often?

   Regular, once a day.

BLANK NO. 13   SERIES II, FORM B.

12. What knowledge of sexual physiology had you before marriage?
    b) how did you obtain it?

    Good deal. "Told by the [loveliest?] woman I ever knew who
    had been married about 2 years."

13. Number of times married. If more than once additional blanks
    will be furnished you to answer the following questions
    separately in regard to each marriage?

    Once

14. Number of years married?

    Almost 7.

15. Do you habitually sleep with your husband? b) **what** reasons
    for so doing or not?

    (a) No. Not since first year.

    (b) **No because of children. The babies disturb the husband
    and he can not sleep again.**

16. Number of conceptions?

    2

17. Number of children? State in connection with each, a) date
    of birth? b) sex? c) whether healthy or not? d) note any
    characteristic and the cause. e) note either immediate or
    after effect on your health of the birth of each of your
    children. f) give time of first menstruation after birth
    of each child.

    [First child]

        (a) [He was born on] June 10, '87--9 mo. & 8 days after
            marriage.

        (b) boy

        (c) very healthy, has had congestion of lungs twice.

        (d) came near having quick consumption, reduced from 125

BLANK NO. 13   SERIES II, FORM B.

            to 90 lbs. Dyspepsia after birth.

        (f) Weaned at 13 or 14 months, menstruated at once.
            Great trouble with breasts.

    [Second child]

        (a) 28 Apr. 1892.

        (b) boy

        (c) very healthy

        (d)

        (e) Severe labour, hemorrhage, bladder trouble induced
            by use of catheter, bacteria caused bladder trouble.

        (f) Weaned at one year. Menstruated 2 or 3 days later.

18. Did conception occur by choice or accident?

    Accident

    [First child] Not deliberate choice, knew it would result.

    [Second child] Deliberate, long hoped for, planned for,
    for 2 years.

19. Habit of intercourse, average number of times per week?

    1 on average.

    per month?

    per year?

    No special regularity but sometimes more sometimes less but
    the average for a year [is] 1 **per wk. First year [of marriage],
    oftener.**

20. Was intercourse held during pregnancy? If so, how often?

    Not so often.

    (b) Had you any desire for it during this period?

BLANK NO. 13   SERIES II, FORM B.

>>Yes. Usual time in the month when period would have come. If slept alone never would desire.

21 At other times have you any desire for intercourse?

>>Yes.

>>(a) How often?

>>>Just before & after menstruation.

>>(b) At what time in relation to your menses?

22. Is intercourse agreeable to you or not?

>>Yes.

>>Do you always have a venereal orgasm?

>>Not always.

>>1. - When you do,

>>(a) Effect immediately afterwards?

>>>Sleep, quieted.

>>(b) Effect next day?

>>2. - When you do not,

>>(a) Effect immediately afterwards?

>>>Nervous, fidgety. Not sleepy.

>>(b) Effect next day?

23. What do you believe to be the true purpose of intercourse?

>>(a) Necessity to man?

>>>Yes. Much more to man than woman.

>>necessity to woman?

>>>Yes.

BLANK NO. 13   SERIES II, FORM B.

   (b) Pleasure?

       Yes.

   (c) Reproduction?

       Yes.

   (d) What other reasons beside reproduction are sufficient to
       warrant intercourse?

       Natural instinct & not satisfied [meaning unclear],
       necessary to married happiness. "Oh but I believe in
       temperance in it."

24. Have you ever used any means to prevent conception? a) if
    so, what?

    Syringe

    (b) Effect on your health?

        None

25. What, to you, would be an ideal habit?

    Once a week

BLANK NO. 14   SERIES II, FORM B.

Your Father:

1. Nationality, if American, of what descent?
   American

2. Home in city or country before marriage?
   City

3. Home in city or country after marriage?
   City

4. Age when married?
   28

5. Occupations before your birth?
   Preaching
   (b) After your birth?
       Preaching

6. Health previous to your birth?
   Good, so far as I know.
   (b) After your birth?
       Probably good.

7. Number of children living?
   (a) Boys: 3
   (b) Girls: 4

8. Number of children dead; give age at time of death and cause:
   Two boys. First died a few hours after birth from premature

BLANK NO. 14   SERIES II, FORM B.

   birth. Second in infancy from scarlet fever.

 9. If your father is living, give his age and present health,
    if dead, age at death and cause?

    Forty nine - R.R. accident.

10. Name any diseases in his family:

    I know very little about the family.

Your Paternal Grandfather: home in city or country?
City.

 1. Age when married?

 2. Occupations?

    City business of some sort.

 3. Health?

 4. Number of children?

    Number reaching maturity?

    4

Your Paternal Grandmother: home in city or country?

 1. Age when married?

    Young.

 2. Occupations?

    Before the day of Ladies' occupations.

BLANK NO. 14   SERIES II, FORM B.

   3. Health?

   4. Age and cause of death?
      About 42. Some acute throat disease

Your Mother:
   1. Nationality, if American of what descent?
      Scotch Irish.

   2. Home in city or country before marriage?
      City
     (b) Home in city or country after marriage?
        City

   3. Occupations before her marriage?
      Home work.
     (b) After her marriage?
        Rearing children.

   4. Note any prenatal influences before your birth:

   5. Her health previous to your birth?
     (b) After your birth?
        She was always "well."

   6. Number of miscarriages?
      1

BLANK NO. 14   SERIES II, FORM B.

   7. Her age if living and present health? if not, age at time of
      death and cause?

      Seventy - good.

   8. How was your mother's health affected by the climacteric
      (change of life)?

      Not at all.

   9. Name any diseases in her family:

Your Maternal Grandfather: home in city or country?
New town

   1. Age when married?

   2. Occupations?

      Physician

   3. Health?

      Good

   4. Number of children?

      10

      (b) Number reaching maturity?

         9

Your Maternal Grandmother: home in city or country?

   1. Age when married?

   2. Occupations?

155

BLANK NO. 14   SERIES II, FORM B.

   3. Health?
   Good.

   4. Age and cause of death?
   92. "Old age."

Your Husband: nationality, if American, of what descent?
German descent

   1. Date of birth?
   1859

   2. Early life in city or country?
   City.

   3. Height?
   Five feet, five in.

   4. Weight?
   135 lbs.

   5. Muscular or weak?
   Muscular.

   6. Where educated? degrees if any?
   Butler, Ind. State U. - M.A., Ph.D., etc.

   7. If a college man, has he been athletic?
   Slightly

BLANK NO. 14   SERIES II, FORM B.

    8. Complexion?

       Neither dark nor fair.

    9. Temperament?

       Nervous

   10. Does he use tobacco?

       No

   11. Occupations?

       Teaching & work of Naturalist.

   12. Health?

       Good.

   13. Diseases in his family: Nervous Disorders? Rheumatism?
       Consumption? Dyspepsia? Varicose Veins? Heart Disease?
       Hernia? Habitual Constipation? Catarrh?

Yourself:

    1. Date of birth?

       1849

    2. Early life in city or country?

       Town.

    3. Height?

       5 ft. 4 in.

    4. Weight?

       124 lbs.

BLANK NO. 14   SERIES II, FORM B.

5. Complexion?

   Fair

6. Temperament?

7. Where educated? give degrees if any?

   B.A., W[estern] F[emale] S[eminary], Oxford, Ohio.

8. Occupations before marriage? a) in city or country? b) time spent in each?

   Teaching. Cities & towns.

9. Diseases in your family? from father or mother's side? Nervous Disorders? Rheumatism? Consumption? Dyspepsia? Varicose Veins? Heart Disease? Hernia? Habitual Constipation? Catarrh?

   Constipation from both sides.

10. General health before marriage? b) since marriage? Paralysis? Brain Fever? Chronic Headache? Nervous Prostration? Catarrh? Hernia? Dyspepsia? Habitual Constipation? Inflammation of Bowels? Pleurisy? Bronchitis? Shortness of Breath? Spitting Blood? Consumption? Laryngitis? Tonsillitis? Insomnia? Rheumatism? Pneumonia? Jaundice? Varicose Veins?

    Have never had any chronic disorder. Health generally good both before and since marriage.

11. Menstruation:

    First menstruation at what age? And when thoroughly established?

    About fifteen.

BLANK NO. 14   SERIES II, FORM B.

Present condition as regards menstruation:

(a) How frequent?

Once in four weeks.

(b) Is it regular or not?

Regular.

(c) Amount? how many napkins?

Six

(d) Duration?

Five days

(e) Pain or not? at what time as to the flow?

No pain.

(f) Is there any leucorrhoea (whites)? character?

None.

Amount?

Constant or occasional?

(g) Have you pain either frequently or habitually in the head, small of the back? abdomen or limbs?

No.

(h) Disease or trouble in Uterus (womb) or other pelvic organs?

None.

(i) Habit of bowels; how often?

Once a day.

12. What knowledge of sexual physiology had you before marriage? b) how did you obtain it?

I was fairly well acquainted with female structure from books. Knew nothing of male structure.

BLANK NO. 14   SERIES II, FORM B.

13. Number of times married. If more than once additional blanks will be furnished you to answer the following questions separately in regard to each marriage?

    Once

14. Number of years married?

    Ten

15. Do you habitually sleep with your husband? b) what reasons for so doing or not?

    Yes. Preference.

16. Number of conceptions?

    Three

17. Number of children? State in connection with each, a) date of birth? b) sex? c) whether healthy or not? d) note any characteristic and the cause. e) note either immediate or after effect on your health of the birth of each of your children. f) give time of first menstruation after birth of each child.

    [First child]

        (a) July 3d 1885.

        (b) Girl, vigorous.

        (e) Recovered quickly.

        (f) One month after birth of child.

    [Second child]

        (a) July 26, 1886.

        (b) Girl.

        (c) Healthy but not as strong as elder.

        (e) Loss of nervous force.

        (f) One month.

BLANK NO. 14   SERIES II, FORM B.

   [Third child]
      (a) June 28, 1891.
      (b) Boy.
      (c) Healthy & <u>strong</u>.
      (e) No effect.
      (f) One month.

18. Did conception occur by choice or accident?
    Both.

19. Habit of intercourse, average number of times per week?
    per month?
    Two or three
    per year?

20. Was intercourse held during pregnancy? If so, how often?
    Yes. Occasionally.
    (b) Had you any desire for it during this period?
    Yes.

21. At other times have you any desire for intercourse?
    Yes.
    (a) How often?
        Occasionally through the month.
    (b) At what time in relation to your menses?
        No especial time.

22. Is intercourse agreeable to you or not?
    Yes.

BLANK NO. 14   SERIES II, FORM B.

Do you always have a venereal orgasm?

Generally.

1. - When you do

(a) Effect immediately afterwards?

No noticeable effect.

(b) Effect next day?

None.

2. - When you do not

(a) Effect immediately afterwards?

None.

(b) Effect next day?

23. What do you believe to be the true purpose of intercourse?

(a) Necessity to man? to woman?

(b) Pleasure?

(c) Reproduction?

(d) What other reasons beside reproduction are sufficient to warrant intercourse?

Pleasure and Reproduction. I consider this appetite as ranking with other natural appetites, and like them to be indulged legitimately and temperately. I consider it illegitimate to risk bringing children into the world under any but most favorable circumstances.

24. Have you ever used any means to prevent conception? a) if so, what?

Confining intercourse to the latter part of my month.

b) Effect on your health?
25. What, to you, would be an ideal habit?

Such as I have - Where intercourse is only held when mutually

BLANK NO. 14   SERIES II, FORM B.

desired, and when no crime will be committed against possible
children.

BLANK NO. 15   SERIES II, FORM B.

Date: January, 1893.

Your Father:
   1. Nationality; if American, of what descent?
      American. English descent.

   2. Home in city or country before marriage?
      Country to age of 21, city from 21 to 28.

   3. Home in city or country after marriage?
      Country towns and villages.

   4. Age when married?
      28.

   5. Occupation before your birth?
      Minister.
      (b) After your birth?
          Minister.

   6. Health previous to your birth?
      Good.
      (b) After your birth?
          Good up to his 46th year.

   7. Number of children living?
      (a) Boys: 2.
      (b) Girls: 6.

BLANK NO. 15   SERIES II, FORM B.

   8. Number of children dead; give age at time of death and cause.
      (a) Boys: 1. This boy died a few hours after birth. I do
          not know exact cause.
      (b) Girls:

   9. If your father is living, give his age and present health,
      if dead, age at death and cause?

      Present age 61, health rather poor, as a result of a general
      break-down of nervous prostration which occurred when he was
      46, and as a direct result of overwork and overstrain.

   10. Name any diseases in his family.

       Heart disease.

Paternal Grandfather: home in city or country?
Country village & country.
   1. Age when married?

      Young.

   2. Occupations?

      Apothecary, Physician.

   3. Health?

      Good.

   4. Number of children?

      9 (at least).

      Number reaching maturity?

      3.

BLANK NO. 15					SERIES II, FORM B.

Your Paternal Grandmother: home in city or country?
Country & country village after marriage, city before.

   1. Age when married?

      Probably somewhere near twenty.

   2. Occupations?

      Housewife and mother.

   3. Health?

      Great vitality. Nervous temperament which caused constant nervous headaches. Late in life had some heart trouble.

   4. Age and cause of death?

      Died when about 75 or over. Cause of death said to be "old age" -- that is no special disease, I think.

Your Mother:

   1. Nationality; if American, of what descent?

      American, English descent &, <u>far</u> back, from Welsh.

   2. Home in city or country before marriage?

      Country.

     (b) Home in city or country after marriage?

        Country towns & villages.

   3. Occupations before her marriage?

      Studying, i.e., going to school.

     (b) After her marriage?

        Housewife & mother.

BLANK NO. 15   SERIES II, FORM B.

   4. Note any prenatal influences before your birth.

   5. Her health previous to your birth?
      (b) After your birth?
          Good.

   6. Number of miscarriages?
      None.

   7. Her age if living, and present health? if not, age at time of death and cause?

      Present age 52, health fair. She has never been robust or muscular. She has no disease, except hay-fever.

   8. How was your mother's health affected by the climacteric (change of life)?

      She had serious hemorrhages which weakened her much, and these continued for half-a-dozen years perhaps. When they ceased she became rather stronger than during these six years.

   9. Name any diseases in her family.

Your Maternal Grandfather: home in city or country?

Town and country village

   1. Age when married?

      Married 3 times, my grandmother was his second wife.

   2. Occupations?

      Lawyer, minister, banker.

BLANK NO. 15   SERIES II, FORM B.

   3. Health?

   4. Number of children?
      12 by 3 wives. 6 I think by my grandmother.
      (b) Number reaching maturity?
         8 or more. All six of my grandmother's children reached maturity.

Your Maternal Grandmother: home in city or country?
Town & country village.
   1. Age when married?

   2. Occupations?
      Housewife & mother.

   3. Health?

   4. Age and cause of death?
      Died at 32 of puerperal fever after birth of 6th child.

Your Husband: nationality; if American, of what descent?
American, Scotch and <u>I suppose</u> English.
   1. Date of birth?
      March 8, 1860.

   2. Early life in city or country?
      Country.

BLANK NO. 15   SERIES II, FORM B.

3. Height?

   About 5 ft. 5 or 6 inches.

4. Weight?

   About 150 or 160 lbs.

5. Muscular or weak?

   Medium, inclining to muscular.

6. Where educated? degrees if any?

   Rushford High School & Cornell University B.A., Ph.D.

7. If a college man, has he been athletic?

   No.

8. Complexion?

   Neither blond nor brunette, between the two.

9. Temperament?

   Non-nervous.

10. Does he use tobacco?

    No.

11. Occupations?

    Teacher, Registrar.

12. Health?

    Good at present, has always been good except for an attack of nervous-prostration three years ago which lasted some months, and from which he is but just recovering completely.

BLANK NO. 15   SERIES II, FORM B.

13. Diseases in his family: Nervous Disorders? Rheumatism?
    Consumption? Dyspepsia? Varicose Veins? Heart Disease?
    Hernia? Habitual Constipation? Catarrh?

    His mother died of consumption, considered an accidental
    case, not hereditary.

Yourself:

1. Date of birth?

    Dec. 26, 1860.

2. Early life in city or country?

    Country proper, and country villages.

3. Height?

    5 ft.

4. Weight?

    125 to 132 lbs.

5. Complexion?

    Between light and dark.

6. Temperament?

    Nervous.

7. Where educated? give degrees if any?

    Private girl's school, & Cornell University B.S.

8. Occupations before marriage? a) in city or country? b) time spent in each?

    Cataloguing books in libraries, 4 years, country town.

BLANK NO. 15   SERIES II, FORM B.

9. Diseases in your family? from father or mother's side?
   Nervous Disorders? Rheumatism? Consumption? Dyspepsia?
   Varicose Veins? Heart Disease? Hernia? Habitual Constipation? Catarrh?

   Hay fever I inherit from my mother.

10. General health before marriage? b) since marriage? Paralysis? Brain Fever? Chronic Headache? Nervous Prostration? Catarrh? Hernia? Dyspepsia? Habitual Constipation? Inflammation of Bowels? Pleurisy? Bronchitis? Shortness of Breath? Spitting Blood? Consumption? Laryngitis? Tonsillitis? Insomnia? Rheumatism? Pneumonia? Jaundice? Varicose Veins?

    Good both before and since. My health has always been good except for nervous prostration lasting a year, occurring when I was 22 or 23 and traceable directly to an unusual nervous strain. I have no disease except hay fever.

11. Menstruation:

    First menstruation at what age? and when thoroughly established?

    14; 14.

    Present condition as regards menstruation:

    (a) How frequent?

        Periods of 28 days.

    (b) Is it regular or not?

        Regular.

    (c) Amount? how many napkins?

        Perhaps ten or a dozen, rather copious flow.

    (d) Duration?

        5 to 6 days.

BLANK NO. 15   SERIES II, FORM B.

(e) Pain or not? at what time as to the flow?

Never pain except slight headache if I overdo the first day or two.

(f) Is there any leucorrheoa (whites)? character?

None.

Amount?

Constant or occasional?

(g) Have you pain either frequently or habitually in the head, small of the back? abdomen or limbs?

No. Slight headaches <u>if</u> <u>I</u> <u>overdo</u>, not otherwise.

(h) Disease or trouble in Uterus (womb) or other pelvic organs?

None.

(i) Habit of bowels; how often?

12. What knowledge of sexual physiology had you before marriage? b) how did you obtain it?

At 12 years my mother told me the facts about menstruation, and the physiology of childbirth. I knew nothing of sexual connection until I was perhaps 16 or 18 when I read about it in the textbooks to which we were referred when we studied physiology. A few months before my marriage a wise woman friend told me about the various ways of "regulating conception" in use, theories concerning the sexual relations, etc., and referred me to one or two books on the subject. These books I read before I was married.

13. Number of times married. If more than once additional blanks will be furnished you to answer the following questions separately in regard to each marriage?

Once.

14. Number of years married?

6.

BLANK NO. 15   SERIES II, FORM B.

15. Do you habitually sleep with your husband? b) what reasons for so doing or not?

   Yes. We sleep together from the choice of both of us and because of the companionship, rest, and pleasure which come with our being together.

16. Number of conceptions?

   2.

17. Number of children? State in connection with each, a) date of birth? b) sex? c) whether healthy or not? d) note any characteristic and the cause. e) note either immediate or after effect on your health of the birth of each of your children. f) give time of first menstruation after birth of each child.

   2 children.

   [First child]

      (a) April 4, 1889.

      (b) boy

      (c) healthy

      (d) Was unusually sensitive to noise during his infancy which might possibly be due to my being much disturbed by noise in the apartment house where we lived before his birth.

      (e) I noticed no material difference in my health before & after.

      (f) About 10 or 12 weeks after birth altho' I nursed him.

   [Second child]

      (a) April 15, 1893.

      (b) girl

      (c) healthy

      (d) Haven't noticed any.

BLANK NO. 15				SERIES II, FORM B.

(e) None.

(f) About 8 or ten weeks although I was nursing her.

18. Did conception occur by choice or accident?

Choice.

19. Habit of intercourse, average number of times per week? per month? per year?

There has been no uniform habit. No intercourse took place at all the first year of marriage. Then intercourse perhaps once a week until conception occurred. During the months when my husband had nervous prostration no intercourse at all. No intercourse while my first child was nursing. At other times intercourse perhaps twice a month or thrice.

20. Was intercourse held during pregnancy? If so, how often?

None.

(b) Had you any desire for it during this period?

No.

21. At other times have you any desire for intercourse?

Yes.

(a) How often?

I have observed no uniform recurrence of desire.

(b) At what time in relation to your menses?

I have often felt desire somewhat more strongly directly after the stopping of menses, not always, and I have also had the desire at the times most distant from menses. I think the strongest desire has been usually just after close of menses.

BLANK NO. 15   SERIES II, FORM B.

22. Is intercourse agreeable to you or not?

   It is agreeable when I wish it--would be unbearable if I did not.

   Do you always have a venereal orgasm?

   No. I have had but one during my whole married life, that one not complete and occasioned by my husband's being very near to me but not by intercourse.

   1. - When you do,

   (a) Effect immediately afterwards?

   (b) Effect next day?

   2. - When you do not,

   (a) Effect immediately afterwards?

   Ten minutes to half an hour afterward I feel as usual, physically.

   (b) Effect next day?

   None whatever.

23. What do you believe to be the true purpose of intercourse?

   (a) Necessity to man? to woman?

   It is my belief and my experience that intercourse is not to the comparatively normal man and woman necessary in the way in which food & drink are necessary. Whatever "necessity" there is is the same for man and woman alike and is a spiritual not a physical impulsion.

   (b) Pleasure

   (c) Reproduction?

   Both [pleasure and reproduction].

   (d) What other reasons beside reproduction are sufficient to warrant intercourse?

   The desire of both husband and wife for this expression of their union seems to me the first and highest reason for intercourse. The desire for offspring is a secondary, incidental, although entirely worthy motive but could never to me make intercourse right unless the mutual desire were also present.

24. Have you ever used any means to prevent conception? b) if so, what?

Only the means of refraining from intercourse at the times when conception is most liable to take place.

(b) Effect on your health?

Refraining from all intercourse for as long as a year has not apparently affected my health one way or the other.

25. What, to you, would be an ideal habit?

In general terms the ideal habit would be that which should most perfectly and completely serve as the physical expression of the spiritual union of husband and wife. My husband and I have not found yet what to us is an ideal habit. We believe in intercourse for its own sake -- we wish it for ourselves and spiritually miss it, rather than physically, when it does not occur, because it is the highest, most sacred expression of our oneness. On the other hand there are sometimes long periods when we are not willing to incur even a slight risk of pregnancy, and then we deny ourselves the intercourse, feeling all the time that we are losing that which keeps us closest to each other.

I wish to say that this need is absolutely spiritual so far as we can judge, possibly reacting somewhat upon the physical organization. We do not find health impaired in any way by the self denial.

BLANK NO. 16 B   SERIES II, FORM B.

Date: [Jany - January?] 4, 1892.

Your Father:

1. Nationality, if American, of what descent?

   American. English-Scotch

2. Home in city or country before marriage?

   Country

3. Home in city or country after marriage?

   Country

4. Age when married?

   24 [first marriage].

5. Occupations before your birth?

   Farmer, wrote for publication. Ed[itor of] paper, lecturer, especially social questions.

   (b) After your birth?

   [Woman was] youngest child. [Father's occupations] same as 5 [a].

6. Health previous to your birth?

   Good

   (b) After your birth?

   Good until recently, severe mental work [caused] great nervousness. Has writer's palsy.

7. Number of children living?

   (a) Boys: 2

BLANK NO. 16 B   SERIES II, FORM B.

    (b) Girls: 4

  8. Number of children dead; give age at time of death and cause
    (a) Boys: One boy, about 22.
    (b) Girls:

  9. If your father is living, give his age and present health, if dead, age at death and cause?

    68, comfortable except for weakness of age and palsy.

  10. Name any diseases in his family.

    In general good health in family.

Your Paternal Grandfather: home in city or country?
Small town almost country.

  1. Age when married?

    [Twice] married.

  2. Occupations?

    Farmer

  3. Health?

    Good

    Age 90 at death

  4. Number of children?

    4 or 5.

    Number reaching maturity?

BLANK NO. 16 B   SERIES II, FORM B.

Your Paternal Grandmother: home in city or country?

    1. Age when married?   **1st wife.**

    2. Occupations?

    3. Health?

    4. Age and cause of death?

Your Mother:

    1. Nationality, if American of what descent?

    American. German descent

    2. Home in city or country before marriage?

    Small town.

    (b) After marriage?

        Mostly country.

    3. Occupations before her marriage?

    Married young. Housekeeper

    (b) After her marriage?

        Housekeeper

    4. Note any prenatal influences before your birth.

    Interest in newer religious thought, breaking away from old traditions, **economy**.   Worked very hard. <u>Gloomy</u>.

    ...Children born with[in] 2 or 3 years of each other. Born[?] after 15 years of married life.

    5. Her health previous to your birth?

BLANK NO. 16 B   SERIES II, FORM B.

   Not naturally strong, frail physique(?).

   (b) After your birth?

       Very weak.

6. Number of miscarriages?

7. Her age if living and present health? if not, age at time of death and cause?

   62. Poor health.

8. How was your mother's health affected by the climacteric (change of life)?

   Sad effect. All troubles emphasized. Head, deafness in one ear, discharge from ear. Memory defected. [Prolapsus] Indigestion.

9. Name any diseases in her family.

Your Maternal Grandfather: home in city or country?

Small town

1. Age when married?

   Young

2. Occupations?

   Minister

3. Health?

   Not robust.

4. Number of children?

   7

BLANK NO. 16 B   SERIES II, FORM B.

   (b) Number reaching maturity?

      All

Your Maternal Grandmother: home in city or country?
Country

   1. Age when married?

      Young

   2. Occupations?

      Housewife

   3. Health?

      Good

   4. Age and cause of death?

      Middle age. Mourned to death for husbands.

Your Husband: nationality, if American, of what descent?
American

   1. Date of birth?

      1861

   2. Early life in city or country?

      Small town

   3. Height?

   4. Weight?

BLANK NO. 16 B   SERIES II, FORM B.

5. Muscular or weak?

   Reasonably strong but not muscular.

6. Where educated? degrees if any?

   Wisconsin University.

7. If a college man, has he been athletic?

   Not athletic tho' played baseball.

8. Complexion?

   Fair.

9. Temperament?

   Nervous.

10. Does he use tobacco?

    No. No stimulants.

11. Occupations?

    Student and teacher; ...printing office; college professor.

12. Health?

    Medium. Has had bowel trouble.

13. Diseases in his family: Nervous Disorders? Rheumatism? Consumption? Dyspepsia? Varicose Veins? Heart Disease? Hernia? Habitual Constipation? Catarrh?

    Dyspepsia, habitual constipation,and catarrh. [Father had] bowel trouble.

BLANK NO. 16 B   SERIES II, FORM B.

Yourself:

1. Date of birth?

   July 6, 1863.

2. Early life in city or country?

   Country and small town.

3. Height?

4. Weight?

   98 - 100 [lbs.]

5. Complexion?

   Brunette

6. Temperament?

   Nervous. (Inclined to [be] gloomy.)

7. Where educated, give degrees if any?

   High school.

8. Occupations before marriage? a) in city or country? b) time spent in each?

   4 yrs. deputy county Treasurer. Town, county seat. 2 1/2 [years?] Deputy Clerk of Court.

9. Diseases in your family? from father or mother's side? Nervous Disorders? Rheumatism? Consumption? Dyspepsia? Varicose Veins? Heart Disease? Hernia? Habitual Constipation? Catarrh?

   Cessation of menstruation (3 of girls.) (two girls about 30.) (about 22) [These notes, apparently by Dr. Mosher, are not explained.]

BLANK NO. 16 B   SERIES II, FORM B.

10. General health before marriage?   b) since marraige?   Paralysis?
    Brain Fever?   Chronic Headache?   Nervous Prostration?   Catarrh?
    Hernia?   Dyspepsia?   Habitual Constipation?   Inflammation of
    Bowels?   Pleurisy?   Bronchitis?   Shortness of Breath?   Spitting
    Blood?   Consumption?   Laryngitis?   Tonsillitis?   Insomnia?
    Rheumatism?   Pneumonia?   Jaundice?   Varicose Veins?

    [Catarrh, occasional constipation, inflammation of bowels,
      pleurisy when very young--5-10 yrs old--and insomnia at times.]

11. Menstruation:

    First menstruation at what age?

    13

    and when thoroughly established?

    At once

    Present condition as regards menstruation (before cessation):

    (a) How frequent?

        Once a month

    (b) Is it regular or not?

        Never exact-- about [once every] 4 to 5 weeks.

    (c) Amount? how many napkins?

        3 days. Never copious, 5 napkins.

    (d) Duration?

        3 days. [She took a partial bath every day in cool water.
        and a full bath with warm water twice a week.]

    (e) Pain or not? at what time as to the flow?

        Slight, 1st day & day before.

    (f) Is there any leucorrhoea (whites)? character?

        Amount?

        Constant or occasional?

BLANK NO. 16 B											SERIES II, FORM B.

(g) Have you pain either frequently or habitually in the head, small of the back? abdomen or limbs?

Common headache in school, always we[a]k back at menstruation. [Pain in] abdomen from bowel trouble. Nervous pain in bowels.

(h) Disease or trouble in Uterus (womb) or other pelvic organs?

Once [for] 2 days [couldn't] lift herself up in bed. Got over it by rest.

(i) Habit of bowels; how often?

Never move of themselves. Has used syringe. Constipation.

12. What knowledge of sexual physiology had you before marriage? b) how did you obtain it?

No knowledge of exact meaning of marriage relation.

13. Number of times married. If more than once additional blanks will be furnished you to answer the following questions separately in regard to each marriage?

2.

14. Number of years married?

18 mo.

15. Do you habitually sleep with your husband? b) what reasons for so doing or not?

Yes. Because of companionship and not wanting to be separated.

16. Number of conceptions?

None.

17. Number of children? State in connection with each, a) date of birth? b) sex? c) whether healthy or not? d) note any characteristic and the cause. e) note either immediate or after effect on your health of the birth of each of your

BLANK NO. 16 B   SERIES II, FORM B.

children. f) give time of first menstruation after birth of each child.

18. Did conception occur by choice or accident?

19. Habit of intercourse, average number of times per week? per month?

    3

    per year?

20. Was intercourse held during pregnancy? If so, how often? b) had you any desire for it during this period?

21. At other times have you any desire for intercourse?

    Yes

    (a) How often?

       3 or 4 times per month.

    (b) At what time in relation to your menses?

22. Is intercourse agreeable to you or not?

    Yes

    Do you always have a venereal orgasm?

    Yes

    1. - When you do,

    (a) Effect immediately afterwards?

       Quiet & calm. Sometimes not altogether restful at once.

    (b) Effect next day?

       No worse & no better.

    2. - When you do not,

BLANK NO. 16 B   SERIES II, FORM B.

    (a) Effect immediately afterwards?

    (b) Effect next day?

23. What do you believe to be the true purpose of intercourse?

    (a) Necessity to man?

        No.

        to woman?

        No.

    (b) Pleasure?

        Yes.

    (c) Reproduction?

        Yes.

    (d) What other reasons beside reproduction are sufficient to warrant intercourse?

24. Have you ever used any means to prevent conception?

    (a) if so, what?

    (b) effect on your health?

25. What, to you, would be an ideal habit?

    As often as perfect happiness and union can be and not to affect health detrimentally.

BLANK NO. 16 A   SERIES II, FORM B.

Your Maternal Grandfather: home in city or country?
   1. Age when married?

   2. Occupations?

   3. Health?

   4. Number of children?
      (b) Number reaching maturity?

Your Maternal Grandmother: home in city or country?
   1. Age when married?

   2. Occupations?

   3. Health?

   4. Age and cause of death?

Your Husband: nationality; if American, of what descent?
American
   1. Date of birth?
      Mar. 30, 1858.

   2. Early life in city or country?
      Small town.

   3. Height?
      Above average.

BLANK NO. 16 A   SERIES II, FORM B.

4. Weight?

   150 [lbs.]

5. Muscular or weak?

   Robust, muscular hardly.

6. Where educated? degrees if any?

   High school [illegible] at Annapolis.

7. If a college man, has he been athletic?

   [Yes]

8. Complexion?

   Fair

9. Temperament?

   Firm, calm.

10. Does he use tobacco?

    No no.

11. Occupations?

    Engineering with tendency to law and abstract [thinking?]. Sedentary.

12. Health?

    Good

13. Diseases in his family: Nervous Disorders? Rheumatism? Consumption? Dyspepsia? Varicose Veins? Heart Disease? Hernia? Habitual Consumption? Catarrh?

    Nervous disorders. Cause of death typhoid fever.

BLANK NO. 16 A   SERIES II, FORM B.

Yourself:

1. Date of birth?

2. Early life in city or country?

3. Height?

4. Weight?

5. Complexion?

6. Temperament?

7. Where educated, give degrees if any?

8. Occupations before marriage? a) in city or country? b) time spent in each?

9. Diseases in your family? from father or mother's side? Nervous Disorders? Rheumatism? Consumption? Dyspepsia? Varicose Veins? Heart Disease? Hernia? Habitual Constipation? Catarrh?

10. General health before marriage? b) after marriage? Paralysis? Brain Fever? Chronic Headache? Nervous Prostration? Catarrh? Hernia? Dyspepsia? Habitual Constipation? Inflammation of Bowels? Pleurisy? Bronchitis? Shortness of Breath? Spitting Blood? Consumption? Laryngitis? Tonsillitis? Insomnia? Rheumatism? Pneumonia? Jaundice? Varicose Veins?

11. Menstruation:

    First menstruation at what age? and when thoroughly established?

BLANK NO. 16 A   SERIES II, FORM B.

Present condition as regards menstruation:

(a) How frequent?

(b) Is it regular or not?

(c) Amount? how many napkins?

(d) Duration?

(e) Pain or not? at what time as to the flow?

(f) Is there any leucorrhoea (whites)? character?

Amount?

Constant or occasional?

(g) Have you pain either frequently or habitually in the head, small of the back? abdomen or limbs?

(h) Disease or trouble in Uterus (womb) or other pelvic organs?

(i) Habit of bowels; how often?

12. What knowledge of sexual physiology had you before marriage? b) how did you obtain it?

13. Number of times married. If more than once additional blanks will be furnished you to answer the following questions separately in regard to each marriage?

14. Number of years married?

   2 yrs. 3 mo.

15. Did   you habitually sleep with your husband?

   Yes.

   (b) What reasons for so doing or not?

16. Number of conceptions?

BLANK NO. 16 A   SERIES II, FORM B.

17. Number of children? State in connection with each, a) date of birth? b) sex? c) whether healthy or not? d) note any characteristic and the cause. e) note either immediate or after effect on your health of the birth of each of your children. f) give time of first menstruation after birth of each child.

18. Did conception occur by choice or accident?

19. Habit of intercourse, average number of times per week? per month? per year?

20. Was intercourse held during pregnancy? If so, how often? b) had you any desire for it during this period?

21. At other times have you any desire for intercourse? a) how often? b) at what time in relation to your menses?

    5 or 6 ?

22. Is intercourse agreeable to you or not?

    Do you always have a venereal orgasm?

    No.

    1. - When you do?

    (a) Effect immediately afterwards?

    (b) Effect next day?

        Lassitude to greater extent.

    2. - When you do not?

    (a) Effect immediately afterwards?

    (b) Effect next day?

23. What do you believe to be the true purpose of intercourse?

    (a) Necessity to man? to woman?

BLANK NO. 16 A   SERIES II, FORM B.

    (b) Pleasure?

    (c) Reproduction?

    (d) What other reasons beside reproduction are sufficient to warrant intercourse?

24. Have you ever used any means to prevent conception? a) if so, what?

    (b) Effect on your health?

25. What, to you, would be an ideal habit?

BLANK NO. 17

[For this questionnaire, we have only the woman's responses in Dr. Mosher's hand. The editors provided the probable questions.]

Date: March 1[8?], 1920

Yourself: nationality, if American, of what descent?
American descent.

1. Home in city or country?

    Lives in country.

2. Which child of parents (1st, 2nd, 3rd, etc)?

    2nd child.

3. Date of birth?

    Aug. 18, 1889.

4. Early life in city or country?

    City.

5. Height?

6. Weight?

7. Where educated, give degrees if any?

    Stanford, A.B., A.M.

8. Occupations before marriage? a) in city or country? b) time spent in each?

    Teacher 3 yrs.

9. General health before marriage? b) since marriage? Paralysis? Brain Fever? Chronic Headache? Nervous Prostration? Catarrh?

BLANK NO. 17

Hernia? Dyspepsia? Habitual Constipation? Inflammation of Bowels? Pleurisy? Bronchitis? Shortness of Breath? Spitting Blood? Consumption? Laryngitis? Tonsillitis? Insomnia? Rheumatism? Pneumonia? Jaundice? Varicose Veins?

General health before marriage excellent.

10. Menstruation:

First menstruation at what age?

16 yrs.

and when thoroughly established?

[1 mo.?]

Present condition as regards menstruation:

(h) Disease or trouble in Uterus (womb) or other pelvic organs?

No pelvic trouble.

(i) Habit of bowels; how often?

Never constipated.

11. What knowledge of sexual physiology had you before marriage? b) how did you obtain it?

What mother told her. **Cowan's "Science of New Life."** Knew what to expect.

12. Number of times married. If more than once additional blanks will be furnished you to answer the following questions separately in regard to each marriage?

Married once.

13. Number of miscarriages?

No miscarriages.

14. Number of children? State in connection with each, a) date

BLANK NO. 17

of birth? b) sex? c) whether healthy or not? d) note any characteristic and the cause. e) note either immediate or after effects on your health of the birth of each of your children. f) give time of first menstruation after birth of each child.

2 children.... Married 10 mo. & 4 days before 1st child.

15. Did conception occur by choice or accident?

    1st [child conceived] because allowed to take chance--[child was] wanted. 2nd [child was] planned for. In each case conception directly after **1st certain [menses]** 2d **3 periods of coitus.** About **10 days probably.**

16. Habit of intercourse, average number of times per week?

    Habit: 1 [time] per wk. Oftener at first.

    per month?

    Oc[casionally?] once [every] 2 wks.

    per year?

17. Was intercourse held during pregnancy? If so, how often?

    During pregnancy: ordinary habit [continued] until 4th month. Then not at all until baby was past 2 mo. old.

    (b) Had you any desire for it during this period?

    No desire during pregnancy but not [unwelcome?].

18. At other times have you any desire for intercourse? a) how often? b) at what time in relation to your menses?

    What time in month--no difference.

19. Is intercourse agreeable to you or not?

    Coitus is agreeable--wants it. Always determined times.

    Do you always have a venereal orgasm?

BLANK NO. 17

Always.

1. When you do,

   (a) Effect immediately afterwards?

   Always relaxed and went to sleep. Always took douche.

   (b) Effect next day?

   Rested & refreshed - a normal natural function.

20. What do you believe to be the true purpose of intercourse?

    (a) Necessity to man?

    Yes.

    to woman?

    Yes.

    (b) Pleasure?

    Yes (if not too frequent).

    (c) Reproduction?

    (d) What other reasons beside reproduction are sufficient to warrant intercourse?

    Sense of completeness, a spiritual completeness which is not gained in [any] other way. Physically necessary to the woman as well as the man for a complete life.

21. Have you ever used any means to prevent conception? a) if so, what?

    Contraceptives: used pastile suppository. Cocoa butter [illegible] & cold water douche.

    (b) Effect on your health?

    No harm.

22. Additional Notes:

BLANK NO. 17

She always regulated frequency and thinks any woman can.

Your Husband:
1. Height?
    5 feet, 10 or 12 inches.

2. Weight?
    185-190 lbs.

3. Muscular or weak?
    Broad shouldered type, slim hipped.

4. Where educated? degrees if any?
    U.C. man.

5. Occupations?
    Civil Engineer.

6. Health?
    Died of influenza before 2nd child was born.

BLANK NO. 18   SERIES II, FORM B.

Your Father:
   1. Nationality, if American, of what descent?
      American. Remote ancestors English.

   2. Home in city our country before marriage?
      Country.

   3. Home in city or country after marriage?
      Country.

   4. Age when married?
      23 -- first marriage.   36 [age at second marriage?]

   5. Occupations before your birth?
      Farmer.
      (b) After your birth?
         Farmer.

   6. Health previous to your birth?
      Good.
      (b) After your birth?
         Good.

   7. Number of children living?
      (a) Boys:
      (b) Girls: [1]

BLANK NO. 18   SERIES II, FORM B.

   8. Number of children dead; give age at time of death and cause.

      (a) Boys

      (b) Girls

         I am the only child my father ever had.

   9. If your father is living, give his age and present health;
      if dead, age at death and cause?

      Age 76. Splendid health.

  10. Name any diseases in his family.

      Consumption (Bronchial)

Your Paternal Grandfather: home in city or country?
Country

   1. Age when married?

      18.

   2. Occupations?

      Farmer & teacher.

   3. Health?

      Splendid health.

   4. Number of children?

      Seven.

      Number reaching maturity?

      All.

200

BLANK NO. 18   SERIES II, FORM B.

Your Paternal Grandmother: home in city or country?
Country.

    1. Age when married?

       18.

    2. Occupations?

    3. Health?

       Very poor. Was nervous & hysterical.

    4. Age and cause of death?

       Bronchial consumption.

Your Mother:

    1. Nationality, if American of what descent?

       American.

    2. Home in city or country before marriage?

       Country.

      (b) Home in city or country after marriage?

       Country.

    3. Occupations before her marriage?

       None -- lived at home.

      (b) After her marriage?

       Kept house & did farm work.

BLANK NO. 18   SERIES II, FORM B.

4. Note any prenatal influences before your birth.

   The millipedes were thick that summer before my birth, and my mother disliked them very much. My aversion to them is absolutely uncontrollable.

5. Her health previous to your birth?

   Good.

   (b) After your birth?

   Good until the turn of life -- and since then she has been an invalid.

6. Number of miscarriages?

   None. One baby died being born.

7. Her age if living, and present health? If not, age at time of death and cause?

   70 years old -- poor health.

8. How was your mother's health affected by the climacteric (change of life)?

   Ruined her health entirely. Has been a nervous invalid for twenty-two years.

9. Name any diseases in her family.

   None.

Your Maternal Grandfather: home in city or country?
Country.

   1. Age when married?

   2. Occupations?

      Farmer.

BLANK NO. 18   SERIES II, FORM B.

    3. Health?

       Good.

    4. Number of children?

       Six.

      (b) Number reaching maturity?

          Five.

Your Maternal Grandmother: home in city or country?
Country.

    1. Age when married?

    2. Occupations?

    3. Health?

       Good.

    4. Age and cause of death?

       Fell from a horse and died of internal injuries at the age of 37 or 38.

Your Husband: Nationality, if American, of what descent?
American.

    1. Date of birth?

       1848.

    2. Early life in city or country?

       City some but mostly country.

BLANK NO. 18   SERIES II, FORM B.

3. Height?

   5 ft. 8 1/2 inches.

4. Weight?

   160 lbs.

5. Muscular or weak?

   Very muscular.

6. Where educated? degrees if any?

   District school. Academy at Fulton, N.Y. Cornell -- B.S.

7. If a college man, has he been athletic?

   Strong but not athletic.

8. Complexion?

   Medium.

9. Temperament?

   Nervous -- melancholy in tendency.

10. Does he use tobacco?

    During the last five years has smoked a very little. Once a day perhaps.

11. Occupations?

    Professor in University.

12. Health?

    Subject to nervous break downs unless cared for very attentively.

BLANK NO. 18   SERIES II, FORM B.

13. Diseases in his family: Nervous Disorders? Rheumatism?
    Consumption? Dyspepsia? Varicose Veins? Heart Disease?
    Hernia? Habitual Constipation? Catarrh?

    Rheumatism

Yourself:

1. Date of birth?

   Sept. 1st, 1855.

2. Early life in city or country?

   Country.

3. Height?

   5 ft. 7 1/2.

4. Weight?

   160 lbs.

5. Complexion?

   Medium -- gray eyes, black hair.

6. Temperament?

   Sanguine - nervous.

7. Where educated, give degrees if any?

   District schools -- **Boarding school mixed.** Cornell
   University -- B.S.

8. Occupations before marriage? a) in city or country? b) time spent in each?

   Taught 1 and 1/2 years in district school.

BLANK NO. 18   SERIES II, FORM B.

9. Diseases in your family? from father or mother's side?
Nervous Disorders? Rheumatism? Consumption? Dyspepsia?
Varicose Veins? Heart Disease? Hernia? Habitual Constipation?

Mother - constipation. Father deaf at fifty from catarrh.

10. General health before marriage? b) since marriage? Paralysis?
Brain Fever? Chronic Headache? Nervous Prostration? Catarrh?
Hernia? Dyspepsia? Habitual Constipation? Inflammation of
Bowels? Pleurisy? Bronchitis? Shortness of Breath? Spitting
Blood? Consumption? Laryngitis? Tonsillitis? Insomnia?
Rheumatism? Pneumonia? Jaundice? Varicose Veins?

[Before marriage] Brain Fever. Nervous Prostration. Habitual
Constipation as a child.

[Since marriage] Inflammation of Bowels.

11. Menstruation:

First menstruation at what age?

14

and when thoroughly established?

16. Excessive at twenty. When at boarding school (16-19)
ran up and down stairs until prolapsis of womb followed.
Troubled with dysmenorrhea [i.e., painful menstruation] from
the first.

Present condition as regards menstruation:

(a) How frequent?

Regular. Three weeks and one or two days.

(b) Is it regular or not?

Regular.

(c) Amount? how many napkins?

Never less than 20.

(d) Duration?

Six days.

(e) Pain or not? at what time as to the flow?

Very little pain, and never except when the membrane is discharged.

(f) Is there any leucorrhoea (acid or alkali)? character?

Amount?

Very little--just before menstruation.

Constant or occasional?

Occasional.

(g) Have you pain either frequently or habitually in the head, small of the back? abdomen or limbs?

No.

(h) Disease or trouble in Uterus (womb) or other pelvic organs?

Subject always to inflammation on the slightest occasion.

(i) Habit of bowels; how often?

Not naturally regular but made so by care--once per day.

12. What knowledge of sexual physiology had you before marriage? b) how did you obtain it?

A good general knowledge of the position and functions of the organs--gathered from various medical books--and a good deal of particular knowledge from my experience with the life on the farm, in seeing **the farm animals during all processes of breeding. Also from very frank talks with my mother.**

13. Number of times married. If more than once additional blanks will be furnished you to answer the following questions separately in regard to each marriage?

Once.

BLANK NO. 18   SERIES II, FORM B.

14. Number of years married?

    Fifteen.

15. Do you habitually sleep with your husband? b) what reasons for so doing or not?

    No. Because my husband is nervous and restless and dislikes sleeping with anyone.

16. Number of conceptions?

    None.

17. Number of children? State in connection with each: a) date of birth? b) sex? c) whether healthy or not? d) note any characteristics and the cause. e) note either immediate or after effect on your health of the birth of each of your children. f) give time of first menstruation after birth of each child.

18. Did conception occur by choice or accident?

19. Habit of intercourse, average number of times per week?

    Twice in the earlier years of married life.

    Per month?

    4 times for the last six years.

    Per year?

20. Was intercourse held during pregnancy? If so, how often? b) had you any desire for it during this period?

21. At other times have you any desire for intercourse? a) how often? b) at what time in relation to your menses?

    No especial desire for intercourse ever. But it seems more natural within ten days after menstruation.

BLANK NO. 18   SERIES II, FORM B.

22. Is intercourse agreeable to you or not?

    Sometimes agreeable, sometimes not, depending on physical condition.

    Do you always have a venereal orgasm?

    Usually.

    1. - When you do?

    (a) Effect immediately afterwards?

        Sometimes a feeling of exhaustion but often followed by wakefulness and nervousness. But the nervousness is more pronounced when there is no venereal orgasm.

    (b) Effect next day?

        None usually.

    2. - When you do not?

    (a) Effect immediately afterwards?

        None.

    (b) Effect next day?

        None.

23. What do you believe to be the true purpose of intercourse?

    (a) Necessity to man? to woman?

        [Man:] Yes, physically. [Woman:] Yes, spiritually.

    (b) Pleasure?

    (c) Reproduction?

    (d) What other reasons beside reproduction are sufficient to warrant intercourse?

        The marriage relation should be nearer than any other. Sexual intercourse is the means which brings this about. Loving relations have a right to exist between married people and these cannot exist in perfection without

BLANK NO. 18SERIES II, FORM B.

sexual intercourse to a moderate degree. This is the result of my experience.

24. Have you ever used any means to prevent conception? a) if so, what?

No. I have always used as a measure of cleanliness an injection of warm water and borax or soap suds--(this or cuticura soap?).

(b) Effect on your health?

Sexual intercourse too often makes me nervous or irritable.

25. What, to you, would be an ideal habit?

To me personally, once a month directly after menstruation. As this would keep alive in me the sense of nearness which I regard indispensable to a happy marriage. But the ideal must be a compromise between two and must be the best for both.

BLANK NO. 19						SERIES II, FORM B.

Date: May 20, 1893.

Your Father:

1. Nationality, if American, of what descent?

    [American of Scotch descent]

2. Home in city or country before marriage?

    Country.

3. Home in city or country after marriage?

    Country.

4. Age when married?

    About 23 or 24.

5. Occupations before your birth?

    Minister. Man of affairs. [Had a] good business. Farming and cattle raising for the sake of his sons.

    (b) After your birth?

    Same.

6. Health previous to your birth?

    (b) After your birth?

7. Number of children living?

    (a) Boys: 2

    (b) Girls: 3

8. Number of children dead; give age at time of death and cause.

BLANK NO. 19   SERIES II, FORM B.

[Mosher notes the violent deaths of two sons: **one** "killed by a horse kick" at 23, the other by a train at 41.]

9. If your father is living, give his age and present health, if dead, age at death and cause?

   [Dead at 75] General debility, breaking down, his people longer lived. Sank away for a year before that time. Not a strong man for many years. Not so well after illness, after birth of daughters. Had some heart trouble but not cause of death.

10. Name any diseases in his family:

    Does not know of any.

Your Paternal Grandfather: home in city or country?
Country.

1. Age when married?

   Young.

2. Occupations?

   Farming, plantation in Missouri & Tenn.

3. Health?

   Excellent as far as known. [He is] very old--nearly 90.

4. Number of children?

   Boys 3, Girls 2.

   Number reaching maturity?

   All.

BLANK NO. 19   SERIES II, FORM B.

Your Paternal Grandmother: home in city or country?
Country.
   1. Age when married?
      About 20. Uncertain.

   2. Occupations?
      Housewife.

   3. Health?
      Good.

   4. Age and cause of death?
      About [8?]5. Old age.

Your Mother:
   1. Nationality, if American, of what descent?
      [American of Dutch-English descent]

   2. Home in city or country before marriage?
      Country.
      (b) Home in city or country after marriage?
          Country.

   3. Occupations before her marriage?
      (b) After her marriage?
          Housewife.

   4. Note any prenatal influences before your birth:

BLANK NO. 19   SERIES II, FORM B.

5. Her health previous to your birth?

   Tremendous will get[s] better of her self? sometimes.

   (b) After your birth?

   Always excellent except at change of life.

6. Number of miscarriages?

   Sure she did not.

7. Her age if living and present health? if not, age at time of death and cause?

   87--almost 88. Health ... excellent, has broken hip which prevents walking but mind and body perfectly sound.

8. How was your mother's health affected by the climacteric (change of life)?

   Not well. Severe attacks of bilious colic, age about 50 or more.

9. Name any diseases in her family:

   Youngest brother died of consumption brought on by exposure & neglect, **only member of family.**

Your Maternal Grandfather: home in city or country?

Country.

1. Age when married?

   About 25.

2. Occupations?

   Farming & stock raising. Land owner.

3. Health?

BLANK NO. 19   SERIES II, FORM B.

   Suppose perfect.

4. Number of children?
   11. 6th child was her mother.
   (b) Number reaching maturity?
   All.

Your Maternal Grandmother: home in city or country?
Country. Dutch descent.
   1. Age when married?
   About 20.

   2. Occupations?
   Housewife.

   3. Health?
   Perfect.

   4. Age and cause of death?
   70. Pneumonia.

Your Husband: nationality, if American, of what descent?
American. Scotch.
   1. Date of birth?
   1826.

   2. Early life in city or country?
   Country.

BLANK NO. 19   SERIES II, FORM B.

3. Height?

   Lacks a little of 6 ft.: 5 [ft.], 11 [in.].

4. Weight?

   155   Formerly, 165-170.

5. Muscular or weak?

   Muscular.

6. Where educated? degrees if any?

   In Missouri.

7. If a college man, has he been athletic?

   Not [a] college [man].

8. Complexion?

   Neither light nor dark, gray eyes.

9. Temperament?

   Even, happy, sanguine, never depressed.

10. Does he use tobacco?

    Yes.

11. Occupations?

    [Mosher's note indicates he was a miner, a teacher, a businessman, and more, with keen judgment.]

12. Health?

    Good, never exuberant, never had an illness since marriage.
    [**Quinzy**]   once or twice.

BLANK NO. 19   SERIES II, FORM B.

13. Diseases in his family: Nervous Disorders? Rheumatism?
    Consumption? Dyspepsia? Varicose Veins? Heart Disease?
    Hernia? Habitual Constipation? Catarrh?

    Slight catarrh. Cancer cause of death of brother--called
    [it] piles [was probably] cancer or something, also bronchial
    [consumption]. Sisters and husband have palsy(?) --trembling.

Yourself:

1. Date of birth?

   1846.

2. Early life in city or country?

   Country.

3. Height?

   5 [ft.], 3 3/4 [in.].

4. Weight?

   160 [lbs.] about.

5. Complexion?

   Blond.

6. Temperament?

   Nervous(?), sanguine--takes good deal to depress.

7. Where educated, give degrees if any?

   Pacific University.

8. Occupations before marriage? a) in city or country? b) time
   spent in each?

BLANK NO. 19   SERIES II, FORM B.

   Country & town.

9. Diseases in your family? from father or mother's side? Nervous
   Disorders? Rheumatism? Consumption? Dyspepsia? Varicose
   Veins? Heart Disease? Hernia? Habitual Constipation?
   Catarrh?

   Brother had Dyspepsia and slight Catarrh. Sister once had
   Habitual Constipation as a result of injury at birth of child.
   [Stricture?] remedied.

10. General health before marriage? b) since marriage? Paralysis?
    Brain Fever? Chronic Headache? Nervous Prostration? Catarrh?
    Hernia? Dyspepsia? Habitual Constipation? Inflammation of
    Bowels? Pleurisy? Bronchitis? Shortness of Breath? Spitting
    Blood? Consumption? Laryngitis? Tonsillitis? Insomnia?
    Rheumatism? Pneumonia? Jaundice? Varicose Veins?

    (a) Catarrh. Chronic cold as a child, took cold very readily.
        No endurance as a girl. Yet perfectly well.

    (b) Pneumonia (fearfully). Cholera morbus, very severe.

11. Menstruation:

    First menstruation at what age?

    About 14.

    and when thoroughly established?

    14.

    Present condition as regards menstruation:

    Regular.

    (a) How frequent?

        One or 2 days short of 4 weeks.

    (b) Is it regular or not?

        Has always been regular.

    (c) Amount? how many napkins?

BLANK NO. 19   SERIES II, FORM B.

        Twice a day or three times. 1 per day after 3rd day.

  (d) Duration?

        7 [days].

  (e) Pain or not? at what time as to the flow?

        [Most pain on 1st day] Severe until after birth of her first child, nausea, vomiting and diarrhoea went with it.

  (f) Is there any leucorrhoea (whites)? character?

        Very slight. Once before birth of one child. Soon cured by a lotion.

        Amount?

        Constant or occasional?

        Once.

  (g) Have you pain either frequently or habitually in the head, small of the back? abdomen or limbs?

  (h) Disease or trouble in Uterus (womb) or other pelvic organs?

  (i) Habit of bowels; how often?

        Regular, usually once, sometimes twice [daily].

12. What knowledge of sexual physiology had you before marriage? b) how did you obtain it?

    "Not the least in the world." [Mosher's quotation marks]

13. Number of times married. If more than once additional blanks will be furnished you to answer the following questions separately in regard to each marriage?

    Once.

14. Number of years married?

    Twenty-seven years.

BLANK NO. 19   SERIES II, FORM B.

15. Do you habitually sleep with your husband?

    Yes (when he is at home).

    (b) What reasons for so doing or not?

        Had always seen it so, and makes husband happier, duty
        as wife. When you think about [it], no objection in her own
        case. Most men would be weaned away from wives without
        it. Sympathy and understanding nearer. To have him all
        to herself and talk over things which could not be done
        in a cold blooded way.

16. Number of children?

    6. 2 months, last; about 31 years [old] at time. Very
    miserable in health at time, despondent, didn't want to have
    it, walked a good deal but nothing that would have hurt if
    she had been ordinarily well. Some discharge of blood as if
    she were [becoming] unwell every 2 or 3 days. Took strong
    physic. Took chill after long ride in carriage & birth took
    place.

17. Number of children? State in connection with each, a) date
    of birth? b) sex? c) whether healthy or not? d) note any
    characteristic and the cause. e) note either immediate or
    after effect on your health of the birth of each of your
    children. f) give time of first menstruation after birth
    of each child.

    [First child]

        (a) Aug., 1867.

        (b) Girl.

        (c) Born healthy, could not nurse it, milk from bottle
            disagreed. Thinks it came from want of vigor. Lived
            7 1/2 months.

        (e) Sick constantly during time of pregnancy, constant
            nausea. (9 mo. period) No strength afterward, almost
            an invalid for a year.

        (f) About 3 mo.

BLANK NO. 19   SERIES II, FORM B.

[Second child]

    (a) 2 years after.

    (b) Girl.

    (c) Born at 8 months, labor produced by severe attack of pneumonia. It lived 48 hours.

    (e) Did not know anyone for 6 wks. Followed by puerperal fever. Never as well since then, not so much vigor.

    (f) Not certain....

[Third child]

    (a) Jan., '72, about 2 1/2 years after [second].

    (b) Girl. Full 9 mo.

    (c) As a child, full of energy but never well. At age of 3, had lung fever, thought she would not live. Teething very severe. Several attacks of lung fever before 3 years of age (over care of mother rather hurt her). Subject to hard illness but seems to have great vitality. Childrens diseases in worst form. At 11 years had diptheria which left her with deafness. Had also a good deal of ear ache & once or twice discharge from ears but hearing not affected. Subject to constant headache since roaring in head is constant. Dreams constantly--sleeps badly.

    (d) Not strong and had run [a] low fever toward end of period from 6 - 9 months, [caused] child to be nervous.

    (e) Up in a month, downstairs in 6 wks.

[Fourth child]

    (a) Less than two years later.

    (b) Boy.

    (c) Lived to be 7 months old. [Died from poor food?], could not get wet nurse. Died of cholera infantum. Most vigorous of all children.

    (e) Never so well before birth of any of children.

    (f) Menstruation came on soon.

BLANK NO. 19   SERIES II, FORM B.

[Fifth child]

(a) 18 months later.

(b) Girl.

(c) Strong & well as a child. Had wet nurse engaged before she was born. Nursed for a year until after teething time. Change of nurse brought on attack of cholera infantum. Childrens diseases not very severe. Measles at about 10 years left her with trouble with eyes and ears. Eyes remedied, about as good as average and ears [got] better, then worse, & then stationary. Growing steadily worse in last year and half. Thinks may have heart trouble or bad circulation. Recently one year ago typhoid fever.

[Sixth child]

Miscarriage.

18. Did conception occur by choice or accident?

Accident. 1st time, 3 or 4th night. [Mosher may be telegraphing that conception occurred the first time the woman had intercourse on the third or fourth night of marriage.]

19. Habit of intercourse, average number of times per week?

2.

per month?

per year?

20. Was intercourse held during pregnancy? If so, how often?

In beginning, one in 2 months or once in a month. Later in pregnancy rarely.... Last 3 months not at all.

(b) Had you any desire for it during this period?

"No difference between that and any other time." [Mosher's quotation marks.]

21. At other times have you any desire for intercourse? a) how often?

BLANK NO. 19   SERIES II, FORM B.

   Not repulsive when with husband, never thinks of it when away.
   Physical response not more than half dozen times when it was
   not suggested from him. Very little pleasure!

   (b) At what time in relation to your menses?

22. Is intercourse agreeable to you or not?

   Sometimes yes, many times no.

   Do you always have a venereal orgasm?

   Few times, but not often, ...many more times no than yes.

   1. - When you do,

   (a) Effect immediately afterwards?

      Don't know. Never noticed.

   (b) Effect next day?

      Never noticed any difference.

   2. - When you do not,

   (a) Effect immediately afterwards?

      Ditto.

   (b) Effect next day?

      Ditto.

23. What do you believe to be the true purpose of intercourse?

   (a) Necessity to man?

      [Yes] No man [is] happy without [intercourse] and [it's]
      a great strain on him to keep himself in restraint all
      the time.

      to woman?

      [It's] healthier to have it in moderation. A woman can
      get along without it, but [it's] natural to her. [It's]
      more necessary to a man than [to a] woman.

BLANK NO. 19   SERIES II, FORM B.

   (b) Pleasure?

       Yes, decidedly with women, but not so great to women [as
       men].

   (c) Reproduction?

       Yes, real purpose. Made pleasurable so it would be
       indulged in, to accomplish purpose of reproduction.

   (d) What other reasons beside reproduction are sufficient to
       warrant intercourse?

       Bond between the sexes, a man more fond of his wife than
       other women, makes people fond and tender.

       A definition of love: that which binds the sexes together.

24. Have you ever used any means to prevent conception?

    Yes.

    (a) If so, what?

        Water, sometimes a solution of [alum?] when near menstrual
        period. Sometimes a little alcohol. A teaspoon of powdered
        alum to a pint of water. Alcohol 1/3 or 1/4. Used as a
        douche. When intercourse came near period & thought there
        was danger. Nothing good to use too often.

    (b) Effect on your health?

        None, perfectly well, regular & strong.

25. What, to you, would be an ideal habit?

    "Now at my time of life--never."

    In prime of life: For a man well developed & vigorous about
    twice a week. For a woman, half as often--twice a month.
    "I was always well and it did not hurt me and I always meant
    to be obliging."

BLANK NO. 20   SERIES II, FORM B.

[For this questionnaire, we have only the woman's responses in Dr. Mosher's hand. The editors provided the questions.]

Date: March 17, 1920.

Nationality: American - English & Scotch ancestry.

Very active out-of-door girl - horseback riding and fishing.

Married when 23 years old.

Husband: American, English descent. Very athletic; brought up on a farm. [Educated at] Stanford [University]. Occupation: Educational - sedentary.

  1. Date of birth?

     1877.

  3. Height?

  4. Weight?

  5. Complexion?

     Medium.

  6. Temperament?

     Sanguine.

  7. Where educated, give degrees if any?

     Stanford, A.B., 1897.

  8. Occupation before marriage? a) in city or country? b) time spent in each?

     Teacher for 2 yrs. before marriage.

BLANK NO. 20   SERIES II, FORM B.

9. Diseases in your family? from father or mother's side? Nervous Disorders? Rheumatism? Consumption? Dyspepsia? Varicose Veins? Heart Disease? Hernia? Habitual Constipation? Catarrh?

   Father nervous **man** - **strong vitality.**

10. General health before marriage? b) since marriage? Paralysis? Brain Fever? Chronic Headache? Nervous Prostration? Catarrh? Hernia? Dyspepsia? Habitual Constipation? Inflammation of Bowels? Pleurisy? Bronchitis? Shortness of Breath? Spitting Blood? Consumption? Laryngitis? Tonsillitis? Insomnia? Rheumatism? Pneumonia? Jaundice? Varicose Veins.

    Good health before [marriage]. Since marriage, much [nervousness?].

11. Menstruation:

    First menstruation at what age?

    Began at 14.

    Present condition as regards menstruation:

    (h) Disease or trouble in Uterus (womb) or other pelvic organs?

        [Slight] hemorrhages when teaching corrected after children were born.

    (i) Habit of bowels; how often?

        Constipation.

12. What knowledge of sexual physiology had you before marriage? b) how did you obtain it?

    Knowledge of sex physiology - hygiene. Inference from hearing and reading. (Mother died in childhood.)

13. Number of times married. If more than once additional blanks will be furnished you to answer the following questions separately in regard to each marriage?

    Once.

BLANK NO. 20											SERIES II, FORM B.

14. Number of years married?

    Married 20 yrs. in June.

15. Do you habitually sleep with your husband? b) what reasons for so doing or not?

    Separate beds & rooms. Since younger child was born. When children were small [illegible] comfortable--began before child was born.

16. Number of conceptions?

    2.

17. Number of children? State in connection with each, a) date of birth? b) sex? c) whether healthy or not? d) note any characteristic and the cause. e) note either immediate or after effect on your health of the birth of each of your children. f) give time of first menstruation after birth of each child.

    2 children.

    [First child]

    (a) 1903.

    (b) Boy.

    (c) Healthy.

    (e) No trouble, care of [illegible] in house told on her. Labor: 12 hr. [Slight?] tear repaired at once. Relatively easy labor; [unintelligible] & prompt recovery. No exhaustion.

    (f) Nursed until 8 mo. Menstr[uation] began soon after.

    [Second child]

    (a) 1907.

    (b) Boy.

    (c) Healthy.

(e) Labor: went to bed at 6 o'clock & baby was born at 2 o'clock. Very easy time with him. Nursed him 11 mo. [Straight?] tear--one stitch at [illegible].

18. Did conception occur by choice or accident?

    Accident.

19. Habit of intercourse, average number of times per week?

    Intercourse about [once per] week more frequent at beginning.

    per month?

    per year?

20. Was intercourse held during pregnancy? If so, how often?

    Less often than usual.

    (b) Had you any desire for it during this period?

    Not before 1st child from time she knew [at] 2 or 3 months. [With second child, intercourse] only during early months.

    [In general,] less often than usual. No desire. Can't remember very well.

21. At other times have you any desire for intercourse? a) how often?

    Very little.

    (b) At what time in relation to your menses?

    Never any special desire unless cultivated. Where omitted would miss it but marriage cultivates it. Perhaps relieves nervousness.

22. Is intercourse agreeable to you or not?

    [More agreeable during the first week after her period.]

BLANK NO. 20   SERIES II, FORM B.

Do you always have a venereal orgasm?

No.

1. - When you do,

(a) Effect immediately afterwards?

(b) Effect next day?

   Notices no difference.

2. - When you do not?

   Does not notice any difference.

23. What do you believe to be the true purpose of intercourse?

(a) Necessity to man?

   Better health.

   to woman?

   Better health.

(b) Pleasure?

   Man [experiences] intense pleasure--[the] greatest he can experience. Woman - personally never has gotten enough out of it to make [pleasure?] a factor.

(c) Reproduction?

   Primary purpose. If it were not for economic conditions would have all the children which came. [Personally] would be glad to have any number--it is so wonderful when you grow old to have many.

(d) What other reasons beside reproduction are sufficient to warrant intercourse?

   Instinct and health make it a necessity.

24. Have you ever used any means to prevent conception? a) if so, what?

   Douches for years. Has fibroid growth & thinks no danger.

BLANK NO. 20   SERIES II, FORM B.

   Time of month--not much danger after 1st [week] after period.

25. What, to you, would be an ideal habit?
   Once a week to keep a man in health.

26. Additional Notes:
   Never conscious of any sex need. Liked society of men.

BLANK NO. 21   SERIES II, FORM B.

Your Father:

1. Nationality, if American, of what descent?

   American, Irish & English.

2. Home in city or country before marriage?

   Country plantation.

3. Home in city or country after marriage?

   Small town in West.

4. Age when married?

   About 23.

5. Occupations before your birth?

   Farmer.

   (b) After your birth?

   Came to California, no occupation but trading.

6. Health previous to your birth?

   Good.

   (b) After your birth?

   Well except dyspepsia.

7. Number of children living?

   (a) Boys: 1.

   (b) Girls: 2.

8. Number of children dead; give age at time of death and cause.

   (a) Boys: 1 died from 1 - 3 years of age, **first wife's child and first child and only.**

BLANK NO. 21   SERIES II, FORM B.

> (b) Girls: 2.

9. If your father is living, give his age and present health, if dead, age at death and cause?

   In California at 40, fever.

10. Name any diseases in his family:

    Dyspepsia.

Your Paternal Grandfather: home in city or country?
Country plantation.

> 1. Age when married?
>
> 2. Occupations?
>
> 3. Health?
>   Good.
>
> 4. Number of children?
>   7 or 8.
>   Number reaching maturity?
>   All.

Your Paternal Grandmother: home in city or country?
Country plantation.

> 1. Age when married?
>
> 2. Occupations?

BLANK NO. 21   SERIES II, FORM B.

   3. Health?
      Fine.

   4. Age and cause of death?
      At least 50 or 55.

Your Mother:
   1. Nationality, if American of what descent?
      American. English, a strain of Irish.

   2. Home in city or country before marriage?
      Country.
      (b) Home in city or country after marriage?
          Country.

   3. Occupations before her marriage?
      (b) After her marriage?
          Embroidered in lace a great deal. Spun. Could do more than any person.

   4. Note any prenatal influences before your birth:

   5. Her health previous to your birth?
      Good.
      (b) After your birth?
          Died 9 days after birth of child of puerperal fever.

   6. Number of miscarriages?
      None.

BLANK NO. 21   SERIES II, FORM B.

7. Her age if living, and present health? if not, age at time of death and cause?

   19 of puerperal fever. Father 40 years of age.

8. How was your mother's health affected by the climacteric (change of life)?

9. Name any diseases in her family:

Your Maternal Grandfather: home in city or country?
Englishman. Country on a plantation in Delaware.

   1. Age when married?

   2. Occupations?

   3. Health?

      Died at 35.

   4. Number of children?

      10, & raised 3 others.

      Number reaching maturity?

      9. 1 died at 8 years.

Your Maternal Grandmother: home in city or country?

   1. Age when married?

      19. 2 times married, 5 [children] by each.

   2. Occupations?

   3. Health?

BLANK NO. 21   SERIES II, FORM B.

   Very delicate baby; better later in life, always delicate.

   4. Age and cause of death?
      8[3?].

Your Husband: nationality, if American, of what descent?
American, English.
   1. Date of birth?
      1828 Oct.

   2. Early life in city or country?
      Country.

   3. Height?
      5 ft., 11 in. in stockings.

   4. Weight?
      165 or 170 [lbs.]

   5. Muscular or weak?
      Muscular.

   6. Where educated? degrees if any?
      N.Y. in an academy.

   7. If a college man, has he been athletic?
      Active but not athletic.

BLANK NO. 21   SERIES II, FORM B.

   8. Complexion?

      Brown eyes & brown hair, dark.

   9. Temperament?

      Nervous, sanguine.

   10. Does he use tobacco?

      Occasionally.

   11. Occupations?

      Lawyer, speculator.

   12. Health?

      Variable, has had hemorrhages of lungs as a young man. Liver trouble.

   13. Diseases in his family: Nervous Disorders? Rheumatism?
       Consumption? Dyspepsia? Varicose Veins? Heart Disease?
       Hernia? Habitual Constipation? Catarrh?

      Nervous Disorders. Weak lungs. Father a smoker, [had] Heart
      Disease. Father & his father's brother & sister had paralysis.

Yourself:

   1. Date of birth?

      1832.

   2. Early life in city or country?

      [Country] until four years old. [Since then in town and city.]

   3. Height?

      5 [ft.], 2 1/2 (?)

BLANK NO. 21   SERIES II, FORM B.

4. Weight?

   102 or 3 lbs.

5. Complexion?

   Hair golden brown & brown eyes; light.

6. Temperament?

   Sanguine, nervous, anxious, melancholy.

7. Where educated, give degrees if any?

   In So[uth] Bend Ind[iana] Academy.

8. Occupations before marriage? a) in city or country? b) time spent in each?

9. Diseases in your family? from father or mother's side? Nervous Disorders? Rheumatism? Consumption? Dyspepsia? Varicose Veins? Heart Disease? Hernia? Habitual Constipation? Catarrh?

   Nervous Disorders. Dyspepsia. Heart Disease (?). Habitual Constipation. No catarrh in father's family.

10. General health before marriage? b) since marriage? Paralysis? Brain Fever? Chronic Headache? Nervous Prostration? Catarrh? Hernia? Dyspepsia? Habitual Constipation? Inflammation of Bowels? Pleurisy? Bronchitis? Shortness of Breath? Spitting Blood? Consumption? Laryngitis? Tonsillitis? Insomnia? Rheumatism? Pneumonia? Jaundice? Varicose Veins?

    (a) Nervous a little. [Chronic Headache?] Nervous Prostration. Catarrh. Dyspepsia. Habitual Constipation. Pleurisy. Bronchitis (?). Shortness of Breath. Laryngitis. "Insomnia. Pneumonia.

    (b) Catarrh. Dyspepsia. Habitual Constipation. Shortness of Breath. Insomnia.

BLANK NO. 21   SERIES II, FORM B.

11. Menstruation:

   First menstruation at what age?

   16.

   and when thoroughly established?

   1 year.

   Present condition as regards menstruation:

   (a) How frequent?

      For years nearly every 3 weeks.

   (b) Is it regular or not?

   (c) Amount? how many napkins?

      Never much. 3 days & slight.

   (d) Duration?

   (e) Pain or not? at what time as to the flow?

      Most at first, [but also] before & all through. Have to be "rubbed to keep breath in me." [No pain?] the last day.

   (f) Is there any leucorrhoea (whites)? character?

      Yes.

      Amount?

      At one time when had prolapsus.

      Constant or occasional?

      Occasional.

   (g) Have you pain either frequently or habitually in the head, small of the back? abdomen or limbs?

      Pain in back of head at times and small of the back.

   (h) Disease or trouble in Uterus (womb) or other pelvic organs?

      Yes, inflammation at times.

BLANK NO. 21   SERIES II, FORM B.

   (i) Habit of bowels; how often?

   Go for days without passage.

12. What knowledge of sexual physiology had you before marriage? b) how did you obtain it?

   Not any to speak of.

13. Number of times married. If more than once additional blanks will be furnished you to answer the following questions separately in regard to each marriage?

   Once married

14. Number of years married?

   35

15. Do you habitually sleep with your husband? b) what reasons for so doing or not?

   Yes. Because it was the habit of people when I married to do so.

16. Number of conceptions?

   3

17. Number of children? State in connection with each, a) date of birth? b) sex? c) whether healthy or not? d) note any characteristic and the cause. e) note either immediate or after effect on your health of the birth of each of your children. f) give time of first menstruation after birth of each child.

   [f] Within six months.

18. Did conception occur by choice or accident?

   Accident.

19. Habit of intercourse, average number of times per week?

BLANK NO. 21   SERIES II, FORM B.

At first twice or three times per week. Later on less often.

per month?

per year?

20. Was intercourse held during pregnancy? If so, how often?

Very seldom.

(b) Had you any desire for it during this period?

No desire in the later months.

21 At other times have you any desire for intercourse? a) how often? b) at what time in relation to your menses?

At such times did not [answer incomplete].

22. Is intercourse agreeable to you or not?

At times.

Do you always have a venereal orgasm?

Not always.

1. When you do?

(a) Effect immediately afterwards?

(b) Effect next day?

Did not think of the effect upon me in relation to it next day.

2. - When you do not?

(a) Effect immediately afterwards?

(b) Effect next day?

Did not notice. Except sometimes felt weak though did not attribute it then to that.

BLANK NO. 21   SERIES II, FORM B.

23. What do you believe to be the true purpose of intercourse?

   (a) Necessity to man? to woman?

      Reproduction

   (b) Pleasure?

   (c) Reproduction?

   (d) What other reasons beside reproduction are sufficient to warrant intercourse?

      Affection, if any [other reason].

24. Have you ever used any means to prevent conception? a) if so, what? b) effect on your health?

25. What, to you, would be an ideal habit?

   Once a month until after the change [menopause] then not at all.

BLANK NO. 22   SERIES II, FORM B.

Date: Sept. 1897.

Your Father:
1. Nationality, if American, of what descent?
   American. English.

2. Home in city or country before marriage?
   City.

3. Home in city or country after marriage?
   City.

4. Age when married?
   Twenty-five (?)

5. Occupations before your birth?
   Physician.
   (b) After your birth?
       Physician.

6. Health previous to your birth?
   Excellent.
   (b) After your birth?
       Excellent.

7. Number of children living:
   (a) Boys: Two.
   (b) Girls: Four.

BLANK NO. 22   SERIES II, FORM B.

   8. Number of children dead; give age at time of death and cause.

      (a) Boys: One boy: dead from fever caused by accidental blow
          upon the head at six(?) mos.

      (b) Girls:

   9. If your father is living, give his age and present health,
      if dead, age at death and cause?

      Sixty. Excellent.

  10. Name any diseases in his family:

      Catarrh. Piles.

Your Paternal Grandfather: home in city or country?
Growing country town.

   1. Age when married?

   2. Occupations?

      Farmer & lawyer.

   3. Health?

      Excellent.

   4. Number of children?

      Eleven.

      Number reaching maturity?

      Eleven.

BLANK NO. 22						SERIES II, FORM B.

Your Paternal Grandmother: home in city or country?
Country.
   1. Age when married?

   2. Occupations?
      Housekeeping.

   3. Health?
      Excellent.

   4. Age and cause of death?

Your Mother:
   1. Nationality, if American of what descent?
      Irish.

   2. Home in city or country before marriage?
      City.
     (b) Home in city or country after marriage?
        City.

   3. Occupations before her marriage?
      Teacher.
     (b) After her marriage?
        Housekeeping.

BLANK NO. 22   SERIES II, FORM B.

4. Note any prenatal influences before your birth.

   None.

5. Her health previous to your birth?

   Excellent.

   (b) After your birth?

   Excellent.

6. Number of miscarriages?

   Two, caused by overwork.

7. Her age if living, and present health? if not, age at time of death and cause?

   Sixty-four. Has heart-trouble and is subject to intense emotional excitement and melancholia.

8. How was your mother's health affected by the climacteric (change of life)?

   The heart-trouble developed together with periods of morbid emotional excitement which have frequently to be quieted by the use of morphine. Climacteric began at about 45.

9. Name any diseases in her family:

Your Maternal Grandfather: home in city or country?

City.

   1. Age when married?

   Twenty-five.

BLANK NO. 22   SERIES II, FORM B.

   2. Occupations?

      Architect.

   3. Health?

      Excellent.

   4. Number of children?

      7.

      (b) Number reaching maturity?

         4.

Your Maternal Grandmother: home in city or country?
City.
   1. Age when married?

      Twenty.

   2. Occupations?

      House family.

   3. Health?

      Good.

   4. Age and cause of death?

      88. I do not know cause of death, but know she was a religious fanatic (R. Catholic), died in a convent and had melancholia.

BLANK NO. 22   SERIES II, FORM B.

Your Husband: nationality, if American, of what descent?
English.

1. Date of birth?

   Nov. 1865.

2. Early life in city or country?

   Country.

3. Height?

   5 ft. 9 in.

4. Weight?

   150 lbs.

5. Muscular or weak?

   Muscular.

6. Where educated? degrees if any?

   Syracuse Univ. M.P.

7. If a college man, has he been athletic?

   Yes.

8. Complexion?

   Fair.

9. Temperament?

   Nervous.

BLANK NO. 22   SERIES II, FORM B.

10. Does he use tobacco or stimulants?

   No.

11. Occupations?

   Teacher & Artist.

12. Health?

   Good.

13. Diseases in his family: Nervous Disorders? Rheumatism? Consumption? Dyspepsia? Varicose Veins? Heart Disease? Hernia? Habitual Constipation? Catarrh?

   Catarrh. I think they are all nervous to the extent of a "disorder" & have delicate stomachs.

Yourself:

   1. Date of birth?

      Jan. 8, 1867.

   2. Early life in city or country?

      City.

   3. Height?

      Five ft. 7 in.

   4. Weight?

      145 lbs.

   5. Complexion?

      Medium.

BLANK NO. 22   SERIES II, FORM B.

6. Temperament?

   Sanguine.

7. Where educated, give degrees if any?

   B.A. Radcliffe.

8. Occupations before marriage? a) in city or country? b) time spent in each?

   Teaching five years in Palo Alto [**California**].

9. Diseases in your family? from father or mother's side? Nervous Disorders? Rheumatism? Consumption? Dyspepsia? Varicose Veins? Heart Disease? Hernia? Habitual Constipation? Catarrh?

   Catarrh from father's side.

10. General health before marriage? b) since marriage? Paralysis? Brain Fever? Chronic Headache? Nervous Prostration? Catarrh? Hernia? Dyspepsia? Habitual Constipation? Inflammation of Bowels? Pleurisy? Bronchitis? Shortness of Breath? Spitting Blood? Consumption? Laryngitis? Tonsillitis? Insomnia? Rheumatism? Pneumonia? Jaundice? Varicose Veins?

    A slight touch of muscular rheumatism after exposure & overwork since I have lived in California, which has almost disappeared since last summer in the Sierras.

11. Menstruation:

    First menstruation at what age? and when thoroughly established?

    Fourteen. Regular from the start.

    Present condition as regards menstruation:

    (a) How frequent?

       Every 28 days.

BLANK NO. 22   SERIES II, FORM B.

(b) Is it regular or not?

   Yes.

(c) Amount? how many napkins?

   About ten.

(d) Duration?

   Five days.

(e) Pain or not? at what time as to the flow?

   Not unless tired; then about twelve hours after the flow begins I suffer from grinding pains that prevent my standing upright for 6 or 8 hrs.

(f) Is there any leucorrhoea (whites)?

   No.

   Amount?

   Constant or occasional?

   Never.

(g) Have you pain either frequently or habitually in the head, small of the back? abdomen or limbs?

   Frequently in the head. Varying from severe headaches (which always accompany menstruation) to sharp shooting pains when tired.

(h) Disease or trouble in Uterus (womb) or other pelvic organs?

   No.

   Have you ever had any <u>pelvic</u> trouble, or been under a physician's care. When and what was the trouble?

   Never.

(i) Habit of bowels; how often?

   One movement a day, after breakfast, very regular.

BLANK NO. 22   SERIES II, FORM B.

12. What knowledge of sexual physiology had you before marriage? b) how did you obtain it?

    General knowledge based on several years work, laboratory & otherwise, in Zoology & Physiology, & a good deal of reading in my father's library (he being a physician). I think I never <u>talked</u> with anybody on the subject except my husband.

13. Number of times married. If more than once additional blanks will be furnished you to answer the following questions separately in regard to each marriage?

    Once.

14. Number of years married?

    One.

15. Do you habitually sleep with your husband? b) what reasons for so doing or not?

    No. 1. More comfortable alone as to bed-clothes & room.
    2. Consider it more wholesome for anybody to sleep alone.
    3. To avoid temptation of too frequent intercourse.

    How long after marriage did first intercourse occur?

    Ten days.

16. Number of conceptions?

    One.

17. Number of children? State in connection with each: a) date of birth? b) sex? c) whether healthy or not? d) note any characteristic and the cause. e) note either immediate or after effect on your health of the birth of each of your children. f) give time of first menstruation after birth of each child.

    One [child].

    (a) May 25, 1897.

BLANK NO. 22   SERIES II, FORM B.

    (b) Girl.

    (c) Healthy.

    (d)

    (e) I had no local trouble, but great weakness owing to prolonged labor from which I still (3 1/2 mos.) feel the effect in gradually diminishing backaches, which were very severe the first six weeks after the labor.

    (f) Three months.

18. Did conception occur by choice or accident?

We believe that it dated from a time chosen by my husband as one that would probably result in pregnancy though I did not know his thought at the time.

19. Habit of intercourse, average number of times per week? per month? per year?

The circumstances of our one year of married life have been too varied to average a "habit." The following has been the case: Married June 10,1896; from June to January I suppose we averaged twice a week, after that (pregnancy having begun in August) there was no more intercourse until after the birth of the child (May 25); about four weeks after this date we were together for about two weeks during which intercourse occurred nearly every night.

20. Was intercourse held during pregnancy? If so, how often? b) had you any desire for it during this period?

    (b) I did not desire it during pregnancy at all.

21. At other times have you any desire for intercourse? a) how often? b) at what time in relation to your menses?

Before the birth of my child I never craved it, & often felt averse to it even during the early months of our married life. After the birth I cared for it, but as I was not menstruating I cannot answer b).

22. Is intercourse agreeable to you or not?

After it has begun, yes. If too long continued it wearies me.

Do you always have a venereal orgasm?

Never but once or twice.

1. - When you do,

(a) Effect immediately afterwards?

Do not notice any.

[Mosher's Note:] When she cares physically for it, [she has a] general sense of well being and relaxation & inclination to sleep. If she does not care physically for it, [she] is much more high strung & nervous. If intercourse is too much prolonged, she ceases to care for it, & becomes more & more nervous.

(b) Effect next day?

Do not notice any. Effects if any are always nervous.

2. - When you do not,

(a) Effect immediately afterwards?

During the first six months of our intercourse I usually felt wearied & "distasteful" afterward; even when the act itself had been very pleasant; those last two weeks when I really enjoyed it, I felt contented & physically at rest afterwards.

(b) Effect next day?

Do not notice any.

23. What do you believe to be the true purpose of intercourse?

(a) Necessity to man? to woman?

From my own thinking I have always believed that there was no more <u>necessity</u> for it in a healthy, pure-minded, actively-employed man than for a woman of the same

BLANK NO. 22   SERIES II, FORM B.

description as far as mere exercise of physical function goes.

(b) Pleasure?

In its right place and a minor purpose.

(c) Reproduction?

Yes, main reason.

(d) What other reasons beside reproduction are sufficient to warrant intercourse?

In the married condition my ideas as to the reasons for it have changed materially from what they were before marriage. I then thought reproduction was the only object & that once brought about [i.e., after conception], intercourse should cease. But in my experience the habitual bodily expression of love has a deep psychological effect in making possible complete mental sympathy & perfecting the spiritual union that must be the lasting "marriage" after the passion of love has passed away with the years.

24. Have you ever used any means to prevent conception? a) if so, what?

No.

(b) Effect on your health?

25. What, to you, would be an ideal habit?

To have it take place not more than from four to six times a month & then at the period that conception is least likely to take place (and ideally I should never have it take place then). Aside from that I should have intercourse entered upon for the purpose of reproduction with deliberate design on both sides in time and circumstances most favorable physically and spiritually for the accomplishment of an immensely important act. It amounts to separating times and objects of intercourse into (a) that of expression of love between man & woman (that act is frequently simply the extreme of causes of love's passion, which it would be a pity to limit it to once in two or three years) and (b) that of carrying on our share in the perpetuation of the race, which should be done carefully & prayerfully.

BLANK NO. 23				SERIES II, FORM B.

Date: March 28, 1920 [The date actually appears below]

Your Father:

1. Nationality, if American, of what descent?
   Eng[lish].

2. Home in city or country before marriage?

3. Home in city or country after marriage?

4. Age when married?

5. Occupations before your birth?
   Farmer.
   (b) After your birth?

6. Health previous to your birth?
   Good.
   (b) After your birth?
       2 [times] married.

7. Number of children living?
   (a) Boys:
   (b) Girls: 3.

8. Number of children dead; give age at time of death and cause.
   (a) Boys:
   (b) Girls:

BLANK NO. 23   SERIES II, FORM B.

   9. If your father is living, give his age and present health,
      if dead, age at death and cause?

  10. Name any diseases in his family:

Your Paternal Grandfather: home in city or country?

   1. Age when married?

   2. Occupations?

   3. Health?

   4. Number of children?

      Number reaching maturity?

Your Paternal Grandmother: home in city or country?

   1. Age when married?

   2. Occupations?

   3. Health?

   4. Age and cause of death?

Your Mother:

   1. Nationality, if American of what descent?

      American of English descent.

   2. Home in city or country before marriage?

      Country.

BLANK NO. 23   SERIES II, FORM B.

   (b) Home in city or country after marriage?

3. Occupations before her marriage?

   Teacher.

   (b) After her marriage?

   No.

4. Note any prenatal influences before your birth:

5. Her health previous to your birth?

   Good.

   (b) After your birth?

   Good.

6. Number of miscarriages?

7. Her age if living and present health? if not, age at time of death and cause?

   [Dead of] cancer at 57 when she [subject] was 13 years old.

8. How was your mother's health affected by the climacteric (change of life)?

   [Does] not know.

9. Name any diseases in her family:

Your Maternal Grandfather: home in city or country?

   1. Age when married?

   2. Occupations?

BLANK NO. 23   SERIES II, FORM B.

   3. Health?

   4. Number of children?
      (b) Number reaching maturity?

Your Maternal Grandmother: home in city or country?
   1. Age when married?

   2. Occupations?

   3. Health?

   4. Age and cause of death?

Your Husband: nationality, if American, of what descent?
   1. Date of birth?

   2. Early life in city or country?

   3. Height?

   4. Weight?

   5. Muscular or weak?

   6. Where educated? degrees if any?

   7. If a college man, has he been athletic?

   8. Complexion?

BLANK NO. 23   SERIES II, FORM B.

   9. Temperament?

   10. Does he use tobacco?

   11. Occupations?

   12. Health?

   13. Diseases in his family: Nervous Disorders? Rheumatism?
       Consumption? Dyspepsia? Varicose Veins? Heart Disease?
       Hernia? Habitual Constipation? Catarrh?

[Date:] March 28, 1920.

Yourself:

   1. Date of birth:

      18th Dec. 1864.

   2. Early life in city or country?

      Country.

   3. Height?

      5 ft. 4 in.

   4. Weight?

      125.   (115 **over.**)

   5. Complexion?

      Medium.

   6. Temperament?

BLANK NO. 23   SERIES II, FORM B.

Matter of fact.

7. Where educated, give degrees if any?

   2 yrs. Cornell Univ. Married and student at Swarthmore.

8. Occupations before marriage? a) in city or country? b) time spent in each?

   Teaching very short time.

9. Diseases in his family? from father or mother's side? Nervous Disorders? Rheumatism? Consumption? Dyspepsia? Varicose Veins? Heart Disease? Hernia? Habitual Constipation? Catarrh?

   Father - Rheumatism. Mother died of cancer.

10. General health before marriage? b) since marriage? Paralysis? Brain Fever? Chronic Headache? Nervous Prostration? Catarrh? Hernia? Dyspepsia? Habitual Constipation? Inflammation of Bowels? Pleurisy? Bronchitis? Shortness of Breath? Spitting Blood? Consumption? Laryngitis? Tonsillitis? Insomnia? Rheumatism? Pneumonia? Jaundice? Varicose Veins?

    Good, [illegible] not strong. Clothes very bad--heavy & tight clothes. Treated for [illegible] after marriage. Corset and waist put on by doctor and clothes supported--began to feel better.

11. Menstruation:

    First menstruation at what age? and when thoroughly established?

    About 14 years.--[doesn't remember]

    Present condition as regards menstruation:

    Ceased [in] 1912 when 48.

    (a) How frequent?

        28 - 35 days.

BLANK NO. 23   SERIES II, FORM B.

    (b) Is it regular or not?

        Fairly reg[ular] within those limits.

    (c) Amount? how many napkins?

        Moderately.

    (d) Duration?

        7 (3). [Maximum and minimum days duration?]

    (e) Pain or not? at what time as to the flow?

        Mod[erate] pain [for a few hours] at the beginning.

    (f) Is there any leucorrhoea (whites)? character?

        [Yes]

        Amount?

        Considerable.

        Constant or occasional?

    (g) Have you pain either frequently or habitually in the head, small of the back? abdomen or limbs?

    (h) Disease or trouble in Uterus (womb) or other pelvic organs?

        Displacement which yielded to [treatment?] after her heavy clothes were supported. '84 - '85 trouble. In '86 many new & fine clothes in latest fashion.

12. What knowledge of sexual physiology had you before marriage? b) how did you obtain it?

    None. May have read a book or two but does not remember.

13. Number of times married. If more than once additional blanks will be furnished you to answer the following questions in regard to each marriage?

14. Number of years married?

    34 years.

BLANK NO. 23   SERIES II, FORM B.

15. Do you habitually sleep with your husband? b) what reasons
    for so doing or not?

    No. In beginning yes--changed to separate beds because they
    did not sleep well, when 2nd child was born about 18 yrs. ago.

16. Number of conceptions?

    3.

17. Number of children? State in connection with each, a) date
    of birth? b) sex? c) whether healthy or not? d) note any
    characteristic and the cause. e) note either immediate or
    after effect on your health of the birth of each of your
    children. f) give time of first menstruation after birth
    of each child.

    [First child]

        (a) 1896.

        (b) Girl.

        (c) Healthy;very vital & nervous temperament.

        (e) After birth better health. Nursed child 9 mo.

        (f) Does not remember.

    [Second child]

        (a) 1902.

        (b) Girl.

        (c) 8 lbs., not strong.

        (e) Nursed child for short period, had much trouble about
            food. Mother had **threatened eclampsia.** Mother's
            health O.K.

18. Did **conception** occur by **choice** or **accident?**

    [First child was] wanted but not **planned for especially.**
    [Second child was an] accident.

BLANK NO. 23 SERIES II, FORM B.

19. Habit of intercourse, average number of times per week? per month? per year?

    [First ten years] once per month or less, always about that because of depletion of husband. Wife never conscious of need for more frequent [intercourse]. Husband had pyorrhea in recent years & was too depleted. Little intercourse for several years--wife felt forlorn & spiritual lack but no physical need.

20. Was intercourse held during pregnancy? If so, how often? b) had you any desire for it during this period?

21. At other times have you any desire for intercourse? a) how often? b) at what time in relation to your menses?

22. Is intercourse agreeable to you or not?

    Spiritual nearness, does not care physically--cares more now than in beginning because she loves husband infinitely more.

    Do you always have a venereal orgasm?

    Never.

    1. - When you do,

    (a) Effect immediately afterwards?

        Keyed up after and more stimulated.

    (b) Effect next day?

        No effect.

    2. - When you do not,

    (a) Effect immediately afterwards?

    (b) Effect next day?

23. What do you believe to be the true purpose of intercourse?

    (a) Necessity to man?

        Yes.

BLANK NO. 23   SERIES II, FORM B.

              to woman?

              No.

      (b) Pleasure?

              Yes.

      (c) Reproduction?

              Yes--not always.

      (d) What other reasons beside reproduction are sufficient to warrant intercourse?

              Pleasure man gets--and the pleasure of the intimacy with the one you love.

24. Have you ever used any means to prevent conception? a) if so, what?

    [A Mosher note indicates that the woman practiced no birth control beyond "refraining altogether," especially during the "mid-menstrual season." The woman had no knowledge of a "sterile period." She avoided work just before her period. For the first ten years of her marriage she went for "two or three years at a time with no intercourse; [she] would not do it again," which could mean either 1.) I'll never have intercourse again, or 2.) I'll never forego it for 2 or 3 yrs at a time.]

25. What, to you, would be an ideal habit?

    Once a month.

Does not remember whether periods were prolonged.

Menopause: menstrual flow increased; 1911 several terrific sick headaches (2 or 3). Very little trouble after it was over.

No thought or consciousness of sex need or sex life before married. Before marriage attracted to men; totally unconscious of sex need, but looks back and recognizes that certain men stirred in her sex attraction.

BLANK NO. 24   SERIES II, FORM B.

Your Father:

1. Nationality, if American, of what descent?

   German descent

2. Home in city or country before marriage?

   Childhood in country

3. Home in city or country after marriage?

   City.

4. Age when married?

   21 yrs.

5. Occupations before your birth?

   Shoemaker

   (b) After your birth?

   Shoemaker

6. Health previous to your birth?

   Good

   (b) After your birth?

   Good

7. Number of children living?

   (a) Boys: 0

   (b) Girls: 4

8. Number of children dead; give age at time of death and cause.

   (a) Boys:

BLANK NO. 24   SERIES II, FORM B.

   (b) Girls:

9. If your father is living, give his age and present health,
   if dead, age at   death and cause?

   53 yrs. Health [is] fair.

10. Name any diseases in his family:

Your Paternal Grandfather: home in city or country?
Country

   1. Age when married?

   2. Occupations?

      Farmer

   3. Health?

   4. Number of children?

      10

      Number reaching maturity?

      9

Your Paternal Grandmother: home in city or country?
Country

   1. Age when married?

   2. Occupations?

      Farmer's wife--[she has been a widow so long she is] practically
      a farmer herself.

BLANK NO. 24   SERIES II, FORM B.

   3. Health?

      Good up to 75 yrs.

   4. Age and cause of death?

      83. Paralysis.

Your Mother:

   1. Nationality: if American of what descent?

      Scotch, English, Welsh

   2. Home in city or country before marriage?

      Town

      (b) Home in city or country after her marriage?

          Town

   3. Occupations before her marriage?

      (b) After her marriage?

   4. Note any prenatal influences before your birth?

   5. Her health previous to your birth?

      (b) After your birth?

          She had for several years falling of the womb; immediate
          cause, or time first appeared, I do not know.

   6. Number of miscarriages?

   7. Her age if living, and present health? if not, age at time
      of death and cause?

      32 yrs. Congestion of Bowels.

BLANK NO. 24   SERIES II, FORM B.

8. How was your mother's health affected by the climacteric (change of life)?

9. Name any diseases in her family:

   Dyspepsia

Your Maternal Grandfather: home in city or country?
Country

   1. Age when married?

      22?

   2. Occupations?

      Gunsmith

   3. Health?

      Fair

   4. Number of children?

      6

     (b) Number reaching maturity?

        6

Your Maternal Grandmother: home in city or country?
City

   1. Age when married?

      18

   2. Occupations?

BLANK NO. 24   SERIES II, FORM B.

   3. Health?

      Dyspeptic

   4. Age and cause of death?

      84; Pneumonia

Your Husband: nationality, if American, of what descent?
American. Swiss-German [descent].

   1. Date of birth?

      Aug. 30, 1862.

   2. Early life in city or country?

      Country

   3. Height?

      6 feet.

   4. Weight?

      145 lbs.

   5. Muscular or weak?

      Muscular

   6. Where educated? degrees if any?

      Ind[iana] University, A.M.

   7. If a college man, has he been athletic?

      Baseball to some extent.

BLANK NO. 24   SERIES II, FORM B.

   8. Complexion?

      Dark

   9. Temperament?

      (Not nervous to any great degree)

   10. Does he use tobacco?

       NO!

   11. Occupations?

       Farm life - teacher. Indefatigable worker.

   12. Health?

       Good with care; has to husband his strength. Grippe, special
       cause.

   13. Diseases in his family: Nervous Disorders? Rheumatism?
       Consumption? Dyspepsia? Varicose Veins? Heart Disease?
       Hernia? Habitual Constipation? Catarrh?

'ourself:

   1. Date of birth?

      Nov. 15, 1862

   2. Early life in city or country?

      City

   3. Height?

      5 feet, 4 inches.

BLANK NO. 24   SERIES II, FORM B.

4. Weight?

   171 lbs.

5. Complexion?

   Neither fair nor dark.

6. Temperament?

   Nervous

7. Where educated, give degrees if any?

   Indiana University.

8. Occupations before marriage? a) in city or country? b) time spent in each?

   An old fashioned training in housewifely arts and [the] too practical use of same, lasting nearly through my nineteenth year. Began teaching at seventeen and taught nearly six years before marriage.

9. Diseases in your family? from father or mother's side? Nervous Disorders? Rheumatism? Consumption? Dyspepsia? Varicose Veins? Heart Disease? Hernia? Habitual **constipation**? Catarrh?

   Dyspepsia, habitual **constipation**, catarrh

10. General health before marriage? b) since marriage? Paralysis? Brain Fever? Chronic Headache? Nervous Prostration? Catarrh? Hernia? Dyspepsia Habitual Constipation? Inflammation of Bowels?   Pleurisy? Bronchitis? Shortness of Breath? Spitting Blood? Consumption? Laryngitis? Tonsillitis   Insomnia? Rheumatism? Pneumonia? Jaundice? Varicose Veins?

    General health before marriage was good although I overworked at teaching and again as student. Since marriage aside from state of health incident to childbearing and nursing, my health has been good except possibly for a growing tendency to nervousness. Grippe at 30 was followed by rheumatism and pleurisy.

11. Menstruation:

First menstruation at what age? and when thoroughly established?

First menstruation at 12 yrs. 6 mos.; a year or less later.

Present condition as regards menstruation:

(a) How frequent?

30 or 31 days.

(b) Is it regular or not?

Grippe on three occasions has produced irregularity -- long delays; ordinarily regular.

(c) Amount? how many napkins?

Amount medium; 6 to 8

(d) Duration?

4 to 6 days

(e) Pain or not?   at what time as to the flow?

Seldom any pain since childbearing. When it occurs it generally precedes and attends the first day. When experiencing no pain, often feel weaker and more nervous in the second day. Duration is shorter and amount less as I grow older.

(f) Is there any leucorrhoea (whites)? character?

Have had leucorrhoea, teaching, when overstrained.

Amount?

Never enough to demand a napkin except for <u>nicety</u> with respect [to outer] clothing.

Constant or occasional?

Very   occasionally.

BLANK NO. 24   SERIES II, FORM B.

    (g) Have you pain either frequently or habitually in the head, small of the back? abdomen or limbs?

    (h) Disease or trouble in Uterus (womb) or other pelvic organs?

    My physician says that the womb and vagina are much enlarged and there is retroversion of womb, and double laceration incurred in child bearing. Seldom have any consciousness of those organs.

    (i) Habit of bowels; how often?

    [Frequent?]; two and three evacuations daily.

12. What knowledge of sexual physiology had you before marriage? b) how did you obtain it?

    Learned everything I know from good sources and in a pure and sacred way. Had access to **Cowan's** Science of a New Life, [Dr. George] Naphey's **Physical Life of Woman** and from best pages of [Orson Squire] **Fowler.**

13. Number of times married. If more than once additional blanks will be furnished you to answer the following questions separately in regard to each marriage?

14. Number of years married?

    Nearly seven

15. Do you habitually sleep with your husband? b) what reasons for so doing or not?

    Have slept with my husband except during greater part of pregnancy. Chief reason for occupying same bed is that we are yet in the phase of "getting along." Personally I prefer to sleep alone always.

16. Number of conceptions?

    Three

BLANK NO. 23   SERIES II, FORM B.

17. Number of children? State in connection with each, a) date
    of birth? b) sex? c) whether healthy or not? d) note any
    characteristic and the cause. e) note either immediate or
    after effect on your health of the birth of each of your
    children. f) give time of first menstruation after birth of
    each child.

    [First child]

        (a) April 25, 1888.

        (b) Son.

        (c) Strong and robust; has developed into a bright and
            very happy child, truly a "love-child."

        (d) Has a tendency to nervousness which I account for
            largely by my having taught through the fifth month
            of that pregnancy beginning with the second month.

        (f) Menstruated sixth month.

        (e) I never regained my shape after first birth and
            increased a good deal in weight, say 20 or 25 lbs.
            Was allowed to eat heartily the first three days and
            had a great excess of milk. My general health was
            excellent until my second conception.

    [Second child]

        (a) Jan. 4, 1890.

        (b) Daughter.

        (c) Apparently healthy and vigorous inclined to sleep more
            than first child. Very well until the fifth month when
            showed a decided derangement of bowels followed by
            nervous **affections**,   later convulsions of light
            character, associated with teething seemingly. The
            nervous system still so seriously deranged at two and
            a half that we decided there was no longer reason to
            hope dentition was the cause. Finally took her to New
            York where she was operated on, her case being described
            as arrested cerebral development due to a too early
            ossification of the bones of the skull. She neither
            walked nor talked. The operation proving fatal, she
            died at the age of 3 yrs. 3 wks.

        (d) The first three months of the second pregnancy I
            suffered greatly from nervousness, nursing first child
            perhaps six wks. after conception. We have always
            wondered greatly if the daughter's sad development were

BLANK NO. 24   SERIES II, FORM B.

influenced by the sickness mentioned above or by prenatal
conditions. Dr. Hammond of N.Y. said it was by no means necessarily
prenatal influence, that such change might occur in children
much older and perfectly normal.

(a) July 9, 1891.

(b) Son.

(c) A large child (12 lbs.), proclaimed the finest new born
child ever seen by doctor, nurse and alas! undertaker.
He had an obstruction in breathing and lived only 10
hours.

(e) After this birth I regained robust health slowly but
increased rapidly in weight gaining 30 lbs. in 3 mo.
time.

18. Did conception occur by choice or accident?

I may say that first one did; second one did not, & third
by accident.

19. Habit of intercourse, average number of times per week?

Per month?

Three or four.

Per year?

20. Was intercourse held during pregnancy? If so, how often?
b) had you any desire for it during this period?

Very rarely to both.

21 At other times have you any desire for intercourse? a) how
often? b) at what time in relation to your menses?

Generally desire precedes and follows menstruation -- always
through fertile period.

BLANK NO. 24   SERIES II, FORM B.

22. Is intercourse agreeable to you or not?

   Do you always have a venereal orgasm?

   I have been very much in love with my husband and have ... rather cultivated the passion, to effect the "compromise" in this direction that must come in every other when people marry. Except at first conception, I had hardly experienced an orgasm until the fifth or sixth year of married life. It does not occur now half the time, but makes intercourse in a sense more agreeable. It makes it also more exhausting, if at all intense.

   1. - When you do,

   (a) Effect immediately afterwards?

   (b) Effect next day?

      I have seldom if ever found the reaction affecting me the next day.

   2. - When you do not,

   (a) Effect immediately afterwards?

      Effects when at all intense (which is very seldom) the nervous system, noticeably at the base of the brain and in lumbar region.

   (b) Effect next day?

23. What do you believe to be the true purpose of intercourse?

   (a) Necessity to man?

      ?

      to woman?

      To none that I have known.

   (b) Pleasure?

   (c) Reproduction?

   (d) What other reasons beside reproduction are sufficient to warrant intercourse?

      I have thought a good deal about it and am not sure that reproduction is the only function. The marital relation when <u>mutual</u> begets a certain bond of love and sympathy that <u>is</u> certainly peculiar only to those happily mated.

24. Have you ever used any means to prevent conception? a) if so, what?

   Withdrawal.

   (b) Effect on your health?

25. What, to you, would be an ideal habit?

   My ideas have undergone some modification through experience. I most heartily wish there were no accidental conceptions. I believe the world would take a most gigantic stride toward high ethical conditions, if every child brought into the world were the product of pure love and conscious choice.
   I cannot recognize as true marriage, that relation unaccompanied by a strong desire for children. Platonic love from this point of view is almost as far removed from my standard as marriage, that is a form of so called legalized prostitution.
   To a girl about to marry I feel like imposing this test. "Seriously is your lover the man of all men, to whose children you would like to be mother? Do you want children?" Any womanly girl will be repelled by a dislike for children in a man. I believe our future sociology, and ethics,and poetry must find in the <u>family</u> its most vital theme.
   I cannot be a strong temperance woman for I do not know intemperance as a reality; and the same is true of abuses of the marital relation. My own experience in bearing children in close succession is probably due to an unusually long period of fertility, rather than excess.
   First child was conceived immediately before the monthly period and the second after the eighteenth day from first appearance of menses.

BLANK NO. 25   SERIES II, FORM B.

Date: Feb. 12, 1896

Your Father:
  1. Nationality, if American, of what descent?
     American, French descent

  2. Home in city or country before marriage?
     Country

  3. Home in city or country after marriage?
     Country

  4. Age when married?
     About 32.

  5. Occupations before your birth?
     Physician
     (b) After your birth?
        Physician

  6. Health previous to your birth?
     Good
     (b) After your birth?
        Good

  7. Number of children living?
     (a) Boys: 2
     (b) Girls: 4

BLANK NO. 25				SERIES II, FORM B.

   8. Number of children dead; give age at time of death and cause?

      (a) Boys:

      (b) Girls: One of scarlet fever.   One of **brain fever.**

   9. If your father is living, give his age and present health, if dead, age at death and cause?

      Age 74. Has some rheumatism.

  10. Name any diseases in his family:

      His father & mother died of heart disease, but they were both over 50.

Your Paternal Grandfather: home in city or country?

Country.

   1. Age when married?

     Don't know.

   2. Occupations?

     Physician.

   3. Health?

     Don't know.

   4. Number of children?

     7

     Number reaching maturity?

     6

BLANK NO. 25   SERIES II, FORM B.

Your Paternal Grandmother: home in city or country?
Country.
    1. Age when married?

    2. Occupations?
            House-keeper.

    3. Health?

    4. Age and cause of death?
    Over 50. Heart disease.

Your Mother:
    1. Nationality, if American of what descent?
    American, English descent.

    2. Home in city or country before marriage?
    Country.
      (b) Home in city or country after marriage?
        Country

    3. Occupations before her marriage?
    Lived with her people.
      (b) After her marriage?
        House-keeper.

    4. Note any prenatal influences before your birth:

BLANK NO. 25   SERIES II, FORM B.

5. Her health previous to your birth?

   Not good.

   (b) After your birth?

   Not good.

6. Number of miscarriages?

   One.

7. Her age if living and present health? if not, age at time of death and cause?

   Died when about 33, six months after I was **born, of blood** poisoning, a swelling came between her breasts, which would not come to a head.

8. How was your mother's health affected by the climacteric (change of life)?

9. Name any diseases in her family:

Your Maternal Grandfather: home in city or country?
Country.

1. Age when married?

   Don't know.

2. Occupations?

   Farmer.

3. Health?

   Good

BLANK NO. 25   SERIES II, FORM B.

    4. Number of children?

       5

      (b) Number reaching maturity?

         5

Your Maternal Grandmother: home in city or country?
Country

    1. Age when married?

      Don't know.

    2. Occupations?

      House keeper.

    3. Health?

      Good.

    4. Age and cause of death?

      Still living, at the age of 92.

Your Husband: nationality, if American, of what descent?
[Fifth child born of both parents]

    1. Date of birth?

      Aug. 1866

BLANK NO. 25   SERIES II, FORM B.

2. Early life in city or country?
   Country

3. Height?
   6 feet, 7 inches

4. Weight?
   174 lbs.

5. Muscular or weak?
   Muscular

6. Where educated? degrees if any?
   Syracuse University, B.A., M.A.

7. If a college man, has he been athletic?
   Yes.

8. Complexion?
   Light

9. Temperament?
   Slightly nervous

10. Does he use tobacco? or stimulants?
    No.

11. Occupations?
    Teacher

BLANK NO. 25   SERIES II, FORM B.

12. Health?

    Good.

13. Diseases in his family: Nervous Disorders? Rheumatism? Consumption? Dyspepsia? Varicose Veins? Heart Disease? Hernia? Habitual Constipation? Catarrh?

    Mother somewhat nervous.

Yourself:

1. Date of birth?

   Jan. 22, 1866

   [Fourth child born of both parents.]

2. Early life in city or country?

   Country.

3. Height?

   5 ft., 5 in.

4. Weight?

   158 lbs.

5. Complexion?

   Medium.

6. Temperament?

   Somewhat nervous.

7. Where educated, give degrees if any?

   Cortland, New York. Graduated from a normal school.

BLANK NO. 25   SERIES II, FORM B.

8. Occupations before marriage? a) in city or country? b) time
    spent in each?

    Teacher in the country.

9. Diseases in your family? from father or mother's side? **Nervous
    Disorders? Rheumatism? Consumption? Dyspepsia? Varicose
    Veins? Heart Disease? Hernia? Habitual Constipation? Catarrh?**

10. General health before marriage? b) since marriage? **Paralysis?
    Brain Fever? Chronic Headache? Nervous Prostration? Catarrh?
    Hernia? Dyspepsia? Habitual Constipation? Inflammation of
    Bowels? Pleurisy? Bronchitis? Shortness of Breath? Spitting
    Blood? Consumption? Laryngitis? Tonsillitis? Insomnia?
    Rheumatism? Pneumonia? Jaundice? Varicose Veins?**

    Good.

    (b) Good.

11. Menstruation:

    First menstruation at what age?

    When 13 1/2 years old.

    and when thoroughly established?

    Six months later.

    Present condition as regards menstruation:

    (a) How frequent?

    (b) Is it regular or not?

        Not regular. Anywhere from 4 to 7 weeks. Have gone 10
        weeks.

285

BLANK NO. 25   SERIES II, FORM B.

   (c) Amount? how many napkins?

       About 12.

   (d) Duration?

       7 days.

   (e) Pain or not? at what time as to the flow?

       During the first two days, sometimes I have more or less pain. Since my baby came I have much less pain than before he was born.

   (f) Is there any leucorrhoea (whites)? character?

       Sometimes I have colorless leucorrhoea after menstruation.

       Amount?

       Very slight

       Constant or occasional?

       Occasional. When I take cold or become very tired.

   (g) Have you pain either frequently or habitually in the head, small of the back? abdomen or limbs?

       No.

       Any pain or other trouble before marriage?

       No.

   (h) Disease or trouble in Uterus (womb) or other pelvic organs?

       No.

   (i) Habit of bowels; how often?

       Once a day.

12. What knowledge of sexual physiology had you before marriage? b) how did you obtain it?

    I had studied physiology in the Normal School. During one of the vacations I read some of my father's medical books. With that and what was taught in the school I had a fair

BLANK NO. 25   SERIES II, FORM B.

knowledge of sexual physiology of the female. Of the male I knew but very little if anything.

12B How long after marriage was 1st intercourse?

Two weeks.

13. Number of times married. If more than once additional blanks will be furnished you to answer the following questions separately in regard to each marriage?

Once.

14. Number of years married?

4 years, 7 months.

15. Do you habitually sleep with your husband?

No.

(b) What reasons for so doing or not?

After baby came, we soon found we could get more sleep by each having a room. If the baby awakened in the night it disturbed my husband. My husband is not a good sleeper & if he wanted a light to read it disturbed me.

16. Number of conceptions?

One.

17. Number of children? State in connection with each, a) date of birth? b) sex? c) whether healthy or not? d) note any characteristic and the cause. e) note either immediate or after effect on your health of the birth of each of your children. f) give time of first menstruation after birth of each child.

[One child]

(a) April 16, 1893.

(b) Male.

(c) Healthy.

BLANK NO. 25   SERIES II, FORM B.

   (d)

   (e) My health was not good for the first year. I think the
       cause was over anxiety for the baby.

   (f) 24 days, then again six weeks later. My mother and a
       sister menstruated within six weeks after their first
       child was born.

18. Did conception occur by choice or accident?

    Accident. 15 days after menstruation.

19. Habit of intercourse, average number of times per week? per
    month?

    Once a month, or once between the menstrual period.

    Per year?

20. Was intercourse held during pregnancy? If so, how often?

    No.

    (b) Had you any desire for it during this period?

        No.

21. At other times have you any desire for intercourse? a) how
    often?

    Sometimes, but not often, a caress from my husband will cause
    me to think of it. It is hardly enough to call it a desire.

    (b) At what time in relation to your menses?

        Sometimes a day or so after menstruation.

22. Is intercourse agreeable to you or not?

    Yes. But there are times when it would not be.

    Do you always have a venereal orgasm?

    No.

BLANK NO. 25   SERIES II, FORM B.

1. - When you do,

(a) Effect immediately afterwards?

One of exhaustion & I want to be quiet and go to sleep.

(b) Effect next day?

No effect.

2. - When you do not,

(a) Effect immediately afterwards?

Very slight exhaustion.

(b) Effect next day?

No effect.

23. What do you believe to be the true purpose of intercourse?

(a) Necessity to man?

No.

to woman?

No.

(b) Pleasure?

(c) Reproduction?

Yes.

(d) What other reasons beside reproduction are sufficient to warrant intercourse?

When I was first married a caress or even a touch of the hand from my husband would cause much colorless leucorrhoea. The entire lower part of my abdomen became very sore. This continued for two weeks until the first intercourse. A day or so after that the soreness was entirely gone and I was not troubled with leucorrhoea. While I was pregnant & for about six months after there was no trouble or desire for intercourse. As I became strong & well the same symptoms that I had when first married appeared **again. For the first two weeks of our married life my husband suffered from soreness even more than I.**

BLANK NO. 25					SERIES II, FORM B.

24. Have you ever used any means to prevent conception? a) if so, what?

   The only thing we have ever done to prevent conception is for neither of us to have an orgasm.

   (b) Effect on your health?

25. What, to you, would be an ideal　　habit?

   Not to desire intercourse, except for reproduction.

BLANK NO. 26   SERIES II, FORM B.

Your Father:
1. Nationality, if American, of what descent?
   American, English descent.

2. Home in city or country before marriage?
   Country.

3. Home in city or country after marriage?
   Both.

4. Age when married?
   25.

5. Occupations before your birth?
   Farmer.
   (b) After your birth?
   Pharmacist.

6. Health   previous to your birth?
   Not strong.
   (b) After your birth?
   Never a well man.

7. Number of children living?
   (a) Boys: 1
   (b) Girls: 2

8. Number of children dead; give age at time of death and cause?
   (a) Boys: One boy died at 4 years & 4 mo. of Typhoid fever.

BLANK NO. 26   SERIES II, FORM B.

   (b) Girls:

9. If your father is living, give his age and present health,
   if dead, age at death and cause?

   Died at 66 yrs. 8 mo. of Angina Pectoris.

10. Name any diseases in his family:

    Heart disease.

Your Paternal Grandfather: home in city or country?

  1. Age when married?
     30
  2. Occupations?

     Lawyer

  3. Health?

     Good.

  4. Number of children?

     11

     Number reaching maturity?

     9

Your Paternal Grandmother: home in city or country?
City.

  1. Age when married?

     25

  2. Occupations?

BLANK NO. 26   SERIES II, FORM B.

   3. Health?

      Good

   4. Age and cause of death?

      87. Paralysis.

Your Mother:

   1. Nationality, if American of what descent?

      American, English descent.

   2. Home in city or country before marriage?

      Country

      (b) Home in city or country after marriage?

          Both.

   3. Occupations before her marriage?

      Sewing.

      (b) After her marriage?

   4. Note any prenatal influences before your birth:

      Cause for anxiety through business reversal.

   5. Her health previous to your birth?

      Good.

      (b) After your birth?

          Good.

   6. Number of miscarriages?

BLANK NO. 26   SERIES II, FORM B.

    One.

    7. Her age if living and present health? if not, age at time of
       death and cause?

       70 years old.   Health delicate.

    8. How was your mother's health affected by the climacteric
       (change of life)?

       Much improved.

    9. Name any diseases in her family:

       Consumption.

Your Maternal Grandfather: home in city or country?
Country

    1. Age when married?

       23

    2. Occupations?

       Farmer

    3. Health?

       Delicate until 55.   Since [then] very well.   Now 95.

    4. Number of children?

       9

       (b) Number reaching maturity?

           6

BLANK NO. 26   SERIES II, FORM B.

Your Maternal Grandmother: home in city or country?
Country

    1. Age when married?

       22

    2. Occupations?

    3. Health?

       Very good

    4. Age and cause of death?

       86 -- Paralysis.

Your Husband: nationality, if American, of what descent?

        English

    1. Date of birth?

       Aug. 1, 1855

    2. Early life in city or country?

       Country

    3. Height?

       6 feet, 2 inches

    4. Weight?

       160 lbs.

    5. Muscular or weak?

       Muscular

BLANK NO. 26   SERIES II, FORM B.

   6. Where educated? degrees if any?

      Dartmouth College, B.A., 1876

   7. If a college man, has he been athletic?

      No.

   8. Complexion?

      Dark complexion.

   9. Temperament?

      Even.

   10. Does he use tobacco?

       No.

   11. Occupations?

       Principal of High School.

   12. Health?

       <u>Excellent</u>. Died from effect of accident April 2, 1888.

   13. Diseases in his family: Nervous Disorders? Rheumatism?
       Consumption? Dyspepsia? Varicose Veins? Heart Disease?
       Hernia? Habitual Constipation? Catarrh?

Yourself:

   1. Date of birth?

      Feb. 8, 1859

   2. Early life in city or country?

BLANK NO. 26   SERIES II, FORM B.

   Country

3. Height?

   5 ft., 3 1/2 in.

4. Weight?

   145 [lbs.]

5. Complexion?

   Light

6. Temperament?

   Even.

7. Where educated, give degrees if any?

   Wellesley College, B.A., 1881

8. Occupations before marriage? a) in city or country? b) time spent in each?

   Teacher. 2 yrs. in country, 4 yrs. in city.

9. Diseases in your family? from father or mother's side? Nervous Disorders? Rheumatism? Consumption? Dyspepsia? Varicose Veins? Heart Disease? Hernia? Habitual Constipation? Catarrh?

   Heart disease from father's side. Tendency to Dyspepsia from both sides.

10. General health before marriage? b) since marriage? Paralysis? Brain Fever? Chronic Headache? Nervous Prostration? Catarrh? Hernia? Dyspepsia? Habitual Constipation? Inflammation of Bowels? Pleurisy? Bronchitis? Shortness of Breath? Spitting Blood? Consumption? Laryngitis? Tonsillitis? Insomnia? Rheumatism? Pneumonia? Jaundice? Varicose Veins?

BLANK NO. 26   SERIES II, FORM B.

   (a) Health good but not robust.
   (b) Health good but not robust.

11. Menstruation:
   First menstruation at what age?
   14 yrs.
   And when thoroughly established?
   14 yrs.
   Present condition as regards menstruation:
   (a) How frequent?
       Once in 28 days.
   (b) Is it regular or not?
       Regular.
   (c) Amount? how many napkins?
       10 - 12.
   (d) Duration?
       5 days.
   (e) Pain or not?
       Very little pain, if any.
       At what time as to the flow?
       At the beginning.
   (f) Is there any leucorrhoea (whites)? character?
       A little.
       Amount?
       Constant or occasional?
       Occasional.

BLANK NO. 26					SERIES II, FORM B.

(g) Have you pain either frequently or habitually in the head, small of the back? abdomen or limbs?

No.

(h) Disease or trouble in Uterus (womb) or other pelvic organs?

Retroversion of the uterus.

(i) Habit of bowels; how often?

Daily.

12. What knowledge of sexual physiology had you before marriage? b) how did you obtain it?

Very little - obtained from reading physiology and Naphey's book on women. (I cannot give the title.)

13. Number of times married. If more than once additional blanks will be furnished you to answer the following questions separately in regard to each marriage?

Once.

14. Number of years married?

Nine months.

15. Do you habitually sleep with you husband? b) what reasons for so doing or not?

I did.

16. Number of conceptions?

None.

17. Number of children? State in connection with each, a) date of birth? b) sex? c) whether healthy or not? d) note any characteristic and the cause. e) note either immediate or after effect on your health of the birth of each of your children. f) give time of first menstruation after birth of each child.

BLANK NO. 26   SERIES II, FORM B.

18. Did conception occur by choice or accident?

19. Habit of intercourse, average number of times per week?

    Once.

    per month?

    Three times.

    per year?

20. Was intercourse held during pregnancy? If so, how often?
    b) had you any desire for it during this period?

21. At other times had you any desire for intercourse? a) how often? b) at what time in relation to your menses?

    Yes. After the menses.

22. Is intercourse agreeable to you or not?

    Yes.

    Do you always have a venereal orgasm?

    No.

    1. - When you do,

    (a) Effect immediately afterwards?

    (b) Effect next day?

    2. - When you do not,

    (a) Effect immediately afterwards?

    (b) Effect next day?

23. What do you believe to be the true purpose of intercourse?

    (a) Necessity to man? to woman?

    (b) Pleasure?

BLANK NO. 26   SERIES II, FORM B.

    (c) Reproduction?

    (d) What other reasons beside reproduction are sufficient to
        warrant intercourse?

        Reproduction and pleasure.

24. Have you ever used any means to prevent conception?   a) if
    so, what?

    Incomplete intercourse.

    (b) Effect on your health?

        Not good.

25. What, to you, would be an ideal habit?

BLANK NO. 27   SERIES II, FORM B.

[Dr. Mosher noted that the answers to this questionnaire began here.]

12. What knowledge of sexual physiology had you before marriage? b) how did you obtain it?

    None. Ran away 1 mo. after marriage. Sent back by parents & told to behave.

13. Number of times married. If more than once additional blanks will be furnished you to answer the following questions separately in regard to each marriage?

    2.

14. Number of years married?

    11.

15. Do you habitually sleep with your husband? b) what reasons for so doing or not?

16. Number of conceptions?

17. Number of children? State in connection with each, a) date of birth? b) sex? c) whether healthy or not? d) note any characteristic and the cause. e) note either immediate or after effect on your health of the birth of each of your children. f) give time of first menstruation after birth of each child.

18. Did conception occur by choice or accident?

    Accident.

19. Habit of intercourse, average number of times per week? per month? per year?

    3 times a week [or] oftener if she would submit. With 1st husband never conceived if intercourse was omitted for 14 days after menstruation.

BLANK NO. 27   SERIES II, FORM B.

20. Was intercourse held during pregnancy? If so, how often?

    Same [as before pregnancy] up to 6 months.

    (b) Had you any desire for it during this period?

        None. Caused excruciating pain during later mos.

21. At other times have you any desire for intercourse? a) how often? b) at what time in relation to your menses?

    Agreeable occasionally. About once in 2 wks.

22. Is intercourse agreeable to you or not?

    Sometimes.

    Do you always have a venereal orgasm?

    1. - When you do,

    (a) Effect immediately afterwards?

        Always wide awake and very nervous.

    (b) Effect next day?

    2. - When you do not,

    (a) Effect immediately afterwards?

    (b) Effect next day?

23. What do you believe to be the true purpose of intercourse?

    (a) Necessity to man?

        ?

        To woman?

        No.

    (b) Pleasure?

        [Yes]

BLANK NO. 27   SERIES II, FORM B.

   (c) Reproduction?

   [Yes]

   (d) What other reasons beside reproduction are sufficient to
       warrant intercourse?

   Necessary to keep home together and keep man satisfied.

24. Have you ever used any means to prevent conception? a) if
    so, what?

   Douches of all kinds.

   (b) Effect on your health?

   Bad. 1 elect[rical?] treatment, not an abortion.

25. What, to you, would be an ideal habit?

   Once in 2 wks omitting 14 days after menstruation to avoid
   conception.

BLANK NO. 28   SERIES II, FORM B.

Your Father:

   1. Nationality, if American, of what descent?

      Scotch

   2. Home in city or country before marriage?

      College Town

   3. Home in city or country after marriage?

      [Unintelligible]

   4. Age when married?

      25

   5. Occupations before your birth?

      Government Service founding system of public schools.

      (b) After your birth?

          Educational

   6. Health previous to your birth?

      Good, but overworked.

      (b) After your birth?

          Student [of medicine and theology], missionary. Died at 55--killed by [a] horse.

   7. Number of children living?

      (a) Boys: 1

      (b) Girls: 5 (1 invalid from prenatal cause [unintelligible]. Nervous Dyspepsia.)

BLANK NO. 28   SERIES II, FORM B.

   8. Number of children dead; give age at time of death and cause.

      (a) Boys: Killed by horse & aneurism [at] 33, 2 in infancy.
          1 at 53 yrs. from overwork causing paralysis.

      (b) Girls: Asthma [at] 58

   9. If your father is living, give his age and present health,
      if dead, age at death and cause?

      55 yrs. killed by horse.

  10. Name any diseases in his family:

      All trouble came from nervous system.

Your Paternal Grandfather: home in city or country?

Farmer owning land in **Susquehanna C.[ounty]**.

   1. Age when married?

      30

   2. Occupations?

      Prof. [of] math in a college & farmer.

   3. Health?

      Homesickness. Had 10 children. Did not drink to excess
      until later. Died at 63 or 64.

   4. Number of children?

      10

      Number reaching maturity?

      10. 1 died **insane with measles at 22 years.**

BLANK NO. 28   SERIES II, FORM B.

Your Paternal Grandmother: home in city or country?
Penna.
   1. Age when married?
      23

   2. Occupations?
      Housewife

   3. Health?
      Good health

   4. Age and cause of death?
      Suddenly, sudden stroke of paralysis.

Your Mother:
   1. Nationality, if American of what descent?
      Scotch

   2. Home in city or country before marriage?
      [Country]
      (b) Home in city or country after marriage?
          Teaching missionary work.

   3. Occupations before her marriage?
      Several years teaching.
      (b) After her marriage?
          Teaching missionary. **9th [child] of mother.**

BLANK NO. 28   SERIES II, FORM B.

4. Note any prenatal influences before your birth:

   [The subject's] 14 mo. older brother died. Her mother had hard time recuperat[ing]. ...

5. Her health previous to your birth?

   Good.

   (b) After your birth?

   Next child 14 mo. after.

6. Number of miscarriages?

7. Her age if living and present health? if not, age at time of death and cause?

   8[6?] yr. 5 mo. Splendid health until last year [when a] fall from [a] carriage caused her death.

8. How was your mother's health affected by the climacteric (change of life)?

   7 yrs, almost an invalid, could not stand any confusion.

9. Name any diseases in her family:

   Nervous weaknesses. Father's sister had cancer from **bruise**. She died insane; she was a deaf mute.

Your Maternal Grandfather: home in city or country?

Country

1. Age when married?

   Mature

2. Occupations?

   Farmer in [Massachusetts]

BLANK NO. 28   SERIES II, FORM B.

   3. Health?

      Excellent

   4. Number of children?

      3

      (b) Number reaching maturity?

          3. 1 died of pneumonia & consumption result from childbirth.

Your Maternal Grandmother: home in city or country?
Country

   1. Age when married?

      Mature

   2. Occupations?

      Spinning, weaving, housekeeping. Daughter of **Captain in** Rev[olutionary] War.

   3. Health?

      Good

   4. Age and cause of death?

      72 dysentery

Your Husband: nationality, if American, of what descent?
American

   1. Date of birth?

      1828

BLANK NO. 28   SERIES II, FORM B.

2. Early life in city or country?

   City. Clerk

3. Height?

   5 feet, 10 1/2 inches

4. Weight?

   202 lbs.

5. Muscular or weak?

   Flesh, good muscle undeveloped.

6. Where educated? degrees if any?

   Watertown, Literary & Religious Institute, N.Y. Left at 14.

7. If a college man, has he been athletic?

   No

8. Complexion?

   [Illegible] blond.

9. Temperament?

   Nervous (appears phlegmatic)

10. Does he use tobacco?

    40 yrs., stopped short, better   ever since.

11. Occupations?

    Merchant

BLANK NO. 28   SERIES II, FORM B.

12. Health?

    Good average health, constipation, & catarrh condition of
    stomach, 66 yrs. & looks not more than 55.

13. Diseases in his family: Nervous Disorders? Rheumatism?
    Consumption? Dyspepsia? Varicose Veins? Heart Disease?
    Hernia? Habitual Consumption? Catarrh?

    Nervous dyspepsia, [sister? had] heart disease, habitual
    constipation, catarrh. Mother died of Bronchial Consumption.

Yourself:

  1. Date of birth?

     1844

  2. Early life in city or country?

     Town, **Honolulu**

  3. Height?

     5 ft, 2 1/2 in.

  4. Weight?

     150 [lbs.]

  5. Complexion?

     [Illegible] blond.

  6. Temperament?

     Nervous.

  7. Where educated, give degrees if any?

     [Walker?] College.

BLANK NO. 28					SERIES II, FORM B.

8. Occupations before marriage?   a) in city or country?   b) time spent in each?

   Teacher in country 6 mo.

9. Diseases in your family? from father or mother's side? Nervous Disorders? Rheumatism? Consumption? Dyspepsia? Varicose Veins? Heart Disease? Hernia? Habitual Constipation? Catarrh?

   [Father had nervous disorders. Mother's father had rheumatism in his old age. Habitual Constipation. Catarrh.]

10. General health before marriage? b) since marriage? Paralysis? Brain Fever? Chronic Headache? Nervous Prostration? Catarrh? Hernia? Dyspepsia? Habitual Constipation? Inflammation of Bowels? Pleurisy? Bronchitis? Shortness of Breath? Spitting Blood? Consumption? Laryngitis? Tonsillitis? Insomnia? Rheumatism? Pneumonia? Jaundice? Varicose Veins?

    Good [health before marriage], [but] not strong in early life. [Unnatural?] nervous prostration. Tonsillitis. Nursed all her children until they were 16 mo. [old and about to walk?].

11. Menstruation?

    First menstruation at what age?

    13 1/2

    and when thoroughly established?

    At once though suffered pain.

    Present condition as regards menstruation:

    (a) How frequent?

        Irreg. 1 in 5 mo. 2 - 3 - 5 mo. Time lengthening slowly.

    (b) Is it regular or not?

    (c) Amount? how many napkins?

        Growing less & less. In youth 5--now 2.

(d) Duration?

5

(e) Pain or not? at what time as to the flow?

Pain due to [clots?] at first. After 1st child's birth no pain.

(f) Is there any leucorrhoea (whites)? character?

At beginning of change of life.

Amount?

Constant or occasional?

(g) Have you pain either frequently or habitually in the head, small of the back? abdomen or limbs?

Overwork brings pain in back of neck.

(h) Disease or trouble in Uterus (womb) or other pelvic organs?

Lacerated at birth of child due to too rapid birth. Never been [illegible] overheated climbing stairs incessently. Ulceration of uterus lasted a year, electricity, & local applications.

(i) Habit of bowels; how often?

Reg[ular].

12. What knowledge of sexual physiology had you before marriage? b) how did you obtain it?

Ignorant, when water broke did not know but for books when in bed with her first child.

13. Number of times married. If mcre than once additional blanks will be furnished you to answer the following questions separately in regard to each marriage?

Once

14. Number of years married?

27

BLANK NO. 28   SERIES II, FORM B.

15. Do you habitually sleep with your husband? b) what reasons
    for so doing or not?

    Yes. (Always.) Convenience.

16. Number of conceptions?

    Son. Daughter lived (son lived 2 yrs. died on steamer).
    Miscarriage (1 mo.). Didn't know of condition until foetus
    passed. Flowed 10 days. Daughter ([Illegible] miscarriage
    putting up curtains. Foetus passed again, [but] did not
    hurt her).

17. Number of children? State in connection with each, a) date
    of birth? b) sex? c) whether healthy or not? d) note any
    characteristic and the cause. e) note either immediate or
    after effect on your health of the birth of each of your
    children. f) give time of first menstruation after birth
    of each child.

    [First child]

        (a) April 10, 1868, born in Paris, 14 mo. after marriage.

        (b) Son.

        (c) 7 mo. child. Too much travel warm bath brought birth
            prematurely. Born big head, no body, no nails, no
            eyebrows, no lashes, wet nursed. Very nervous.
            Nursed until 16 mo. old.

        (e) Small child - had court physician. Did not know what
            the breaking of water [meant], thought she had neuralgia.

        (f) Menstruated immediately.

    [Second child]

        (a) Sept. 20, 1870.

        (b) Daughter.

        (c) Very healthy 11 lbs. Gained information before this
            child was born.

        (e) Health excellent. Health especially good during
            pregnancy. Grew younger with each child.

BLANK NO. 28   SERIES II, FORM B.

   (f)

[Third child]

   (a) June 14, 1875.

   (b) Son.

   (c) Healthy, [but] died [at] 2 yrs. [due to] teething.

   (e) Health good.

   (f) Menst. about 5 or 6 wks after birth.

[Fourth child--miscarriage]

[Fifth child]

   (a) Aug. 17, 1879.

   (b) Daughter.

   (c) Healthy, extra fine. Well until 7 yrs. old. Just
       [recovered from] chicken pox. Put on night dress
       with hose with cold water on abdomen [?]. Next day
       had fearful pain in abdomen. 10 days very ill.
       Pains in abdomen from that time to this in ovarial
       region. Began to mens. at 13 1/2. Pain. Mens. 5
       times [illegible]. Stopped mens. after 14 mo. for
       4 times. Never since. May have taken cold while in
       country. Old pain came back & grew worse & worse.
       Nausea. Medicine burned child's stomach until little
       drops of blood came from stomach. Put in hospital.
       Pumped out stomach. Pumped out stomach until the blood
       came from ears by inexperienced intern. Knees cold.
       Blood increasing. Doctors changed many times. Local
       examination. Ovaries small--prolapsed. Has been fed
       through rectum for nearly a year.

   [Sixth child--miscarriage]

18. Did conception occur by choice or accident?

   Not preconcerted. Willingness.

BLANK NO. 28   SERIES II, FORM B.

19. Habit of intercourse, average number of times per week? per month? per year?

    Early [in marriage] 1 per week. Late [in marriage] 1 per mo. or 2 mo.

20. Was intercourse held during pregnancy? If so, how often? b) had you any desire for it during this period?

    Yes. 1 in 2 wks (indifferent)

21. At other times have you any desire for intercourse? a) how often? b) at what time in relation to your menses?

    When away never had any desire to get back in [that?] life. Never conscious of any desire but readily responded.

22. Is intercourse agreeable to you or not?

    Agreeable

    Do you always have a venereal orgasm?

    Not always

    1. - When you do,

    (a) Effect immediately afterwards?

        Sleep

    (b) Effect next day?

    2. - When you do not,

    (a) Effect immediately afterwards?

        (No not when tired -- no effect)

    (b) Effect next day?

23. What do you believe to be the true purpose of intercourse?

    (a) Necessity to man?

        Yes.

316

BLANK NO. 28   SERIES II, FORM B.

>   to woman?
>
>   Relief to nervous system.
>
>   (b) Pleasure?
>
>   Yes but not much. But no special inter[est?].
>
>   (c) Reproduction?
>
>   Primarily
>
>   (d) What other reasons beside reproduction are sufficient to warrant intercourse?
>
>   Healthy for both.

24. Have you ever used any means to prevent conception? a) if so, what?

    Try period of immunity--did not work. Then repulsion. 3) Earlier used <u>hot</u> syringe.

    (b) Effect on your health?

    Had pain next day.

25. What, to you, would be an ideal habit?

    Separate beds. Special occasion each time. Man should court wife each time. 1 per wk or 1 in 2 wks.

26. Additional Notes:

    Has not menstruated.

    Old Grecian law if husband did not come to her once a wk.

    1st intercourse 1st night--no trouble. [Mosher's comment probably concerns the woman's wedding night.]

BLANK NO. 29   SERIES II, FORM B.

Date: Mar., 29, 1920

Your Father:

1. Nationality, if American, of what descent?

   Am[erican]. Scotch Irish Dutch

2. Home in city or country before marriage?

   Country

   [He was the] youngest son of 15 children.

3. Home in city or country after marriage?

   City

4. Age when married?

   32 yrs.

5. Occupations before your birth?

   Physician. <u>Son of</u> <u>Middle Border</u> by Hamlin Garland describes her father's life. Youngest son of 15 children.

   (b) After your birth?

6. Health previous to your birth?

   Good

   (b) After your birth?

   Good

7. Number of children living?

   (a) Boys: 1

   (b) Girls: 1

BLANK NO. 29   SERIES II, FORM B.

8. Number of children dead; give age at time of death and cause.

   (a) Boys:

   (b) Girls:

9. If your father is living, give his age and present health, if dead, age at death and cause?

10. Name any diseases in his family:

Your Paternal Grandfather: home in city or country?

   1. Age when married?

   2. Occupations?

   3. Health?

   4. Number of children?

      (b) Number reaching maturity?

Your Paternal Grandmother: home in city or country?

   1. Age when married?

   2. Occupations?

   3. Health?

   4. Age and cause of death?

BLANK NO. 29   SERIES II, FORM B.

Your Mother:

1. Nationality, if American of what descent?

   [American. English] and Dutch.

2. Home in city or country before marriage?

   City. (Conn.) Age 23 at marriage.

   (b) Home in city or country after marriage?

3. Occupations before her marriage?

   Studied music.

   (b) After her marriage?

   No.

4. Note any prenatal influences before your birth:

5. Her health previous to your birth?

   Married 5 yrs. before daughter's birth.

   (b) After your birth?

   Happiest time of her life.

6. Number of miscarriages?

   1 (1st)

7. Her age if living and present health? if not, age at time of death and cause?

   55 -- frail

8. How was your mother's health affected by the climacteric (change of life)?

   Miserable. Headaches every 2 wks.

BLANK NO. 29   SERIES II, FORM B.

   9. Name any diseases in her family:

Your Maternal Grandfather: home in city or country?

   1. Age when married?

   2. Occupations?

   3. Health?

   4. Number of children?
      (b) Number reaching maturity?

Your Maternal Grandmother: home in city or country?

   1. Age when married?

   2. Occupations?

   3. Health?

   4. Age and cause of death?

Your Husband: nationality, if American, of what descent?
[American]

   1. Date of birth?
      1891

   2. Early life in city or country.
      City.

BLANK NO. 29   SERIES II, FORM B.

   3. Height?

      5 feet, 6 or 7 inches

   4. Weight?

      150 lbs.

   5. Muscular or weak?

      Not athletic but strong

   6. Where educated? degrees if any?

      Stanford.

   7. If a college man, has he been athletic?

      No.

   8. Complexion?

      Medium

   9. Temperament?

      Nervous

  10. Does he use tobacco?

      No.

  11. Occupations?

      Office

  12. Health?

      Good

BLANK NO. 29   SERIES II, FORM B.

13. Diseases in his family: Nervous Disorders? Rheumatism?
    Consumption? Dyspepsia? Varicose Veins? Heart Disease?
    Hernia? Habitual Constipation? Catarrh?

Yourself: March 29, 1920.

   1. Date of birth?

      Apr. 1892

   2. Early life in city or country?

      City

   3. Height?

   4. Weight?

   5. Complexion?

      Medium

   6. Temperament?

      Nervous.

   7. Where educated, give degrees if any?

      A.B., Stanford, 1914

   8. Occupations before marriage? a) in city or country? b) time
      spent in each?

      Married next fall [after college graduation:] Oct. 14, 1914.

   9. Diseases in your family? from father or mother's side? Nervous Disorders? Rheumatism? Consumption? Dyspepsia? Varicose Veins? Heart Disease? Hernia? Habitual Constipation? Catarrh?

BLANK NO. 29   SERIES II, FORM B.

10. General health before marriage? b) since marriage? Paralysis?
    Brain Fever? Chronic Headache? Nervous Prostration? Catarrh?
    Hernia? Dyspepsia? Habitual Constipation? Inflammation of
    Bowels? Pleurisy? Bronchitis? Shortness of Breath? Spitting
    Blood? Consumption? Laryngitis? Tonsillitis? Insomnia?
    Rheumatism? Pneumonia? Jaundice? Varicose Veins?

    Good. Op[eration] for Dermoid Cyst of Ovary.

    (b) Good. Pleurisy & Pneumonia.

11. Menstruation:

    First menstruation at what age?

    About 11 yrs. old.

    and when thoroughly established?

    Estab. at once.

    Present condition as regards menstruation:

    Reg[ular]

    (a) How frequent?

        Every 4 wks often 5 wks.

    (b) Is it regular or not?

        Irreg[ular]?

    (c) Amount? how many napkins?

        Abund[ant]

    (d) Duration?

        7 (5). [Maximum and minimum days duration?]

    (e) Pain or not? at what time as to the flow?

        Pain 1st day, less now than before marriage. **Weak** when
        delayed very nervous. Pain in back, helped by osteopathy.

    (f) Is there any leucorrhoea (whites)? character?

        Yes. Mid mo[nth].

BLANK NO. 29   SERIES II, FORM B.

Amount?

Constant or occasional?

(g) Have you pain either frequently or habitually in the head, small of the back? abdomen or limbs?

(h) Disease or trouble in Uterus (womb) or other pelvic organs?

Op[eration] for Dermoid Cyst of ovary before marriage--Jan. 1914.

(i) Habit of bowels; how often?

Daily

12. What knowledge of sexual physiology had you before marriage? b) how did you obtain it?

Read "What a Girl Should Know." Full knowledge--talked with 2 doctors.

13. Number of times married. If more than once additional blanks will be furnished you to answer the following questions separately in regard to each marriage?

14. Number of years married?

5 1/2 yrs since 1914

15. Do you habitually sleep with your husband? b) what reasons for so doing or not?

Yes. Like it, enjoy it--only time for being together.

16. Number of conceptions?

2

17. Number of children? State in connection with each, a) date of birth? b) sex? c) whether healthy or not? d) note any characteristic and the cause. e) note either immediate or after effect on your health of the birth of each of your children. f) give time of first menstruation after birth of

BLANK NO. 29   SERIES II, FORM B.

each child.

[First child]

   (a) Dec. 19, 1915

   (b) Boy

   (c) Very healthy. Nursed 9 mo.

   (d) Persistent like father; reasoning;

   (e) Health improved.

   (f) Following Sept. once [illegible] about Easter.

[Second child]

   (a) Apr. 21, 1919

   (b) Boy

   (c) Very healthy. [Illegible] colic and mother got more tired when nursing him.

   (e) Gen. health good. Was nervous, too much care. Got up when 9 days doing things. Felt so well.

   (f) Mens. began at end of 8 mo. First mens. 8 mo.

   Got **magazine** out 2 wks after birth and nursed a friend's baby with her own after her own baby was a wk. old. 3 [times] & 1 bottle taken from breast. 3 wks after birth went to Univ. Taking older child with her and also put magazine thro' press. Was somewhat nervous. Went to mountains with baby who had accident and was very sick with only country doctor to help her & away from many comforts.

18. Did conception occur by choice or accident?

   [First child] Accident.

   [Second child] Planned

19. Habit of intercourse, average number of times per week?

   per month?

3 - 4 times during safe period.

per year?

20. Was intercourse held during pregnancy? If so, how often? b) had you any desire for it during this period?

   Yes until about 7th month; frequency not nearly so often as ordinarily.

   (b) No desire, [but] not disagreeable.

21. At other times have you any desire for intercourse? a) how often? b) at what time in relation to your menses?

   Yes. Occasionally.

   (b) Oc[casionally?] at menstrual period but in mid month. Much stronger when 2nd child was conceived which was near menst[rual] period.

22. Is intercourse agreeable to you or not?

   Yes.

   Do you always have a venereal orgasm?

   Not always.

   1. - When you do,

   (a) Effect immediately afterwards?

   Always relaxation and satisfied.

   (b) Effect next day?

   Relaxed next day. Calmer. Gets more tired by night if she is overworked.

   2. - When you do not,

   (a) Effect immediately afterwards?

   (b) Effect next day?

BLANK NO. 29   SERIES II, FORM B.

23. What do you believe to be the true purpose of intercourse?

   (a) Necessity to man?

   Yes. (Less nervous tension & very [different?] after.)

   to woman?

   Yes. Less nervous tension & very [different?] after, especially when she has felt the need.

   (b) Pleasure?

   A higher purpose than physical enjoyment. Simply--sweeps you out of everything that is [commonplace?] and every day. A strength to go on. Union, which brings something to both.

   (c) Reproduction?

   Yes.

   (d) What other reasons beside reproduction are sufficient to warrant intercourse?

   If people are to live together as married people your bond must be strengthened. It makes a more close bond and reproduction is the highest tie.

24. Have you ever used any means to prevent conception? a) if so, what?

   Yes. Douches, [**boracic?**] sol., bi-chloride sol. & always use capsule beforehand [i.e., before intercourse] and one or the other douche after. Mid month period. Formerly did not use mid month [**Carl Degler suggests that "mid month" may refer to a method--intercourse during the so-called safe period**].

   (b) Effect on your health?

   None.

25. What, to you, would be an ideal habit?

   Several times during mid month.

Never conscious of any physical sex need before marriage.

BLANK NO. 29   SERIES II, FORM B.

Was too busy in college to sit about with girls and talk; therefore, does not know as much as she might. They talked of marriage & number of children they hoped to have but in a way quite different from present girl[s]. "Things seem to be less sacred, and much more open and free."

[Dr. Mosher's notes at the end of the questionnaire may reflect her interest in the effects of surgical ovary removal upon fertility. She noted that this woman's right ovary had been removed, but that later she had borne two sons. Mosher also noted that another woman, a "friend," had given birth to a boy and a girl after the removal of an ovary.]

BLANK NO. 30   SERIES II, FORM B.

Date: Apr. 20, 1920

Your Father:
   1. Nationality, if American, of what descent?
      Am[erican]. Scotch Irish.

   2. Home in city or country before marriage?

   3. Home in city or country after marriage?
      Small town

   4. Age when married?
      19

   5. Occupations before your birth?
      Retail lumber.
      (b) After your birth?

   6. Health previous to your birth?
      Good
      (b) After your birth?
         Very energetic

   7. Number of children living?
      (a) Boys: 1
      (b) Girls: 1

   8. Number of children dead; give age at time of death and cause.
      (a) Boys: 1 died [at 43?] of T.B.

BLANK NO. 30   SERIES II, FORM B.

   (b) Girls: [Illegible] T.B. at 32

9. If your father is living, give his age and present health,
   if dead, age at death and cause?

   Death from Cerebro Meningitis

10. Name any diseases in his family:

Your Paternal Grandfather: home in city or country?

   1. Age when married?

   2. Occupations?

   3. Health?

   4. Number of children?

      Number reaching maturity?

Your Paternal Grandmother: home in city or country?

   1. Age when married?

   2. Occupations?

   3. Health?

   4. Age and cause of death?

Your Mother:

   1. Nationality, if American of what descent?

      English [French?]

BLANK NO. 30   SERIES II, FORM B.

   2. Home in city or country before marriage?

      (b) Home in city or country after marriage?

   3. Occupations before her marriage?

      (b) After her marriage?

   4. Note any prenatal influences before your birth:

   5. Her health previous to your birth?

      Good. Always [threatened with?] heart [trouble?].

      (b) After your birth?

   6. Number of miscarriages?

      None(?)

   7. Her age if living and present health? if not, age at time of death and cause?

      [Still living at 80 yrs. Well for age.]

   8. How was your mother's health affected by the climacteric (change of life)?

      At 52 yrs., palpitation greater.

   9. Name any diseases in her family:

Your Maternal Grandfather: home in city or country?

   1. Age when married?

   2. Occupations?

   3. Health?

BLANK NO. 30								SERIES II, FORM B.

   4. Number of children?

      (b) Number reaching maturity?

Your Maternal Grandmother: home in city or country?

   1. Age when married?

   2. Occupations?

   3. Health?

   4. Age and cause of death?

Your Husband: nationality, if American, of what descent?
Am[erican]. English ... New England

   1. Date of birth?

      1847

   2. Early life in city or country?

      Small town

   3. Height?

      5 ft., 11 in.

   4. Weight?

      175 [lbs.]

   5. Muscular or weak?

      Medium

BLANK NO. 30   SERIES II, FORM B.

6. Where educated? degrees if any?

   Stanford

7. If a college man, has he been athletic?

   Not athletic. Tennis[?], golf. Runner[?].

8. Complexion?

   Sanguine

9. Temperament?

   Nervous

10. Does he use tobacco?

    No. Except as a child until 13.

11. Occupations?

    Lawyer - Teacher   [illegible]

12. Health?

    T.B.

13. Diseases in his family: Nervous Disorders? Rheumatism?
    Consumption? Dyspepsia? Varicose Veins? Heart Disease?
    Hernia? Habitual Constipation? Catarrh?

    T.B. mother and brother. Consumption.

Yourself:

1. Date of birth?

   Dec. 20, 1874

BLANK NO. 30   SERIES II, FORM B.

2. Early life in city or country?

   Small town

3. Height?

   5 ft., 5 1/2 in.

4. Weight?

   150 [lbs. average].

5. Complexion?

   [Blond?]

6. Temperament?

   Sanguine. Intellectually a pessimist; emotionally [an] optimist.

7. Where educated, give degrees if any?

   A.B., Stanford, 1895. [Illegible] for J.D.

8. Occupations before marriage? a) in city or country? b) time spent in each?

   Married Sept. 1896

9. Diseases in your family? from father or mother's side? Nervous Disorders? Rheumatism? Consumption? Dyspepsia? Varicose Veins? Heart Disease? Hernia? Habitual Constipation? Catarrh?

   Consumption, Heart Disease.

10. General health before marriage? b) since marriage? Paralysis? Brain Fever? Chronic Headache? Nervous Prostration? Catarrh? Hernia? Dyspepsia? Habitual Constipation? Inflammation of Bowels? Pleurisy? Bronchitis? Shortness of Breath? Spitting Blood? Consumption? Laryngitis? Tonsillitis? Insomnia? Rheumatism? Pneumonia? Jaundice? Varicose Veins?

BLANK NO. 30   SERIES II, FORM B.

　　　Good.

　　　(b) Good. Rheumatism after [illegible] 1908.

11. Menstruation:

　　　First menstruation at what age?

　　　At 15.

　　　and when thoroughly established?

　　　Estab. [after] about a year.

　　　Present condition as regards menstruation:

　　　Menopause.

　　　(a) How frequent?

　　　　　[Irregular. Varies between 24 and 38 days?]

　　　(b) Is it regular or not?

　　　　　Formerly reg[ular].

　　　(c) Amount? how many napkins?

　　　(d) Duration?

　　　(e) Pain or not? at what time as to the flow?

　　　(f) Is there any leucorrhoea (whites)? character?
　　　　　Amount?

　　　　　Constant or occasional?

　　　(g) Have you pain either frequently or habitually in the head,
　　　　　small of the back? abdomen or limbs?

　　　　　No.

　　　(h) Disease or trouble in Uterus (womb) or other pelvic organs?

　　　(i) Habit of bowels; how often?

　　　　　Reg[ular]

BLANK NO. 30   SERIES II, FORM B.

12. What knowledge of sexual physiology had you before marriage?
    b) how did you obtain it?

    Class work in sex hygiene; intellectual curious[ity]. No
    consciousness of sex desire until married. No sex consciousness.

13. Number of times married. If more than once additional blanks
    will be furnished you to answer the following questions
    separately in regard to each marriage?

14. Number of years married?

    24

15. Do you habitually sleep with your husband? b) what reasons
    for so doing or not?

    No. [They slept together for] possibly 3 yrs. because no
    extra room.

16. Number of conceptions?

    3

17. Number of children? State in connection with each, a) date
    of birth? b) sex? c) whether healthy or not? d) note any
    characteristic and the cause. e) note either immediate or
    after effect on your health of the birth of each of your
    children. f) give time of first menstruation after birth
    of each child.

    [First child]

        (a) Apr. 20, 1899

        (b) Boy

        (c) Healthy, but not rugged. Wt. 8 lbs., 3 oz. Constipation;
            scarlet fever, ill 36 hrs; [died] at 4 years.

        (e) Normal labor, 6-7 hrs. natural; 3 wks. later went on
            as usual.

        (f) When stopped nursing. (Nursed until 9 mo. old.)

BLANK NO. 30   SERIES II, FORM B.

   [Second child]

   (a) May 6, 1901.

   (b) Girl.

   (c) Very **husky** baby, 8 lb. 6 oz.; at 1 yr. 25 lbs.

   (e) Good. Normal labor about 2 - 2 1/2 hrs. Only slight ext[ernal] tear 1 - 2 stitches. Nursed until 7 mo. not fully weaned until 8 or 9 mo. Health good.

   (f) Mens[truated] after weaning.

   [Third child] **Premature 7 mo.**

   (a) Mar. 15, 1904.

   (c) Child perfect. Difficulty with [umbilical] cord. Hermorrhage--even doctor could not **cure.** 33% anemia; probably cause[d] loss of child.

   (e) **8 weeks in bed.**

18. Did conceptions occur by choice or accident?

    Willingness, no def[inite] plan. [They] plan when [they] don't want [children].

19. Habit of intercourse, average number of times per week? per month? per year?

    Earlier perhaps 1 in 2 wks. Now 1 [per] mo.

20. Was intercourse held during pregnancy? If so, how often?

    1 - 3 times during pregnancy.

    (b) Had you any desire for it during this period?

        No always [agreeable?] though.

21. At other times have you any desire for intercourse?

    Yes, sometimes.

BLANK NO. 30   SERIES II, FORM B.

     (b) At what time in relation to your menses?

     Near period but not every period.

22. Is intercourse agreeable to you or not?

    Yes.

    Do you always have a venereal orgasm?

    Always.

    1. - When you do,

    (a) Effect immediately afterwards?

       Relaxed **quiet** sleep.

    (b) Effect next day?

       Tired next day.

    2. - When you do not,

    (a) Effect immediately afterwards?

    (b) Effect next day?

23. What do you believe to be the true purpose of intercourse?

    (a) Necessity to man?

       No.

       To woman?

       No.

    (b) Pleasure?

       Yes(?), but not necessarily a legitimate one.

    (c) Reproduction?

       Yes.

BLANK NO. 30   SERIES II, FORM B.

   (d) What other reasons beside reproduction are sufficient to
       warrant intercourse?

       A **sense**   of intimacy not to be had in any other way;
       especially when people cannot be affectionate without
       going full course. Serves as a bond above even physical
       pleasure.

24. Have you ever used any means to prevent conception? a) if
    so, what?

    Plain water douche; practically always.

    (b) Effect on your health?

        None.

25. What, to you, would be an ideal habit?

    Not to restrict [intercourse] to reproduction but limit [it]
    to times when not pressed with work; when time for pleasure.
    Intellectually restrict to reproduction, say 2 - 3 [times] a
    year.

(Father married 3 times; 2nd wife probably unfair to husband)
Husband: men who are successful in world are abstemious. [Illegible]
Thinks he has abnormal desire : **about 2 wks. or so.**

Husband's sister unmarried; ulcer of [stomach?]; love's quirk; colon
removed; lived a month; nerves worked hardest; domestic raised to
marry; [illegible].

BLANK NO. 31

SERIES II, FORM B.

[First three pages missing from ms.]

Date: [1913]

Yourself:

1. Date of birth?

    Apr. 27, 1856.

2. Early life in city or country?

    Country

3. Height?

    Almost 5 ft., 6 in.

4. Weight?

    150 lbs.

5. Complexion?

    Dark.

6. Temperament?

7. Where educated, give degrees if any?

    Vassar, A.B.

8. Occupations before marriage? a) in city or country? b) time spent in each?

    2 yrs. teaching in City Private School.

9. Diseases in your family? from father or mother's side? Nervous Disorders? Rheumatism? Consumption? Dyspepsia? Varicose

BLANK NO. 31   SERIES II, FORM B.

Veins? Heart Disease? Hernia? Habitual Constipation? Catarrh?

[Two brothers had tuberculosis.]

10. General health before marriage? b) since marriage? Paralysis? Brain Fever? Chronic Headache? Nervous Prostration? Catarrh? Hernia? Dyspepsia? Habitual Constipation? Inflammation of Bowels? Pleurisy? Bronchitis? Shortness of Breath? Spitting Blood? Consumption? Laryngitis? Tonsillitis? Insomnia? Rheumatism? Pneumonia? Jaundice? Varicose Veins?

Very good [health both before and after marriage]. [Tendency for] constipation.

11. Menstruation:

First menstruation at what age?

About 15 yrs.

and when thoroughly established?

At once.

Present condition as regards menstruation:

Passed menopause [at 48 years old?].

(a) How frequent?

28 days.

(b) Is it regular or not?

Regular

(c) Amount? how many napkins?

Scanty.

(d) Duration?

5 (3). [Maximum and minimum days duration?]

(e) Pain or not? at what time as to the flow?

No. Flushed[?].

BLANK NO. 31   SERIES II, FORM B.

   (f) Is there any leucorrhoea (whites)? character?
       No.
       Amount?

       Constant or occasional?

   (g) Have you   pain either frequently or habitually in the
       head, small of the back? abdomen or limbs?

   (h) Disease or trouble in Uterus (womb) or other pelvic
       organs?

       No.

   (i) Habit of bowels; how often?

       [Tendency for constipation]

12. What knowledge of sexual physiology had you before marriage?
    b) how did you obtain it?

    Vague idea.

13. Number of times married. If more than once additional blanks
    will be furnished you to answer the following questions
    separately in regard to each marriage?

14. Number of years married?

    30 1/2 (June 1883)

15. Do you habitually sleep with your husband? b) what reasons
    for so doing or not?

16. Number of conceptions?

    3

17. Number of children? State in connection with each, a) date
    of birth? b) sex? c) whether healthy or not? d) note any
    characteristic and the cause. e) note either immediate or
    after effect on your health of the birth of each of your
    children. f) give time of first menstruation after birth
    of each child.

343

BLANK NO. 31   SERIES II, FORM B.

[First child]

    (a) Oct. 29, 1884.

    (b) Girl.

    (c) Very healthy; nursed 4 mo.

    (e) (Restless & much care & worn out with care.)

    (f) Mens[truation] 5 mo. later.

[Second child]

    (a) Aug. 4, 1886.

    (b) Boy.

    (c) Delicate & difficult to feed. Takes cold easily-- nursed 6 wks. Thinks [weaned?] too soon.

    (e) Did not sleep during pregnancy. Did not know how to care for children. Ignorant. Overworked. Appendix removed at 14.

    (f) Mens[truation] overdue.

[Third child]

    (a) Nov. 12, 1890.

    (b) Boy.

    (c) Very strong, much endurance. Normal birth. Nursed 3 mo.

    (e) Thinks she had fully recovered strength after birth of first 2 children.

18. Did conception occur by choice or accident?

    Accident, but glad to have it occur.

19. Habit of intercourse, average number of times per week?

    1 - 2

    per month?

BLANK NO. 31   SERIES II, FORM B.

per year?

20. Was intercourse held during pregnancy?
    During earlier mo[nths].
    If so, how often?
    Less frequent [than before conception].
    (b) Had you any desire for it during this period?
        Yes.

21. At other times have you any desire for intercourse?
    Yes.
    (a) How often?
        When not too tired. 2 [times] weekly.
    (b) At what time in relation to your menses?
        Before.

22. Is intercourse agreeable to you or not?
    Yes.
    Do you always have a venereal orgasm?
    Yes.
    1. - When you do,
    (a) Effect immediately afterwards?
        Relax.
    (b) Effect next day?
    2. - When you do not,
    (a) Effect immediately afterwards?
    (b) Effect next day?
        No.

BLANK NO. 31   SERIES II, FORM B.

23. What do you believe to be the true purpose of intercourse?

   (a) Necessity to man?

   Yes more.

   To woman?

   Yes.

   (b) Pleasure?

   Yes.

   (c) Reproduction?

   Yes.

   (d) What other reasons beside reproduction are sufficient to warrant intercourse?

   [Necessity and pleasure] to both.

24. Have you ever used any means to prevent conception? a) if so, what?

   Withdrawal.

   (b) Effect on your health?

   No.

25. What, to you, would be an ideal habit?

   About twice a week.

[Husband? is] athletic--baseball pitcher.

BLANK NO. 32   SERIES II, FORM B.

[Dr. **Mosher** notes that the first three pages are unused. Illegible word follows "unused."]

Date: Dec. 15, 191[7?].

Yourself:

Father's parentage French, English, German, Dutch.

1. Date of birth:

   Apr. 28, 1878.

2. Early life in city or country?

   City.

3. Height?

   5 ft., 4 in.

4. Weight?

   112 - 115 [lbs].

5. Complexion?

   Dark.

6. Temperament?

7. Where educated, give degrees if any?

8. Occupations before marriage? a) in city or country? b) time spent in each?

   School teacher 2 yrs.

9. Diseases in your family? from father or mother's side? Nervous Disorders? Rheumatism? Consumption? Dyspepsia? Varicose Veins? Heart Disease? Hernia? Habitual Constipation? Catarrh?

BLANK NO. 32   SERIES II, FORM B.

10. General health before marriage? b) since marriage? Paralysis?
    Brain Fever? Chronic Headache? Nervous Prostration? Catarrh?
    Hernia? Dyspepsia? Habitual Constipation? Inflammation of
    Bowels? Pleurisy? Bronchitis? Shortness of Breath? Spitting
    Blood? Consumption? Laryngitis? Tonsillitis? Insomnia?
    Rheumatism? Pneumonia? Jaundice? Varicose Veins?

    Perfect [health before and after marriage]. Pneumonia at 16
    or 17. Mild case of diphtheria.

11. Menstruation:

    First menstruation at what age?

    About 12.

    and when thoroughly established?

    From [beginning].

    Present condition as regards menstruation:

    Reg[ular].

    (a) How frequent?

        About 27 days.

    (b) Is it regular or not?

        Regular. 4 (2). [Maximum and minimum days duration?]

    (c) Amount? how many napkins?

        1. Scanty.

    (d) Duration?

        4 (2).

    (e) Pain or not? at what time as to the flow?

        [No pain]

    (f) Is there any leucorrhoea (whites)? character?

        No.

BLANK NO. 32   SERIES II, FORM B.

         Amount?

         Constant or occasional?

    (g) Have you pain either frequently or habitually in the head,
         small of the back? abdomen or limbs?

         No.

    (h) Disease or trouble in Uterus (womb) or other pelvic organs?

         Curettage 7 yrs. ago.

    (i) Habit of bowels; how often?

         No [habit].

12. What knowledge of sexual physiology had you before **marriage?**
    b) how did you obtain it?

       2 mo. before [marriage] told by sister-in-law.

13. Number of times married. If more than once additional blanks
    will be furnished you to answer the following questions
    separately in regard to each marriage?

14. Number of years married?

15. Do you habitually sleep with your husband? b) what **reasons**
    for so doing or not?

16. Number of conceptions?

       2 yrs. after marriage had a 6 wks. foetus after missing
       menst[ruation for] 6 wks--**no flow and popped out no pain no**
       symptoms. Had been under great nervous & physical [strain].
       No curettage at time.

17. Number of children? State in connection with each, a) date
    of birth? b) sex? c) whether healthy or not? d) note any
    characteristic and the cause. e) note either immediate or
    after effect on your health of the birth of each of your
    children. f) give time of first menstruation after birth of
    each child.

349

BLANK NO. 32

SERIES II, FORM B.

[First child]

    (a) Oct. 17, 1911.

    (b) Girl.

    (c) Perfectly healthy.

    (d) Easy labor. Nursed baby for 12 mo.

    (e) Mens[truated in the] 13th mo.

[Second child]

    (a) Nov. 14, 1913.

    (b) Boy.

    (c) Perfectly healthy.

    (d) Easier labor. Nursed.

18. Did conception occur by choice or accident?

Choice and accident.

19. Habit of intercourse, average number of times per week?

2 - 3

per month?

per year?

20. Was intercourse held during pregnancy? If so, how often?

Yes - irregularly. Never in 1st month because of nausea. [Then once or twice every two weeks.]

    (b) Had you any desire for it during this period?

    No.

21. At other times have you any desire for intercourse?

BLANK NO. 32   SERIES II, FORM B.

   No.
   (a) How often?
   (b) At what time in relation to your menses?
       Less objectionable.

22. Is intercourse agreeable to you or not?
    Not.
    Do you always have a venereal orgasm?
    Occasionally. **Not usually.** [**Slower than husband?**]
    1. - When you do?
    (a) Effect immediately afterwards?
        Always sleepy. Does own work. May be tired. More amiable after.
    (b) Effect next day?
    2. - When you do not?
    (a) Effect immediately afterwards?
    (b) Effect next day?

23. What do you believe to be the true purpose of intercourse?
    (a) Necessity to man?
        No.
        To woman?
        No.
    (b) Pleasure?
        To man - occasionally. Like animal once or twice a year.
    (c) Reproduction?
        Yes.

BLANK NO. 32   SERIES II, FORM B.

   (d) What other reasons beside reproduction are sufficient to
       warrant intercourse?

       Husband's pleasure demands it & therefore prefers to
       want   it herself.

24. Have you ever used any means to prevent conception? a) if
    so, what?

    1st few yrs. douche of warm water before time of menstruation.
    Husband withdrawal.

    (b) Effect on your health?

       None.

25. What, to you, would be an ideal habit?

    Man & woman so mated both should want it at same time.
    [Illegible] **Physically no dif.**

BLANK NO. 33   SERIES II, FORM B.

Your Father:

1. Nationality, if American, of what descent?

   American, Scotch-Irish descent.

2. Home in city or country before marriage?

   Country and small town.

3. Home in city or country after marriage?

   Small town.

4. Age when married?

   19

5. Occupations before your birth?

   Lumber business which was partially outdoor & partially office work. He was also always a great student.

   (b) After your birth?

   The same.

6. Health previous to your birth?

   Good.

   (b) After your birth?

   Good for three or four years.

7. Number of children living?

   (a) Boys: 1

   (b) Girls: 1

8. Number of children dead; give age at time of death and cause:

BLANK NO. 33   SERIES II, FORM B.

　　　　(a) Boys:

　　　　(b) Girls: 1 - died at 32, of consumption.

　　9. If your father is living, give his age and present health,
　　　 if dead, age at death and cause?

　　　　Died at age of 41 of cerebral meningitis, brought on by
　　　　overwork.

　 10. Name any diseases in his family:

　　　　There   were one or two cases of consumption, but I think
　　　　it would not be called a family disease. There is   tendency
　　　　to nervous trouble.

Your Paternal Grandfather: home in city or country?

Small town.

　　1. Age when married?

　　　 23.

　　2. Occupations?

　　　 Merchant & Post Master.

　　3. Health?

　　　 Good.

　　4. Number of children?

　　　 10

　　　 Number reaching maturity?

　　　 8

BLANK NO. 33   SERIES II, FORM B.

Your Paternal Grandmother: home in city or country?
Country.

    1. Age when married?

       Do not know.

    2. Occupations?

    3. Health?

       Good so far as I know.

    4. Age and cause of death?

       Died at 37. Do not know cause.

Your Mother:

    1. Nationality, if American of what descent?
American, English descent.

    2. Home in city or country before marriage?

       Small town.

       (b) Home in city or country after marriage?

          Small town.

    3. Occupations before her marriage?

       Teaching.

       (b) After her marriage?

          Housekeeping.

    4. Name any prenatal influences before your birth:

BLANK NO. 33   SERIES II, FORM B.

   5. Her health previous to your birth?

      Good.

      (b) After your birth?

         Good.

   6. Number of miscarriages?

      None that I know of.

   7. Her age if living and present health? if not, age at time of death and cause?

      She is now 58 yrs. old and is fairly well.

   8. How was your mother's health affected by the climacteric (change of life)?

      She was quite ill during that period. Having always had sympathetic palpitation of the heart, it was much worse at that time, but is as well now as before that period.

   9.   Name any diseases in her family:

      One brother had consumption.

Your Maternal Grandfather: home in city or country?
Country.

   1. Age when married?

      20 yrs. about.

   2. Occupations?

      Farming.

   3. Health?

      Good.

BLANK NO. 33   SERIES II, FORM B.

   4. Number of children?
      7 or 8.
      (b) Number reaching maturity?
         3.

Your Maternal Grandmother: home in city or country?
Country.
   1. Age when married?
      About 27.

   2. Occupations?
      Housekeeping.

   3. Health?
      Good.

   4. Age and cause of death?
      Died at age of 89 of old age.

Your Husband: nationality, if American, of what descent?
American, English & French descent.
   1. Date of birth?
      July 24, 1872.

   2. Early life in city or country?
      City till 9 yrs. old, then in town not thickly populated.

   3. Height?

357

BLANK NO. 33   SERIES II, FORM B.

   6 feet.

4.   Weight?

   150 lbs.

5. Muscular or weak?

   Medium.

6. Where educated? degrees if any?

   Stanford, 1893, A.B.   1896, L.L. B.

7. If a college man, has he been athletic?

   No.

8. Complexion?

   Light.

9. Temperament?

   Moderate.

10. Does he use tobacco or stimulants?

    No.

11. Occupations?

    Teaching.

12. Health?

    Fair.

13. Diseases in his family: Nervous Disorders? Rheumatism? Consumption? Dyspepsia. Varicose Veins? Heart Disease?

BLANK NO. 33   SERIES II, FORM B.

   Hernia?   Habitual Constipation?   Catarrh?
   Consumption and dyspepsia

Yourself:

1. Date of birth:

   Dec. 20, 1874.

2. Early life in city or country?

   Small town until 10, a little larger town later.

3. Height?

   5 feet, 5 1/2 inches.

4. Weight?

   136 lbs.

5. Complexion?

   Light.

6. Temperament?

   Rather high strung, nervous.

7. Where educated, give degrees if any?

   Public school. [Stanford] 1895, A.B.

8. Occupations before marriage? a) in city or country? b) time spent in each?

   Attending school principally. Leisure spent mostly out of doors. I attended public school 5 1/2 hours a day.

BLANK NO. 33   SERIES II, FORM B.

9. Diseases in your family? from father or mother's side? Nervous Disorders? Rheumatism? Consumption? Dyspepsia? Varicose Veins? Heart Disease? Hernia? Habitual Constipation? Catarrh?

   I think there are no diseases in our family which came thro' heredity, unless it be a nervous tendency, but this has never developed into a particular disease. There is a very little consumption on both sides.

10. General health before marriage? b) since marriage? Paralysis? Brain Fever? Chronic Headache? Nervous Prostration? Catarrh? Hernia? Dyspepsia? Habitual Constipation? Inflammation of Bowels? Pleurisy? Bronchitis? Shortness of Breath? Spitting Blood? Consumption? Laryngitis? Tonsillitis? Insomnia? Rheumatism? Pneumonia? Jaundice? Varicose Veins?

    <u>Good</u>   both before & since [marriage].

11. Menstruation:

    First menstruation at what age?

    1st menstruation at 15.

    And when thoroughly established?

    For first year it recurred every 3 wks, & then became thoroughly established every 4 wks.

    Present condition as regards menstruation:

    (a) How frequent?

        Every four wks.

    (b) Is it regular or not?

        Quite   regular, never varies more than a day
        or so.

    (c) Amount? how many napkins?

        Copious - 6 napkins saturated.

BLANK NO. 33   SERIES II, FORM B.

    (d) Duration?

        7 or 8 days.

    (e) Pain or not? at what time as to the flow?

        Seldom any pain whatever.

    (f) Is there any leucorrhoea (whites)? character?

        A little, white in color. Comes during week following menstruation.

        Amount?

        Slight.

        Constant or occasional?

        Occasional.

    (g) Have you pain either frequently or habitually in the head, small of the back? abdomen or limbs?

        No.

        Have you ever had any pelvic trouble & had to go to a physician? When, and what was it?

        No.

    (h) Disease or trouble in Uterus (womb) or other pelvic organs?

        None.

    (i) Habit of bowels; how often?

        Regular, every day once.

12. What knowledge of sexual physiology had you before marriage? b) how did you obtain it?

    Considerable, thro' books also some from my mother & other friends.

13. Number of times married. If more than once additional blanks will be furnished you to answer the following questions separately in regard to each marriage?

BLANK NO. 33   SERIES II, FORM B.

Once.

14. Number of years married?

    1 year.

15. Do you habitually sleep with your husband? b) what reasons for so doing or not?

    I do, because we enjoy it merely from the companionable standpoint, & secondly because it has so far been inconvenient to arrange it otherwise.

16. Number of conceptions?

    None.

17. Number of children? State in connection with each, a) date of birth? b) sex? c) whether healthy or not? d) note any characteristic and the cause. e) note either immediate or after effect on your health of the birth of each of your children. f) give time of first menstruation after birth of each child.

18. Did conception occur by choice or accident?

19. Habit of intercourse, average number of times per week?

    Once

    per month?

    per year?

20. Was intercourse held during pregnancy? If so, how often? b) had you any desire for it during this period?

21. At other times have you any desire for intercourse?

    Yes.

BLANK NO. 33   SERIES II, FORM B.

   (a) How often?

   (b) At what time in relation to your menses?

       Desire is not regular, but often a few days before menstruation.

22. Is intercourse agreeable to you or not?

    Yes.

    Do you always have a venereal orgasm?

    Very nearly always.

    1. - When you do,

    (a) Effect immediately afterwards?

        Nothing particular.

    (b) Effect   next day?

        It is usually fatiguing, that is causes drowsy & stupid feeling.

    2. - When you do not?

    (a) Effect immediately afterwards?

        None.

    (b) Effect next day?

        None.

23. What do you believe to be the true purpose of intercourse?

    (a) Necessity to man?

        To woman?

    (b) Pleasure?

    (c) Reproduction?

        [Yes]

BLANK NO. 33　　　　　　　　　　　　　SERIES II, FORM B.

(d) What other reasons beside reproduction are sufficient to warrant intercourse?

I think the pleasure is sufficient to warrant it provided people are extremely moderate, and do not allow it to injure their health or degrade their best feelings toward each other. This must depend on individual standpoint.

24. Have you ever used any means to prevent conception? a) if so, what?

    I have used simple clean water, with fountain syringe.

    (b) Effect on your health?

    None that I have discovered.

25. What, to you, would be an ideal habit?

    As I now personally see it, I think a habit of intercourse once a month if both desire would be as much of an ideal as I now have. [**This paragraph is crossed out in the original.**]

    Since writing the [paragraph immediately] above I have become convinced that the ideal would be to have no intercourse except for reproduction, but it is often hard to live up to such an ideal. However I think it would be easier for young people to approach it as they grow older, if they had such an ideal.

BLANK NO. 34   SERIES II, FORM B.
Date: Dec. 30, 1897

Your Father:

1. Nationality, if American, of what descent?
   American -- English
   What child of his parents, 1st, 2nd, 3rd, etc?
   First.

2. Home in city or country before marriage?
   Country.

3. Home in city or country after marriage?
   Country.

4. Age when married?
   24.

5. Occupations before your birth?
   Agriculture.
   (b) After your birth?
       Surgeon.

6. Health previous to your birth?
   Good.
   (b) After your birth?
       Good.

7. Number of children living?
   (a) Boys: 1

BLANK NO. 34	SERIES II, FORM B.

   (b) Girls: 3.

8. Number of children dead; give age at time of death and cause.
   (a) Boys: Boy of 6, brain fever. Boy 30 typhoid fever, immediately heart failure.
   (b) Girls: Girl, infant. Girl 19, "Quick" Consumption.
   [Apparently, four of his children died and four lived.]
9. If your father is living, give his age and present health, if dead, age at death and cause?

   Died at 56 with typhoid fever, and heart failure.

10. Name any diseases in his family:

    Are none. All healthy.

Your Paternal Grandfather: home in city or country?
Country.
   1. Age when married?

   2. Occupations?

      Blacksmith.

   3. Health?

      Do not know.

   4. Number of children?

      Number reaching maturity?

Your Paternal Grandmother: home in city or country?
   1. Age when married?

BLANK NO. 34   SERIES II, FORM B.

   2. Occupations?

   3. Health?

   4. Age and cause of death?

Your Mother:

   1. Nationality, if American of what descent?
      What child of her parents, 1st, 2nd, 3rd, etc?

   2. Home in city or country before marriage?
      (b) Home in city or country after marriage?

   3. Occupations before her marriage?
      (b) After her marriage?

   4. Note any prenatal influences before your birth:

   5. Her health previous to your birth?
      (b) After your birth?

   6. Number of miscarriages?

   7. Her age if living and present health? if not, age at time of death and cause?

   8. How was your mother's health affected by the climacteric (change of life)?

   9. Name any diseases in her family:

BLANK NO. 34					SERIES II, FORM B.

Your Maternal Grandfather: home in city or country?
Country.
    1. Age when married?

    2. Occupations?
       Agriculture.

    3. Health?
       Excellent.

    4. Number of children?
       9.
      (b) Number reaching maturity?
         9.

Your Maternal Grandmother: home in city or country?
City.
    1. Age when married?

    2. Occupations?

    3. Health?

    4. Age and cause of death?

Your Husband: nationality, if American, of what descent?
American-Irish.
    1. Date of birth?
       Aug. 12, 1866.

BLANK NO. 34   SERIES II, FORM B.

2. Early life in city or country?
   Country.

3. Height?
   73 inches.

4. Weight?
   190.

5. Muscular or weak?
   Medium.

6. Where educated? degrees if any?
   De Pau University, Stanford, and Johns Hopkins, A.B., A.M.

7. If a college man, has he been athletic?
   No.

8. Complexion?
   Florid.

9. Temperament?
   Reflective.

10. Does he use tobacco or stimulants of any kind?
    No.

11. Occupations?
    Teacher.

BLANK NO. 34   SERIES II, FORM B.

12. Health?

    Good.

13. Diseases in his family: Nervous Disorders? Rheumatism?
    Consumption? Dyspepsia? Varicose Veins? Heart Disease?
    Hernia? Habitual Constipation? Catarrh?

    Consumption and catarrh

Yourself:

1. Date of birth?

   July 9, 1865.

2. Early life in city or country?

   Country.

3. Height?

   69 inches.

4. Weight?

   165 lbs.

5. Complexion?

6. Temperament?

7. Where educated, give degrees if any?

   Stanford, A.B.

8. Occupations before marriage? a) in city or country? b) time spent in each?

   Teacher in village for seven years.

BLANK NO. 34   SERIES II, FORM B.

9. Diseases in your family? from father or mother's side? Nervous Disorders? Rheumatism? Consumption? Dyspepsia? Varicose Veins? Heart Disease? Hernia? Habitual Constipation? Catarrh?

   Heart disease

10. General health before marriage? b) since marriage? Paralysis? Brain Fever? Chronic Headache? Nervous Prostration? Catarrh? Hernia? Dyspepsia? Habitual Constipation? Inflammation of Bowels? Pleurisy? Bronchitis? Shortness of Breath? Spitting Blood? Consumption? Laryngitis? Tonsillitis? Insomnia? Rheumatism? Pneumonia? Jaundice? Varicose Veins?

    Good [before marriage]. Good [since marriage].

11. Menstruation:

    First menstruation at what age?

    And when thoroughly established?

    Present condition as regards menstruation:

    (a) How frequent?

    (b) Is it regular or not?

    (c) Amount? how many napkins?

    (d) Duration?

    (e) Pain or not? at what time as to the flow?

    (f) Is there any leucorrhoea (whites)? character?

        Amount?

        Constant or occasional?

    (g) Have you pain either frequently or habitually in the head, small of the back? abdomen or limbs?

    (h) Disease or trouble in Uterus (womb) or other pelvic organs?

    (i) Habit of bowels; how often?

BLANK NO. 34   SERIES II, FORM B.

12. What knowledge of sexual physiology had you before marriage? b) how did you obtain it?

    What could be known from a good course in zoology and Dr. Wood's course on that subject.

13. Number of times married. If more than once additional blanks will be furnished you to answer the following questions separately in regard to each marriage?

    1.

14. Number of years married?

    2 1/2.

15. Do you habitually sleep with your husband? b) what reasons for so doing or not?

    Yes. I like to be near him and for economic reasons.

16. Number of conceptions?

    One.

17. Number of children? State in connection with each, a) date of birth? b) sex? c) whether healthy or not? d) note any characteristic and the cause. e) note either immediate or after effect on your health of the birth of each of your children. f) give time of first menstruation after birth of each child.

    One.

    (a) June 22, 1896.

    (b) Male.

    (c) Healthy.

    (e) Stronger than for two years.

    (f) Third month after birth.

BLANK NO. 34   SERIES II, FORM B.

18. Did conception occur by choice or accident?

   A combination of the two.

19. Habit of intercourse, average number of times per week? per month? per year?

   A very irregular habit, averaging perhaps 6 or 8 times a month.

20. Was intercourse held during pregnancy? If so, how often?

   Yes. As much as at other times.

   (b) Had you any desire for it during this period?

21. At other times have you any desire for intercourse?

   Yes.

   (a) How often?

   It has no time regulation any more than kissing my husband or baby has.

   (b) At what time in relation to your menses?

22. Is intercourse agreeable to you or not?

   It is.

   Do you always have a venereal orgasm?

   No.

   1. When you do?

   (a) Effect immediately afterwards?

   None.

   (b) Effect next day?

   None.

   2. - When you do not?

BLANK NO. 34   SERIES II, FORM B.

   (a) Effect immediately afterwards?

       None.

   (b) Effect next day?

       None.

23. What do you believe to be the true purpose of intercourse?

    (a) Necessity to man?

        To woman?

    (b) Pleasure?

    (c) Reproduction?

    (d) What other reasons beside reproduction are sufficient to warrant intercourse?

        This is only a matter of opinion and hence not of scientific value, and my opinion on the matter has not yet crystalized.

24. Have you ever used any means to prevent conception? a) if so, what?

    No.

    (b) Effect on your health?

25. What, to you, would be an ideal habit?

BLANK NO. 35   SERIES II, FORM B.

[The editors provided the questions for this questionnaire, incomplete in the original.]

Date: Sept. 1897.

   4. Number of children?

      Number reaching maturity?

Your Paternal Grandmother: home in city or country?

   1. Age when married?

   2. Occupations?

   3. Health?

   4. Age and cause of death?

Your Mother:

   1. Nationality, if American of what descent?

      American. Puritan.

   2. Home in city or country before marriage?

      (b) Home in city or country after marriage?

   3. Occupations before her marriage?

      Teacher.

      (b) After her marriage?

         Teaching and all kinds of housework. Missionary.

   4. Note any prenatal influences before your birth:

BLANK NO. 35   SERIES II, FORM B.

5. Her health before your birth?
   (b) After your birth?

6. Number of miscarriages?
   Five miscarriages in first years of married life. Then boy
   child born. Incompetent physician decided beforehand [I]
   could not have any child. [I was] in labor 57 hours. Pressure
   of head on coccyx, child died. Next year [had] child with
   shoulder presentation. Child died immediately. Same
   physician. Physician did not examine her beforehand; said
   it was an abnormal growth. Bled her in her foot for 4 mo.
   She felt quickening & would not be bled anymore. A little
   more than a year later a boy child was born & lived 10 mo.
   Died of cholera infantum. Her health through pregnancy was
   always good. She was always able to nurse her babies. When
   not pregnant always had **flooding.**

   After death of baby had letter from home saying father
   and 2 sisters were dead. Cried whole year while carrying
   next child. This child was a girl (a blue baby) lived 48
   hours. 14 mo. later another girl born (this child **fills**
   out this blank) 12 years after marriage. After first 2
   confinements labor very short, not more than hour. This
   girl child perfectly healthy and well. Child was washed &
   dressed and laid in a draught by nurse; baby took cold &
   had influenza and nearly died at end of 3 weeks. No childish
   sicknesses. This baby kicked mother in night when between

BLANK NO. 35

1 & 2 yrs old & mother had another miscarriage. Sister born 2 yr. & 9 mo. younger. Mother only had one pain & in labor 2 minutes. This last baby when 2 1/2 years old had first measles & then whooping cough, then younger child had dysentery which caused her death.

Mother after child's death had return of old trouble prolapse. She had been on feet constantly with care of sick child. When second surviving daughter was born, Mother was 35. This was 2 1/2 years after. At 42 became **pregnant again**. Former children had weighed 7 or 7 1/2 lbs. This child was 10 1/2 lbs. (Mother hoped there would be twins.) Birth too rapid, muscle in rectum injured so defoecation was not controlled for rest of life. In bed 1 mo. was well. Baby boy was very delicate, sensitive & nervous. This child was nursed for 2 1/2 yrs. There were no baby foods in those days. Mother began to teach school. Not enough to eat in those days. **Natives** paid 25¢ per week. Taught until over 70 years old. This daughter began to teach at 13 yrs. old.

BLANK NO. 35   SERIES II, FORM B.

   7. Her age if living and present health? if not, age at time
      of death and cause?

      75 years old. Last week [of life she] would wake up for an
      hour. [She] gradually faded away.

   8. How was your mother's health affected by the climacteric
      (change of life)?

   9. Name any diseases in her family:

Your Maternal Grandfather: home in city or country?

   1. Age when married?

   2. Occupations?

   3. Health?

   4. Number of children?

      (b) Number reaching maturity?

Your Maternal Grandmother: home in city or country?

   1. Age when married?

   2. Occupations?

   3. Health?

   4. Age and cause of death?

Your Husband: nationality, if American, of what descent?
American   Puritan

BLANK NO. 35   SERIES II, FORM B.

1. Date of birth?
   1844.

2. Early life in city or country?
   Country. Went to sea [for] 7 years when 14 [years old].

3. Height?
   5 feet, 7 1/2 inches.

4. Weight?
   180 lbs.

5. Muscular or weak?
   Muscular

6. Where educated? degrees if any?
   U.S.

7. If a college man, has he been athletic?
   [Yes]

8. Complexion?
   Blue eyes, brown hair, fair complexion.

9. Temperament?
   Sanguine.

10. Does he use tobacco?
    No.

BLANK NO. 35   SERIES II, FORM B.

11. Occupations?

   Varied. Mental rather than physical. Active.

12. Health?

   Good. Excellent.

13. Diseases in his family: Nervous Disorders? Rheumatism? Consumption? Dyspepsia? Varicose Veins? Heart Disease? Hernia? Habitual Constipation? Catarrh?

   Mother had catarrh. Nervous disorders--the result of patent med[icines] for catarrh. Slight dyspepsia--now.

Yourself:

1. Date of birth?

   June 4, 1844.

2. Early life in city or country?

   Country

3. Height?

   5 ft., 5 1/2 in.

4. Weight?

   135 [lbs]. About 96 - 100 before marriage.

5. Complexion?

   Sallow.

6. Temperament?

7. Where educated, give degrees if any?

   High school.

BLANK NO. 35   SERIES II, FORM B.

8. Occupations before marriage? a) in city or country? b) time spent in each?

    Teacher at 12 & also after marriage for several years. 24 [years old] when married.

9. Diseases in your family? from father or mother's side? Nervous Disorders? Rheumatism? Consumption? Dyspepsia? Varicose Veins? Heart Disease? Hernia? Habitual Constipation? Catarrh?

    Asthma.

10. General health before marriage? b) since marriage? Paralysis? Brain Fever? Chronic Headache? Nervous Prostration? Catarrh? Hernia? Dyspepsia? Habitual Constipation? Inflammation of Bowels? Pleurisy? Bronchitis? Shortness of Breath? Spitting Blood? Consumption? Laryngitis? Tonsillitis? Insomnia? Rheumatism? Pneumonia? Jaundice? Varicose Veins?

    Good health since marriage.

    Typhoid fever. Slight nervous prostration and exhaustion. Habitual constipation--always. Insomnia--at times.

11. Menstruation:

    First menstruation at what age?

    14 1/2.

    and when thoroughly established?

    At once.

    Present condition as regards menstruation:

    Change of life.

    (a) How frequent?

        Month.

    (b) Is it regular or not?

        Regular.

BLANK NO. 35   SERIES II, FORM B.

   (c) Amount? how many napkins?

       Excessive.

   (d) Duration?

       5.

   (e) Pain or not? at what time as to the flow?

       [No pain]

   (f) Is there leucorrhoea (whites)? character?

       Slight.

       Amount?

       Constant or occasional?

       Occasional

   (g) Have you pain either frequently or habitually in the head, small of the back? abdomen or limbs?

   (h) Disease or trouble in Uterus (womb) or other pelvic organs?

       None.

   (i) Habit of bowels; how often?

       Once in 2 days.

12. What knowledge of sexual physiology had you before marriage?

    Slight from girls. Mother taught her that such things were not only not talked about but also not thought of. School child at 14 told [her] what intercourse was. [She] was shocked and didn't believe it.

13. Number of times married. If more than once additional blanks will be furnished you to answer the following questions separately in regard to each marriage?

    Once.

BLANK NO. 35   SERIES II, FORM B.

14. Number of years married?

   Since 1869. 28 1/2 yrs.

15. Do you habitually sleep with your husband? b) what reasons for so doing or not?

   Yes, until last 3 or 4 mo. Then due to not sleeping well, [snoring?] etc. nervousness.

16. Number of conceptions?

   12. 6 miscarriages & 6 children.

17. Number of children? State in connection with each, a) date of birth? b) sex? c) whether healthy or not? d) note any characteristic and the cause. e) note either immediate or after effect on your health of the birth of each of your children. f) give time of first menstruation after birth of each child.

   One miscarriage, then:

   [First child]

      (a) 14 mo. after marriage.

      (b) Girl.

      (c) Wt. 10 lbs. Very healthy.

      (d) Long labor.

      (e) Good.

      (f) 15 mo. then weaned child because of it.

   [Second child]

      (a) 2 1/2 yrs. later.

      (b) Boy.

      (c) When he was 14 mo. old [he] bit mother causing an abcess & so [he was] weaned. He died of cholera infantum.

      (e) Wt. 92 lbs. after weaning both child[ren].

BLANK NO. 35   SERIES II, FORM B.

[Third child]

   (b) Boy (W).

   (c) Nursed 8 mo. Very hearty.

   (f) 9 mo. [Did] not [menstruate?] for 5 yrs. Husband
       ill with melancholia. Great strain on her, then
       [her menstruation was] colorless when [she moved] to
       cold climate. [?] children ill [with] children's
       diseases.

When boy was 15 mo. old, miscarriage brought about by mental
shock.
[Fourth child]

   (a) 1880.

   (b) Boy.

   (c) Lived 6 mo. [then] died of cholera infantum.

[Fifth child]

   (a) [Born one year after death of 4th child]

   (c) (H) weighed 10 1/2 lbs. When H was 9 mo. old, horse
       ran away, and shock caused miscarriage [to mother who
       was again pregnant].

[Sixth child]

   (a) 2 yrs. after H's birth.

   (b) Daughter (M).

   (c) Well.

   (e) Lost much sleep with boys during babyhood.

Three miscarriages in 3 successive years at 45, 46, and 47.
Doctor thought it [was] change of life. Went to bed each
time. No irregularity until about 50 yrs. old. Then
tendency to excessive [bleeding?] & irregularity - now
[bleeds? menstruates?] every] 6 mo. but great relief when it
occurs.

18. Did conception occur by choice or accident?

BLANK NO. 35   SERIES II, FORM B.

[Conceived] after 15th miscarriage because not well[?]. [An accidental conception occurred] just before menstruation. [**The next conception was by choice--she says "willing"--occurred "when there was no reason for not conceiving." One child was] much wanted.**

19. Habit of intercourse, average number of times per week?

    [Average once a week,] sometimes oftener sometimes less often.

    per month?

    per year?

20. Was intercourse held during pregnancy? If so, how often?

    About average. Not so often during last 2 mo.

    (b) Had you any desire for it during this period?

        [Often] more desire than at other times, and she needed it. "Nothing would ease my nervous condition but that."

21. At other times have you any desire for intercourse? a) how often? b) at what time in relation to your menses?

    Yes. Very soon after period, [it is] more agreeable. Sometimes just before [period]. Much of time could have blotted [it] out and never missed it. Then another time wanted it. [She prefers intercourse] when not too tired, just before and just after [menses].

22. Is intercourse agreeable to you or not?

    Yes, when not too tired & conditions are right.

    Do you always have a venereal orgasm?

    Always when she desires. Many times not.

    1. - When you do,

    (a) Effect immediately afterwards?

        Sleepy, relaxed, less nervous, good.

(b) Effect next day?

Feels well.

2. - When you do not,

(a) Effect immediately afterwards?

Nervous strung up not sleepy.

(b) Effect next day?

No effect.

23. What do you believe to be the true purpose of intercourse?

(a) Necessity to man? to woman?

[Yes] Because many [who are] unmarried are too nervous & do not recognize what the cause is.

(b) Pleasure?

[Yes] for purpose of bringing about [**reproduction**].

(c) Reproduction?

[Yes] highest purpose.

(d) What other reasons beside reproduction are sufficient to warrant intercourse?

Individual health: a normal desire and a rational use of it tends to keep people healthier.

24. Have you ever used any means to prevent conception? a) if so, what?

Withdrawal sometimes.

(b) Effect on your health?

None in either [husband or wife?]

25. What, to you, would be an ideal habit?

Once a week or [once every] ten days. When both want it.

BLANK NO. 36   SERIES II, FORM B.
Date: June 21, 1895.

Your Father:

1. Nationality, if American, of what descent?

   German.

2. Home in city or country before marriage?

    Country

3. Home in city or country after marriage?

    City

4. Age when married?

   25.

5. Occupations before your birth?

   Tanner.

   (b) After your birth?

      Wholesale leather dealer.

6. Health previous to your birth?

   Excellent. Suffered from youth from hemorrhoids a result of disease.

   (b) After your birth?

      Excellent with occasional touches of constipation.

7. Number of children living?

   (a) Boys: 1

   (b) Girls: 1

BLANK NO. 36   SERIES II, FORM B.

8. Number of children dead; give age at time of death and cause:

   (a) Boys: 1. Waked from a sound sleep. Vaccinated in the fashion of 25 years ago. Ate a hearty supper. Waked up in night ill, & two days after died in convulsions. Had always been perfectly healthy.

9. If your father is living, give his age and present health, if dead, age at death and cause?

   59. Health very good.

10. Name any diseases in his family:

    Catarrh. One of sisters [had an] enlarged gland in neck.

Your Paternal Grandfather: home in city or country?

Country.

   1. Age when married?

   2. Occupations?

      Farmer.

   3. Health?

      Very good.

   4. Number of children?

      5.

      Number reaching maturity?

      5.

Your Paternal Grandmother: home in city or country?

Country.

BLANK NO. 36   SERIES II, FORM B.

   1. Age when married?

   2. Occupations?
      Housekeeper.

   3. Health?
      Good.

   4. Age and cause of death?
      About 40. Cholera.

Your Mother:

   1. Nationality, if American of what descent?
      German.

   2. Home in city or country before marriage?
       Country
      (b) Home in city or country after marriage?
          City

   3. Occupations before her marriage?
      Teaching school & attending school before 20.
      (b) After her marriage?
          Housekeeper.

   4. Note any prenatal influences before your birth:

   5. Her health previous to your birth?
      Excellent.

BLANK NO. 36　　　　　　　　　　　　　SERIES II, FORM B.

    (b) After your birth?

       Excellent.

6. Number of miscarriages?

   None.

7. Her age if living and present health? if not, age at time of death and cause?

   54. Physical health good. Mentally--religious mania since 47 years old. A twelfth child born when her mother was about 43 years old.

8. How was your mother's health affected by the climacteric (change of life)?

   Menstruated irregularly since 47 years.

9. Name any diseases in her family:

   None except Father's rheumatism when 87 years old. Mother became feeble-minded in her 85th year.

Your Maternal Grandfather: home in city or country?

Country.

1. Age when married?

2. Occupations?

   Farmer.

3. Health?

   Good except rheumatism.

4. Number of children?

BLANK NO. 36   SERIES II, FORM B.

    12.
    (b) Number reaching maturity?
        11. One drowned in infancy.

Your Maternal Grandmother: home in city or country?
Country.
    1. Age when married?

    2. Occupations?
       Housekeeper.

    3. Health?
       Good.

    4. Age and cause of death?
       Old age.

Your Husband: nationality, if American, of what descent?
American, New England.
    1. Date of birth?
       1861.

    2. Early life in city or country?
       Country.

    3. Height?
       6 feet.

BLANK NO. 36							SERIES II, FORM B.

4. Weight?

   156 lbs.

5. Muscular or weak?

   Not muscular.

6. Where educated? degrees if any?

   College, Ph.D.

7. If a college man, has he been athletic?

   No.

8. Complexion?

   Medium.

9. Temperament?

   Nervous.

10. Does he use tobacco?

    Tea & coffee in moderation. [He was the] 10th child. 4 reached maturity.

11. Occupations?

    Teacher only.

12. Health?

    His father died 3 [months] before his birth. His mother used opiates continually to ward off child birth pains. Very delicate up to 3 years old. Partially worked his way through college. Has overworked for 10 yrs. Broke down in 1894 at 32 1/2 yrs. old. Had T.B. & is recovering in 1895.

BLANK NO. 36   SERIES II, FORM B.

13. Diseases in his family: Nervous Disorders? Rheumatism?
    Consumption? Dyspepsia? Varicose Veins? Heart Disease?
    Hernia? Habitual Constipation? Catarrh?

    Mother had consumption and varicose veins. Nervous disorders,
    heart disease, paralysis, cancer, and catarrh [in his family].

Yourself:

1. Date of birth?

   1864.

2. Early life in city or country?

   City

3. Height?

   5 feet, 4 inches.

4. Weight?

   142 lbs.

5. Complexion?

   Light.

6. Temperament?

7. Where educated, give degrees if any?

   College, B.L.

8. Occupations before marriage? a) in city or country? b) time spent in each?

   Taught six months in country. First child, born two years after marriage. Father 27 years. Mother 22 years.

BLANK NO. 36   SERIES II, FORM B.

9. Diseases in your family? from father or mother's side? Nervous Disorders? Rheumatism? Consumption? Dyspepsia? Varicose Veins? Heart Disease? Hernia? Habitual Constipation? Catarrh?

   Nervous disorders and catarrh

10. General health before marriage? b) since marriage? Paralysis? Brain Fever? Chronic Headache? Nervous Prostration? Catarrh? Hernia? Dyspepsia? Habitual Constipation? Inflammation of Bowels? Pleurisy? Bronchitis? Shortness of Breath? Spitting Blood? Consumption? Laryngitis? Tonsilitis? Insomnia? Rheumatism? Pneumonia? Jaundice? Varicose Veins?

   Catarrh before [marriage]. Slight bronchitis Scarlet fever at 5 yrs. left with cough & threatened tendency to consumption, [which] continued through girlhood, [but was] outgrown by 22 years [old].

11. Menstruation:

    First menstruation at what age? and when thoroughly established?

    Between twelve & thirteen.

    Present condition as regards menstruation:

    (a) How frequent?

        Twenty-six days.

    (b) Is it regular or not?

        Two - three days occasional.

    (c) Amount? how many napkins?

        Six to eight.

    (d) Duration?

        About five days.

    (e) Pain or not? at what time as to the flow?

        No pain except little dragging in the back.

BLANK NO. 36   SERIES II, FORM B.

   (f) Is there any leucorrhoea (whites)? character?

   No.

   Amount?

   Constant or occasional?

   (g) Have you pain either frequently or habitually in the head, small of the back? abdomen or limbs?

   [Small of the back] when standing on feet too much.

   (h) Disease or trouble in Uterus (womb) or other pelvic organs?

   None.

   (i) Habit of bowels; how often?

   Loose - usually once a day, sometimes twice a day.

12. What knowledge of sexual physiology had you before marriage? b) how did you obtain it?

   Understood what marriage meant. Obtained information from Mother & future sister-in-law & talked some with future husband.

13. Number of times married. If more than once additional blanks will be furnished you to answer the following questions separately in regard to each marriage?

   Once.

14. Number of years married?

   Nearly seven.

15. Do you habitually sleep with your husband? b) what reasons for so doing or not?

   Yes. Because of the personal comfort and closer companionship thus afforded. Not within last year. ... because of husband's ill health.

BLANK NO. 36   SERIES II, FORM B.

16. Number of conceptions?

    Two.

17. Number of children? State in connection with each, a) date of birth? b) sex? c) whether healthy or not? d) note any characteristic and the cause. e) note either immediate or after effect on your health of the birth of each of your children. f) give time of first menstruation after birth of each child.

    Two children. Girl born Sept. 16, 1889. Boy born Sept. 10, 1891.

    (c) Both very healthy.

    (d) Home conditions trying. Husband away. An attack of bronchitis. Girl had whooping cough.

    (e) Both births left me strong and well; except that I had hemorrhoids.

    (f) After birth of girl five months. After birth of boy eleven months.

18. Did conception occur by choice or accident?

    Accident.

19. Habit of intercourse, average number of times per week?

    per month?

    Three

    per year?

    36 - 40.

20. Was intercourse held during pregnancy? If so, how often? b) had you any desire for it during this period?

    Yes, up to sixth month about three times a month. During the early months--moderate desire.

21. At other times have you any desire for intercourse? a) how often? b) at what time in relation to your menses?

    Yes. Before and after the menses.

22. Is intercourse agreeable to you or not?

    Yes.

    Do you usually have a venereal orgasm?

    Usually.

    1. - When you do?

    (a) Effect immediately afterwards?

    Quieting.

    (b) Effect next day?

    Usually feel exceeding well & in excellent spirits.

    2. - When you do not?

    (a) Effect immediately afterwards?

    Feel tired.

    (b) Effect next day?

    Not noticeable.

23. What do you believe to be the true purpose of intercourse?

    (a) Necessity to man?

    No.

    To woman?

    No.

    (b) Pleasure?

    No.

    (c) Reproduction?

    Yes.

(d) What other reasons beside reproduction are sufficient to warrant intercourse?

The gratification of a normal healthy appetite.

24. Have you ever used any means to prevent conception? a) if so, what?

Yes. A warm water douche recommended by a physician in good standing.

(b) Effect on your health?

So far as one can judge the health has been improved.

25. What, to you, would be an ideal habit?

Total abstinence, with intercourse for reproduction only. Until human nature is different from what it is now, it seems as though such a habit would not be the most healthful for all people. Persons differ as much in this respect as in others, & it seems as though the only way now, is to gain all possible knowledge on the subject, and then the two persons having equal weight in the decision work out their own habit of life.

BLANK NO. 38 **unknown** [sic]   SERIES II, FORM B.

[The editors provided the questions for this questionnaire, incomplete in the original.]

Date: Dec. 20, 1913.

Yourself:

1. Date of birth?

   [Age] 30

2. Early life in city or country?

   City

3. Height?

   About 5 ft., 3 [in.] tall

4. Weight?

   135

5. Complexion?

   Dark

6. Temperament?

   Nervous

7. Where educated, give degrees if any?

   High school.

Italian father. American mother. Husband: very athletic **man** Health before marriage: good. Since [marriage]: good. **Menstrual: normal. No uterine trouble.**

BLANK NO. 38   SERIES II, FORM B.

12. What knowledge of sexual physiology had you before marriage?
    b) how did you obtain it?

    No knowledge.

14. Number of years married?

    12 yrs. Married at 18.

15. 1st intercourse how soon after marriage?

    Immediate. (Left her for 3 mo. next day or so.)

16. Number of conceptions?

    Twice.

17. Number of children? State in connection with each, a) date
    of birth? b) sex? c) whether healthy or not? d) note any
    characteristic and the cause. e) note either immediate or
    after effect on your health of the birth of each of your
    children. f) give time of first menstruation after birth
    of each child.

    [First child]

        (a) 7 mo. child about 10 mo. after.

        (b) Girl.

        (c) Healthy. Died at 2 1/2 yrs of spinal meningitis.

        (f) Nursed it.

    [Second child]

        (a) About 2 yrs. later.

        (b) Girl.

        (c) Healthy. Nursed (Vagina distended at birth of last
            child [and] never has gone back.)

18. Did conception occur by choice or accident?

BLANK NO. 38   SERIES II, FORM B.

Choice.

20. Was intercourse held during pregnancy? If so, how often?
    b) had you any desire for it during this period?

    Not during pregnancy.

21. At other times have you any desire for intercourse? a) how
    often? b) at what time in relation to your menses?

    No.

22. Is intercourse agreeable to you?

    Yes.

    Do you always have a venereal orgasm?

    Yes. Since birth of last child no sensation. [She will
    have an] operation.

23. What do you believe to be the true purpose of intercourse?

    (a) Necessity to man?

        No.

        to woman?

        No.

    (b) Pleasure?

    (c) Reproduction?

        Yes.

    (d) What other reasons beside reproduction are sufficient to
        warrant intercourse?

        Love [is] a spiritual experience.

24. Have you ever used any means to prevent conception? a) if
    so, what?

BLANK NO. 38   SERIES II, FORM B.

No means of prevention.

(b) Effect on your health?

BLANK NO. 40   SERIES II, FORM B.

[The editors provided the questions for this questionnaire, incomplete
in the original.]

Date: Dec. 17, 1913.

Yourself:

1. Date of birth?

   July 14, 1876.

2. Early life in city or country?

   Country.

3. Height?

   5 ft., 4 in.

4. Weight?

   116 [lbs].

5. Complexion?

   Light.

6. Temperament?

   Quick movements but calm temperament....

7. Where educated, give degrees if any?

   Stanford, 3 yrs.

8. Occupations before marriage? a) in city or country? b) time spent in each?

   None.

BLANK NO. 40   SERIES II, FORM B.

9. Diseases in your family? from father or mother's side? Nervous Disorders? Rheumatism? Consumption? Dyspepsia? Varicose Veins? Heart Disease? Hernia? Habitual Constipation? Catarrh?

10. General health before marriage? b) since marriage? Paralysis? Brain Fever? Chronic Headache? Nervous Prostration? Catarrh? Hernia? Dyspepsia? Habitual Constipation? Inflammation of Bowels? Pleurisy? Bronchitis? Shortness of Breath? Spitting Blood? Consumption? Laryngitis? Tonsillitis? Insomnia? Rheumatism? Pneumonia? Jaundice? Varicose Veins?

    Perfect. Excellent health before & after [marriage]. Very athletic. Brought up like a boy.

11. Menstruation:

    First menstruation at what age?

    About 13.

    and when thoroughly established?

    Present condition as regards menstruation:

    (a) How frequent?

        28 days.

    (b) Is it regular or not?

        Reg[ular].

    (c) Amount? how many napkins?

        Scanty very.

    (d) Duration?

        6 (1). [Maximum and minimum days duration?]

    (e) Pain or not? at what time as to the flow?

        No pain--knows no dif[ference].

    (f) Is there any leucorrhoea (whites)? character?

        No.

BLANK NO. 40   SERIES II, FORM B.

   (g) Have you pain either frequently or habitually in the head, small of the back? abdomen or limbs?

   (h) Disease or trouble in Uterus (womb) or other pelvic organs?

   No.

   (i) Habit of bowels; how often?

   Not constipated.

12. What knowledge of sexual physiology had you before marriage? b) how did you obtain it?

   Not any knowledge.

13. Number of times married. If more than once additional blanks will be furnished you to answer the following questions separately in regard to each marriage?

14. Number of years married?

   Married in 1897 - 16 years.

15. Do you habitually sleep with your husband? b) what reasons for so doing or not?

16. Number of conceptions?

   5 conceptions.

17. Number of children? State in connection with each, a) date of birth? b) sex? c) whether healthy or not? d) note any characteristic and the cause. e) note either immediate or after effect on your health of the birth of each of your children. f) give time of first menstruation after birth of each child.

   4 children.

   [First child]

      (a) Apr. 15, 1898.

BLANK NO. 40   SERIES II, FORM B.

    (b) Boy.

    (c) Very healthy (6 lbs). Nursed 9 mo.

    (e) Normal birth. Slight tear. Ten hours of labor.

    (f) Menstruation returned at   4th or 5th week.

[Second child]

    (a) Sept. 1900.

    (b) Boy.

    (c) 6 1/4 lbs.--perfectly healthy. Baby died of cholera infantum in East at 1 yr.

    (e) Nursing 1st baby & did not know she was pregnant until 4 mo. Not knowing she was pregnant she played basketball & rode wheel all day after. Labor 1 hr. from 1st pain. Nursed him 5 mo. and stopped because Dr. said mother was too thin. Had quantities of milk.

    (f) [Menstruction irregular after birth?]

[Third child]

    (a) May 1902.

    (b) Boy.

    (c) 6 1/2 lbs. Nursed him 8 mo. Very healthy. At 8 mo. had whooping cough. 3 or 4 yrs. not strong [due to] asthma. California air cured him & he is very strong now.

    (e) Normal birth. Hemorrhages. Labor [lasted] 2 1/2 hours.

    (f) [Menstruation after birth irregular.]

Miscarriage

    (a) Miscarriage in Sept. 1903 [at] 3 mo.

    (e) Menstr[uation] slight. Twice in bed **some under doctor's** care. Worked hard & rode wheel (as usual during pregnancy). Insufficient care--afterbirth left until 1 wk after. Dr. drunk. Not well for 1 yr.

BLANK NO. 40   SERIES II, FORM B.

[Fourth child]

    (a) Mar. 20, 1905.

    (b) Boy.

    (c) Very healthy. 7 lbs. Nursed 7 mo.

    (e) Labor 3 hrs. 3 or 4 hard pains.

    (f) [Menstruation began 6 weeks after delivery and is irregular.]

18. Did conception occur by choice or accident?

    All accidental conceptions.

19. Habit of intercourse, average number of times per week? per month? per year?

    [For the first six years of marriage intercourse took place] almost every day, sometimes 2 [times] daily. Now: 1 [per] week--2 or 3 [times per] month.

20. Was intercourse held during pregnancy? If so, how often?

    All during pregnancy - somewhat less often. 2 - 3 [times per] wk during 1st [?]. Later perhaps 1 [per] wk.

    (b) Had you any desire for it during this period?

    No desire during pregnancy.

21. At other times have you any desire for intercourse?

    When feels well & not tired.

    (a) How often?

    1 - 2 [times per] month.

    (b) At what time in relation to your menses?

    No relation in regard to periods.

22. Is intercourse agreeable to you or not?

    Not agreeable.

    Do you always have a venereal orgasm?

    No orgasm for years. Does [have orgasms] now. After **coitus** stimulated, more keen. More alive mentally & physically.

    1. - When you do,

       (a) Effect immediately afterwards?

       (b) Effect next day?

    2. - When you do not,

       (a) Effect immediately afterwards?

       (b) Effect next day?

23. What do you believe to be the true purpose of intercourse?

    (a) Necessity to man?

       No.

       to woman?

       No.

    (b) Pleasure?

       If both want it.

    (c) Reproduction?

       Yes.

    (d) What other reasons beside reproduction are sufficient to warrant intercourse?

       A way of showing you care as [with] kisses & caresses. Thinks men have not been properly trained.

24. Have you ever used any means to prevent conception? a) if so, what?

BLANK NO. 40   SERIES II, FORM B.

    Last years - [only had intercourse during] sterile interval.
    Vaseline. Condom(?). Skin[?] used only once.

25. What, to you, would be an ideal habit?

    1 - 2 [times per] month. When acceptable to both [husband
    and wife].

BLANK NO. 41　　　　　　　　　　　　　　　SERIES II, FORM B.

Yourself:

1. Date of birth?

    May 13, 1862

2. Early life in city or country?

    Up to ten years country of Iowa then small city, then S.F., Berkeley, Oakland, till marriage.

3. Height?

    5 ft., 4 in.

4. Weight?

    About 125 pounds

5. Complexion?

    Medium fair

6. Temperament?

    Ardent

7. Where educated, give degrees if any?

    Univ. California B.L.

8. Occupations before marriage? a) in city or country? b) time spent in each?

    Married at twenty, just out of college

9. Diseases in your family? from father or mother's side? Nervous Disorders? Rheumatism? Consumption? Dyspepsia? Varicose Veins? Heart Disease? Hernia? Habitual Constipation? Catarrh?

    None of these. Father died of cancer

BLANK NO. 41   SERIES II, FORM B.

10. General health before marriage? b) since marriage? Paralysis? Brain Fever? Chronic Headache? Nervous Prostration? Catarrh? Hernia? Dyspepsia? Habitual Constipation? Inflammation of Bowels? Pleurisy? Bronchitis? Shortness of Breath? Spitting Blood? Consumption? Laryngitis? Tonsillitis? Insomnia? Rheumatism? Pneumonia? Jaundice? Varicose Veins?

   Good. Have been sick only once in my life. Had typhoid fever in my sophomore year in college. It caused constipation which persisted for fifteen years and was cured by physical exercise.

11. Menstruation:

    First menstruation at what age? and when thoroughly established?

    Began to menstruate at fourteen and a half, and was absolutely regular always until beginning of change of life at fifty.

    Present condition as regards menstruation:

    (a) How frequent?

        Now irregular--skipped three months last time.

    (b) Is it regular or not?

    (c) Amount? how many napkins?

        About five napkins a day but have been examined twice and pronounced all right.

    (d) Duration?

        Lasts five days now, less than three all my life before.

    (e) Pain or not? at what time as to the flow?

        No pain since I bore my first child. Used to suffer some pain the first day.

    (f) Is there any leucorrhoea (whites)? character?

        Some now. Remarkably free from it until now.

        Amount?

        Small amount several days before and after menstruating.

BLANK NO. 41   SERIES II, FORM B.

Constant or occasional?

(g) Have you pain either frequently or habitually in the head, small of the back? abdomen or limbs?

Never had a headache in my life--no pain of any kind.

(h) Disease or trouble in Uterus (womb) or other pelvic organs?

Never

(i) Habit of bowels; how often?

Move once every twenty-four hours sometimes twice.

12. What knowledge of sexual physiology had you before marriage? b) how did you obtain it?

Vague ideas from fellow pupils at school. My mother was a physician but refused to instruct me when I asked questions. I remember well the first time I asked a question which showed that I already had the idea there was something shameful about child bearing. Yet she told me I would read books about it when I was older, and I never asked again.

13. Number of times married. If more than once additional blanks will be furnished you to answer the following questions separately in regard to each marriage?

14. Number of years married?

Over thirty years

15. Do you habitually sleep with your husband? b) what reasons for so doing or not?

Yes, for the comfort of it, and because it keeps us close together. I suppose separate beds are more hygienic, but I believe people drift apart when they do not sleep together.

16. Number of conceptions?

Five. I had one miscarriage between the first two boys, due to working very hard at the time of the illness and death of

BLANK NO. 41   SERIES II, FORM B.

a sister's child, when I did not know that I was pregnant
(6 weeks).

17. Number of children? State in connection with each: a) date
of birth? b) sex? c) whether healthy or not? d) note any
characteristic and the cause. e) note either immediate or
after effect on your health of the birth of each of your
children. f) give time of first menstruation after birth of
each child. g) whether you nursed each child and how long

No. 1 - boy February 11, 1884 Perfectly healthy very bright
and active because I was perfectly well, travelling and
studying abroad up to the moment of his birth. Perfectly
natural birth, caused me little pain, no anaesthetic taken,
and with a month's rest as well as ever. Continued travels
and nursed baby till about fourteen months old. **Menstruated one**
month after weaning.

Mishap I think in August, 1885-no exposure for month following,
but must have conceived immediately after next menstruation,
for the next boy came June 29, 1886. Perhaps he was short
time, for I was not so well this time, worked very hard, at
housework and care of lively boy, constipation very bad,
and when baby came I suffered much more than the first time.
The baby was nervous too, and troublesome, though not really
sick. Nursed till nine months old--weaned him to go to work.
Husband's health poor. Menstruated one month after weaning.
Husband recovered health in a measure. Next boy came May 31st,
1888. I had been working very hard, and was tired, but was
in labor only half an hour, and Dr. Charlotte Blake Brown

said it was as normal as any birth she ever saw. A little
exhausted after it, and had to stop work for two months, but
nursed baby till three months old, then lost milk from
dysentery. I think menstruation followed as in other cases.
Child had bronchitis and pneumonia, but now strong man. Fourth
boy born June 4, 1890. Perfectly well when carrying him, out
of doors, not working last three months, was in labor twenty
minutes. Nursed this boy till fourteen months old. Was only
100 pounds left of me, but well after trip to Hawaii and six
weeks rest.

18. Did conception occur by choice or accident?

    Always an accident. Did not mean to have any children for
    five years in order to study. Practiced rule [of] no
    intercourse ten days after menstruation and three days before,
    which served my mother. [And] douche immediately after
    [intercourse]. Did not answer in my case. French method of
    prevention perfectly successful.

19. Habit of intercourse, average number of times per week?

    Perhaps three times a week for the two weeks supposed to be
    safe.

    per month?

20. Was intercourse held during pregnancy? If so, how often?

    Occasionally.

    (b) Had you any desire for it during this period?

       Generally not, but before birth of third boy did have.
       Can not see that it affected character of this son. He
       is perfectly continent at twenty-five.

BLANK NO. 41   SERIES II, FORM B.

21. At other times have you any desire for intercourse?

    Yes.

    (b) How often? at what time in relation to your menses?

        Always strongest a few days before and after menses.

22. Is intercourse agreeable to you or not?

    Yes

    Do you always have a venereal orgasm?

    No

    1. - When you do,

    (a) Effect immediately afterwards?

        No bad effect. I believe reasonable intercourse conduces to health and I am sure it makes married life the happiest state in the world on account of the spiritual union which results from it.

    (b) Effect next day?

        None--a general sense of well being, contentment and regard for husband. This is true Doctor.

    2. - When you do not,

    (a) Effect immediately afterwards?

        Every wife submits sometimes when perhaps she is not in the mood, but I can see no bad effect. It is as if it had not been. But my husband was absolutely considerate. I do not think I could endure a man who forced it.

    (b) Effect next day?

        None

23. What do you believe to be the true purpose of intercourse?

    (a) Necessity to man? to woman?

        I think women as well as men need this relation during middle life. It makes more normal people.

BLANK NO. 41   SERIES II, FORM B.

   (b) Pleasure?

      Yes

   (c) Reproduction?

      Yes

   (d) What other reasons beside reproduction are sufficient to warrant intercourse?

      Even if there are no children, men love their wives more if they continue this relation, and the highest devotion is based upon it, a very beautiful thing, and I am glad nature gave it to us.

24. Have you ever used any means to prevent conception?

   (a) If so, what?

      Described [earlier]. Husband used French means.

   (b) Effect on your health?

      I could see none. I know it is better to use something than to have the husband withdraw. That is dangerous to his health.

25. What, to you, would be an ideal habit?

   Once a month

26. Are you athletic or not? what kind of exercise?

   Not athletic in a special sense, but very fond of walking and outdoor exercise. Special exercises every night to keep bowels regular also conduce to general health.

27. Husband - college man?

   Yes, graduate U.C.

   Athletic?

   No

BLANK NO. 41   SERIES II, FORM B.

   Sedentary or active life?
   Rather active

BLANK NO. 42   SERIES II, FORM B.

[The editors provided the questions for this blank, incomplete in the original.]

Date: Dec. 2[9?], 1913.

Yourself:

1. Date of birth?

   July 27, 1863. 3rd child of father & mother.

2. Early life in city or country?

   Country. Small town.

3. Height?

   5 ft., 7 in.

4. Weight?

   112.

5. Complexion?

   Light.

6. Temperament?

7. Where educated, give degrees if any?

   Private school.

8. Occupations before marriage? a) in city or country? b) time spent in each?

   None.

9. Diseases in your family? from father or mother's side? Nervous Disorders? Rheumatism? Consumption? Dyspepsia? Varicose

BLANK NO. 42   SERIES II, FORM B.

   Veins? Heart Disease? Hernia? Habitual Constipation? Catarrh?

   None.

10. General health before marriage? b) since marriage? **Paralysis?**
    Brain Fever? Chronic Headache? Nervous Prostration? **Catarrh?**
    Hernia? Dyspepsia? Habitual Constipation? Inflammation of
    Bowels? Pleurisy? Bronchitis? Shortness of Breath? Spitting
    Blood? Consumption? Laryngitis? Tonsillitis? Insomnia?
    Rheumatism? Pneumonia? Jaundice? Varicose Veins?

    Good health before [and since] marriage.

11. Menstruation:

    First menstruation at what age?

    Between 12 - 13.

    and when thoroughly established?

    At once.

    Present condition as regards menstruation:

    (a) How frequent?

        28 days.

    (b) Is it regular or not?

        Reg[ular].

    (c) Amount? how many napkins?

        Usually nine. **Abundant flow**.

    (d) Duration?

        Dur[ation] 6 - 7 days.

    (e) Pain or not? at what time as to the flow?

        V[ery] little pain. Occasional[ly] due to wet feet or
        other indiscretion.

    (f) Is there any leucorrhoea (whites)? character?

BLANK NO. 42   SERIES II, FORM B.

   No.

   Amount?

   Constant or occasional?

   (g) Have you pain either frequently or habitually in the head, small of the back? abdomen or limbs?

   (h) Disease or trouble in Uterus (womb) or other pelvic organs?

   No uterine trouble.

   (i) Habit of bowels; how often?

   Constipation after birth of 3rd child.

12. What knowledge of sexual physiology had you before marriage? b) how did you obtain it?

   No knowledge. Did not know what marriage meant.

13. Number of times married. If more than once additional blanks will be furnished you to answer the following questions separately in regard to each marriage?

14. Number of years married?

   Jan. 21, 1891.

   Husband [is] not athletic.

15. 1st intercourse how soon after marriage?

   Immediately.

16. Number of conceptions?

   6 conceptions.

17. Number of children? 4 State in connection with each, a) date of birth? b) sex? c) whether healthy or not? d) note any characteristic and the cause. e) note either immediate or after effect on your health of the birth of each of your

children. f) give time of first menstruation after birth of each child.

[First child]

(a) June 1893.

(b) Girl.

(c) Healthy. Nursed 9 mo.

(f) Mens[truation] began during nursing.

[Second child]

(a) Oct. 1894.

(b) Girl.

(c) Healthy. 10 lbs. Nursed 9 mo.

[Third child]

(a) July 1897.

(b) Twin boys.

(c) 7 lbs. [One boy] died at birth.

(e) During 9 mo. before twin boys had terrible itching of whole body. No sign of eruption on skin. Labor from Fri. night [?] to Sunday at 8 a.m. Carried boy downstairs at end of 10 days [?] children. Very bad constipation ever since. Perfectly well baby - nursed. Had enough milk for 2. Very fretful baby. No sleep at night until 4 yrs. old. Ate & grew.

Miscarriage 1 yr. after last boy. Brought on by a shock at 5 months--frightful hemorrhage for 2 days. Hair turned white. During Spanish war [she had an] incompetent Dr.(?). [Miscarriage took place during the] first yr. after marriage, due to a fall [when she was] 2 mo. along.

18. Did conception occur by choice or accident?

Accident.

19. Habit of intercourse, average number of times per week?

BLANK NO. 42   SERIES II, FORM B.

    3 to 4 times per week.

    per month?

    per year?

20. Was intercourse held during pregnancy? If so, how often?

    Yes during pregnancy. 2 [times] weekly possibly.

    (b) Had you any desire for it during this period?

    No.

21. At other times have you any desire for intercourse? a) how often?

    Occasionally.

    (b) At what time in relation to your menses?

        Usually before. [And when there is a] feeling of well being and harmony.

22. Is intercourse agreeable to you or not?

    Not always agreeable.

    Do you always have a venereal orgasm?

    Not always orgasm, only occasionally.

    1. - When you do,

    (a) Effect immediately afterwards?

        Relaxed.

    (b) Effect next day?

        Better next day.

    2. - When you do not,

    (a) Effect immediately afterwards?

        More nervous.

BLANK NO. 42   SERIES II, FORM B.

   (b) Effect next day?

23. What do you believe to be the true purpose of intercourse?

   (a) Necessity to man?

      Yes.

      to woman?

      Yes.

   (b) Pleasure?

      Yes.

   (c) Reproduction?

      Yes.

   (d) What other reasons beside reproduction are sufficient to warrant intercourse?

      Shock and destruction of all ideals: When a pure woman is treated by her husband as he has treated the prostitute he has been to before marriage, it becomes loathsome.

24. Have you ever used any means to prevent conception? a) if so, what?

   Yes. Cold douches.

   (b) Effect on your health?

      No effect on health.

25. What, to you, would be an ideal habit?

   When both had desire.

BLANK NO. 43   SERIES II, FORM B.

[The editors provided the questions for this blank, incomplete in the original.]

Date: Dec. 23, 1913.

Yourself:

1. Date of birth?

   May 4, 1857.

2. Early life in city or country?

   Country.

3. Height?

   5 ft. tall.

4. Weight?

   Wt. about 100.

5. Complexion?

   Light (medium).

6. Temperament?

   Not nervous.

7. Where educated, give degrees if any?

   Oswego Normal.

8. Occupations before marriage? a) in city or country? b) time spent in each?

   4 yrs. teaching in [District?] School in Oswego & near Rochester. Burlington, Vt.

BLANK NO. 43   SERIES II, FORM B.

9. Diseases in your family? from father or mother's side? Nervous Disorders? Rheumatism? Consumption? Dyspepsia? Varicose Veins? Heart Disease? Hernia? Habitual Constipation? Catarrh?

   Nothing.

10. General health before marriage? b) since marriage? Paralysis? Brain Fever? Chronic Headache? Nervous Prostration? Catarrh? Hernia? Dyspepsia? Habitual Constipation? Inflammation of Bowels? Pleurisy? Bronchitis? Shortness of Breath? Spitting Blood? Consumption? Laryngitis? Tonsillitis? Insomnia? Rheumatism? Pneumonia? Jaundice? Varicose Veins?

    Frail [before marriage]; no particular trouble. At 17 had scarlet fever no sequelae. Better [since marriage].

11. Menstruation:

    First menstruation at what age?

    Nearly 16 yrs. old.

    and when thoroughly established?

    Established at once.

    Present condition as regards menstruation:

    (a) How frequent?

        Every 4 wks.

    (b) Is it regular or not?

        Reg[ular].

    (c) Amount? how many napkins?

        Profuse flow.

    (d) Duration?

        6 - 7 (3) [Maximum and minimum days duration?]

    (e) Pain or not? at what time as to the flow?

        Before marriage pain the 1st day. After marriage: never.

BLANK NO. 43   SERIES II, FORM B.

   (f) Is there any leucorrhoea (whites)? character?

       Amount?

       Constant or occasional?

   (g) Have you pain either frequently or habitually in the head, small of the back? abdomen or limbs?

   (h) Disease or trouble in Uterus (womb) or other pelvic organs?

       [Pan?] hysterectomy Apr. 1907 (yr. after earthquake) for carcinoma. [Felt] effects of op[eration for] 1 - 2 yrs. Very well since.

   (i) Habit of bowels; how often?

       Always constipated, [a] habit.

12. What knowledge of sexual physiology had you before marriage? b) how did you obtain it?

    At 12 yrs. new school girl told her awful things. Was sleepless for nights & finally went to Mother who did not help much. Married cousin told her just before marriage.

13. Number of times married. If more than once additional blanks will be furnished you to answer the following questions separately in regard to each marriage?

14. Number of years married?

    Married [in] 1885.

    Sedentary husband.

15. 1st intercourse how long after marriage?

    [Took] 2 wks [after her marriage] before [intercourse was] accomplished. Considerate husband.

16. Number of conceptions?

    4

BLANK NO. 43   SERIES II, FORM B.

17. Number of children? State in connection with each, a) date of birth? b) sex? c) whether healthy or not? d) note any characteristic and the cause. e) note either immediate or after effect on your health of the birth of each of your children. f) give time of first menstruation after birth of each child.

   [First child]

   (a) July 1886.

   (b) Girl.

   (c) Healthy. Nursed 11 mo.

   (e) All normal labors, health good.

   (f) Does not remember. Was with child before she stopped nursing 1st child.

   [Second child]

   (a) March 1888.

   (b) Girl.

   (c) Healthy. Nursed 1 yr.

   [Third child]

   (a) June 1890.

   (b) Girl.

   (c) Healthy.

   (Fourth child]

   (a) March 1893.

   (b) Girl.

   (c) Healthy.

18. Did conception occur by choice or accident?

   Accidental conceptions, but welcome.

BLANK NO. 43   SERIES II, FORM B.

19. Habit of intercourse, average number of times per week? per month? per year?

    Irreg. 2 - 3 [times] per wk in early married life up to operation. Sometimes not for wks then perhaps oftener. Now sometimes months.

20. Was intercourse held during pregnancy? If so, how often?

    During early pregnancy less often [than before pregnancy]. About 1st 6 mo. [of pregnancy] about 1 [intercourse] per wk.

    (b) Had you any desire for it during this period?

        Not particularly. Not distasteful. When 2nd child was conceived exquisite pleasure.

21. At other times have you any desire for intercourse? a) how often?

    Yes. Pleasure grew up to time of op[eration].

    (b) At what time in relation to your menses?

        Just after menstrual period--for wk following **anytime.**

22. Is intercourse agreeable to you or not?

    Yes. Sometimes, not always. [More agreeable] after periods.

    Do you always have a venereal orgasm?

    1. - When you do,

    (a) Effect immediately afterwards?

        Rested & refreshed, relaxed. Was good for her.

    (b) Effect next day?

    2. - When you do not,

    (a) Effect immediately afterwards?

        Does not remember.

    (b) Effect next day?

BLANK NO. 43   SERIES II, FORM B.

   Does not remember

23. What do you believe to be the true purpose of intercourse?

   (a) Necessity to man?

   Yes unless he controls his mind. [He] thinks it is good for him.

   to woman?

   Beneficial.

   (b) Pleasure?

   Yes.

   (c) Reproduction?

   Yes.

   (d) What other reasons beside reproduction are sufficient to warrant intercourse?

   Relation brings man and woman closer.

24. Have you ever used any means to prevent conception? a) if so, what?

   Prevention: after 2 or 3 children husband wore **shield** of rubber/[?].

   (b) Effect on your health?

   No effect on health.

25. What, to you, would be an ideal habit?

   Ideal habit·- 1 per wk.

26. Family limited by wish of both.

27. Menopause due to op[eration].

BLANK NO. 44   SERIES II, FORM B.

[The editors provided the questions for this blank, incomplete in the original.]

Date: Dec. 26, 1913.

Yourself:
1. Date of birth:

    Nov. 13, 1871.

    5th child of father & mother.

2. Early life in city or country?

    Country town.

3. Height?

    5 ft., 6 in. tall.

4. Weight?

    120 - 125.

5. Complexion?

6. Temperament?

    Nervous.

7. Where educated, give degrees if any?

    Public Schools - Iowa State University 1 yr.

8. Occupations before marriage? a) in city or country? b) time spent in each?

    No occupation before marriage.

BLANK NO. 44   SERIES II, FORM B.

9. Diseases in your family? from father or mother's side? **Nervous Disorders?** **Rheumatism?** **Consumption?** **Dyspepsia?** **Varicose Veins?** **Heart Disease?** **Hernia?** **Habitual Constipation?** **Catarrh?**

   Nothing.

10. General health before marriage? b) since marriage? **Paralysis?** **Brain Fever?** **Chronic Headache?** **Nervous Prostration?** **Catarrh?** **Hernia?** **Dyspepsia?** **Habitual Constipation?** **Inflammation of Bowels?** **Pleurisy?** **Bronchitis?** **Shortness of Breath?** **Spitting Blood?** **Consumption?** **Laryngitis?** **Tonsillitis?** **Insomnia?** **Rheumatism?** **Pneumonia?** **Jaundice?** **Varicose Veins?**

    Delicate but no special trouble.

    (b) Very good except when in tropics. Better since marriage. [Had] amoebic dysentery.

11. Menstruation:

    First menstruation at what age?

    1st at 13.

    and when thoroughly established?

    Established [within one year?]

    Present condition as regards menstruation:

    (a) How frequent?

       Every 30 days.

    (b) Is it regular or not?

       Reg[ular].

    (c) Amount? how many napkins?

       Mod[erate].

    (d) Duration?

       5 (3) [Maximum and minimum days duration?]

431

BLANK NO. 44   SERIES II, FORM B.

   (e) Pain or not? at what time as to the flow?

       Never any pain. Abd[ominal] breathing.

   (f) Is there any leucorrhoea (whites)? character?

       No.

       Amount?

       Constant or occasional?

   (g) Have you pain either frequently or habitually in the head,
       small of the back? abdomen or limbs?

   (h) Disease or trouble in Uterus (womb) or other pelvic organs?

       No uterine trouble.

   (i) Habit of bowels; how often?

       No constipation.

12. What knowledge of sexual physiology had you before marriage?
    b) how did you obtain it?

    No knowledge. Did not know what marriage meant.

13. Number of times married. If more than once additional blanks
    will be furnished you to answer the following questions
    separately in regard to each marriage?

14. Number of years married?

15. 1st intercourse how long after marriage?

    2 or 3 days after marriage.

16. Number of conceptions?

    4.

17. Number of children? State in connection with each, a) date
    of birth? b) sex? c) whether healthy or not? d) note any

BLANK NO. 44   SERIES II, FORM B.

characteristic and the cause. e) note either immediate or
after effect on your health of the birth of each of your
children. f) give time of first menstruation after birth
of each child.

[First child]

    (a) Oct. 26, 1903.

    (b) Boy.

    (c) Very delicate due to birth in tropics. On [?] 1 mo.
        & could not eat. Grew stronger. Nursed him 6 mo.

    (f) Menstruation in 3 mo. after birth.

[Second child]

    (a) June 17, 1906.

    (b) Girl.

    (c) Very healthy. Conceived 1 mo. after [recovering from?]
        amoebic dysentery. Nursed 6 mo.

    (f) Menstruated 3 mo. after birth.

Miscarriage

    (a) 1909.   **3 yrs. later about 2 mo.** [along].

Miscarriage

    (a) 1912.   **About 6 wks.** [along].

18. Did conception occur by choice or accident?

    1st by choice. All others accidental.

19. Habit of intercourse, average number of times per week? per
month? per year?

    Formerly 2 [times] weekly. Now once in 2 - 3 wks. **Depends
on whether they have leisure.**

20. Was intercourse held during pregnancy? If so, how often?

Rarely with 1st [child] during [entire pregnancy]. Not with 2nd [child].

(b) Had you any desire for it during this period?

With 2nd one yes, not with 1st.

21. At other times have you any desire for intercourse?

Yes.

(a) How often?

(b) At what time in relation to your menses?

Following or preceding menstruation.

22. Is intercourse agreeable to you or not?

Yes.

Do you always have a venereal orgasm?

No. Conscious of suppression on part of woman. Time reaction slower.

1. - When you do,

(a) Effect immediately afterwards?

Rests better when she has orgasm. Temperamental uplift.

(b) Effect next day?

2. - When you do not,

(a) Effect immediately afterwards?

Very little difference.

(b) Effect next day?

23. What do you believe to be the true purpose of intercourse?

(a) Necessity to man?

Yes.

BLANK NO. 44   SERIES II, FORM B.

        to woman?

        Yes.

   (b) Pleasure.

        Very strong. Psychological 2nd.

   (c) Reproduction?

        Yes 1st.

   (d) What other reasons beside reproduction are sufficient to warrant intercourse?

        If women enjoyed intercourse, the demands on them would be much less. Males [have] less desire when [they are] more perfectly satisfied. Intellectual work on part of husband--less leisure. [Intercourse produces] oneness [and is] uplifting like music. [There is] very little that is animal about it. The comradeship of it. [Remainder of response is unintelligible.]

24. Have you ever used any means to prevent conception? a) if so, what?

    After known miscarriage because husband did not wish her to conceive again until she was strong. Douches of bichloride.

    (b) Effect on your health?

    No effect.

25. What, to you, would be an ideal habit?

    When desired by both.

Husband: physically active & strong. Lover of the open - tramping.
Wife: great walker & good climber.

BLANK NO. 45   SERIES II, FORM B.

[The editors provided the questions for this blank, incomplete in the original.]

Date: Dec. 27, 1913.

Yourself:

1. Date of birth?

   Oct. 2d, 1860. Parents about 30.

2. Early life in city or country?

   Small town of 8,000.

3. Height?

   About 5 ft., 8 in.

4. Weight?

   About 150.

5. Complexion?

   Blond.

6. Temperament?

   Very nervous.

7. Where educated, give degrees if any.

   Cornell, 1888, Ph.B.

8. Occupations before marriage? a) in city or country? b) time spent in each?

   Taught before going to college. 2 yrs. teaching before marriage.

BLANK NO. 45   SERIES II, FORM B.

9. Diseases in your family? from father or mother's side? Nervous
   Disorders? Rheumatism? Consumption? Dyspepsia? Varicose
   Veins? Heart Disease? Hernia? Habitual Constipation? Catarrh?

10. General health before marriage? b) since marriage? Paralysis?
    Brain Fever? Chronic Headache? Nervous Prostration? Catarrh?
    Hernia? Dyspepsia? Habitual Constipation? Inflammation of
    Bowels? Pleurisy? Bronchitis? Shortness of Breath? Spitting
    Blood? Consumption? Laryngitis? Tonsillitis? Insomnia?
    Rheumatism? Pneumonia? Jaundice? Varicose Veins?

    Health good [before marriage] except for 2 nervous breakdowns.
    Hysterical & melancholic.

    (b) 1 breakdown immediately after marriage.

11. Menstruation:

    First menstruation at what age?

    1st at 17.

    and when thoroughly established?

    Estab. at once.

    Present condition as regards menstruation:

    Menopause: began 2 yrs. ago. Little irreg. 5 wks. about 2 or
    3 mo. quantity less.

    (a) How frequent?

        28 days.

    (b) Is it regular or not?

        Reg[ular].

    (c) Amount? how many napkins?

        Quantity: abundant but not excessive.

    (d) Duration?

        Dur.: 7 (4)   [Maximum and minimum days duration?]

BLANK NO. 45   SERIES II, FORM B.

   (e) Pain or not? at what time as to the flow?

   No pain.

   (f) Is there any leucorrhoea (whites)? character?

   L[ight?].

   Amount?

   Constant or occasional?

   (g) Have you pain either frequently or habitually in the head, small of the back? abdomen or limbs?

   (h) Disease or trouble in Uterus (womb) or other pelvic organs?

   No uterine trouble.

   (i) Habit of bowels; how often?

12. What knowledge of sexual physiology had you before marriage? b) how did you obtain it?

   Everything. Married at 30.

13. Number of times married. If more than once additional blanks will be furnished you to answer the following questions separately in regard to each marriage?

14. Number of years married?

15. 1st intercourse how soon after marriage?

   At once. 2nd night.

16. Number of conceptions?

   7 conceptions.

17. Number of children? State in connection with each, a) date of birth? b) sex? c) whether healthy or not? d) note any characteristic and the cause. e) note either immediate or

after effect on your health of the birth of each of your children. f) give time of first menstruation after birth of each child.

[First child]

    (a) Nov. 20, 1894 (4th yr. of marriage).

    (b) Boy.

    (c) Very healthy. Tangled cord. Nursed & bottle fed 3 - 4 mo.

    (e) Hard labor. Much torn repaired at time.

    (f) Periods returned at 8 mo.

1st miscarriage

    (a) 1895. Happened after lifting baby. Period missed.

[Second child]

    (a) May 8, 1897.

    (b) Boy.

    (c) Healthy. Nursed 6 mo.

    (e) Hard labor - [?] **presentation.**

    (f) Mens. 7 - 8 mo. (?).

2nd misc[arriage](?)

    (a) 6 wks. without period not sure she miscarried.

[Third child]

    (a) Aug. 30, 1898.

    (b) Girl.

    (c) Healthy. Tangled cord. Nursed 6 mo.

    (e) Easier labor.

    (f) Period 7 to 8 mo.

BLANK NO. 45   SERIES II, FORM B.

[Fourth child]

(a) Sept. 4, 1900.

(b) Boy.

(c) Strong. Nursed 6 mo.

(e) [?[labor.

(f) Period 7 to 8 mo.

[Fifth child]

(a) Nov. 12, 1903.

(b) Girl.

(c) Strong **and well. Nursed 6 mo.**

(e) Labor hard. Economic disaster husband out of work.

(f) Periods at 6 - 7 mo.

18. Did conception occur by choice or accident?

Choice--no precautions.

19. Habit of intercourse, average number of times per week? per month? per year?

Intercourse 3 - 4 times. Av. about 3 [times] weekly.

20. Was intercourse held during pregnancy? If so, how often?

During pregnancy yes, until about 7th mo. [with] about same frequency.

(b) Had you any desire for it during this period?

Yes rather more than other times.

21. At other times have you any desire for intercourse? a) how often?

BLANK NO. 45   SERIES II, FORM B.

Moderate desire, sometimes much [desire]. Never distasteful.

(b) At what time in relation to your menses?

Just before periods desire greater.

22. Is intercourse agreeable to you or not?

Agreeable always.

Do you always have a venereal orgasm?

Does not always have an orgasm. Time reaction much slower than husband. "Clitoris type."

1. - When you do,

(a) Effect immediately afterwards?

[Even?]

(b) Effect next day?

[?] and nervous next day.

2. - When you do not,

(a) Effect immediately afterwards?

(b) Effect next day?

23. What do you believe to be the true purpose of intercourse?

(a) Necessity to man? to woman?

[Both:] Not physical but emotional.

(b) Pleasure?

Yes.

(c) Reproduction?

Incidentally.

(d) What other reasons beside reproduction are sufficient to warrant intercourse?

BLANK NO. 45   SERIES II, FORM B.

Affection much. One man & one woman spiritual significance most vital.

24. Have you ever used any means to prevent conception? a) if so, what?

Yes: a) **cundrum**; b) **woman's shield--pessary** cap--given by Dr. so as not to have withdrawal **because bad for husband.** And she must not have more children; c) withdrawal; d) when they could afford chance **at interval of immunity.**

(b) Effect on your health?

No effect on health.

25. What, to you, would be an ideal habit?

Husband: very athletic earlier.

Menopause: makes no dif[ference] in wife's desire.

BLANK NO. 46   SERIES II, FORM B.

[The editors provided the questions for this blank, incomplete in the original.]

Date: Dec. 27, 1913.

Yourself:

1. Date of birth?

    Sept. 28, 1879. 6th child of father (50 yrs old). 3rd child of mother.

2. Early life in city or country?

    City 7 yrs.

3. Height?

    5 ft., 4 in.

4. Weight?

    Wt. 104.

5. Complexion?

    Dark.

6. Temperament?

    Nervous perhaps.

7. Where educated, give degrees if any?

    Stanford, 1900, A.B.

8. Occupations before marriage? a) in city or country? b) **time** spent in each?

    No occupations.

BLANK NO. 46   SERIES II, FORM B.

9. Diseases in your family? from father or mother's side? Nervous
   Disorders? Rheumatism? Consumption? Dyspepsia? Varicose
   Veins? Heart Disease? Hernia? Habitual Constipation? Catarrh?

   Nothing.

10. General health before marriage? b) since marriage? Paralysis?
    Brain Fever? Chronic Headache? Nervous Prostration? Catarrh?
    Hernia? Dyspepsia? Habitual Constipation? Inflammation of
    Bowels? Pleurisy? Bronchitis? Shortness of Breath? Spitting
    Blood? Consumption? Laryngitis? Tonsillitis? Insomnia?
    Rheumatism? Pneumonia? Jaundice? Varicose Veins?

    Fair [health before marriage]. Pneumonia 2 [times]. Typhoid
    [fever]. Appendicitis. [Health] much better after marriage.

11. Menstruation:

    First menstruation at what age?

    12.

    and when thoroughly established?

    At once.

    Present condtion as regards menstruation:

    (a) How frequent?

        28 days.

    (b) Is it regular or not?

        Reg[ular].

    (c) Amount? how many napkins?

        Abundant.

    (d) Duration?

        7 (4). [Maximum and minimum days duration?]

    (e) Pain or not? at what time as to the flow?

        Backache - before & during 1st [and] 2nd [day]. Depression
        [**before**].

BLANK NO. 46   SERIES II, FORM B.

    (f) Is there any leucorrhoea (whites)? character?

        No.

        Amount?

        Constant or occasional?

    (g) Have you pain either frequently or habitually in the head, small of the back? abdomen or limbs?

    (h) Disease or trouble in Uterus (womb) or other pelvic organs?

        No uterine [problems].

    (i) Habit of bowels; how often?

        Not constipated.

12. What knowledge of sexual physiology had you before marriage? b) how did you obtain it?

    No knowledge. No knowledge [of sexuality or meaning] of marriage.

13. Number of times married. If more than once additional blanks will be furnished you to answer the following questions separately in regard to each marriage?

    1.

14. Number of years married?

    Sept. 1, 1900.

15. 1st intercourse how soon after marriage?

    1st night.

16. Number of conceptions?

    2 conceptions.

BLANK NO. 46   SERIES II, FORM B.

17. Number of children? State in connection with each, a) date of birth? b) sex? c) whether healthy or not? d) note any characteristic and the cause. e) note either immediate or after effect on your health of the birth of each of your children. f) give time of first menstruation after birth of each child.

   [First child]

   (a) May 9, 1901.

   (b) Girl.

   (c) Had typhoid at 2 yrs. old. Stronger now. Delicate child **five weeks too soon. Nursed 9 mo.**

   (f) Menstruated after stopped nursing.

   [Second child]

   (a) May 13, 1903 (1 mo. early).

   (b) Boy.

   (c) Strong. Nursed 4 mo.

   (f) Menstr[uated] within a month or 1 1/2 mo. after his birth.

18. Did conception occur by choice or accident?

   1st accident. 2nd choice.

19. Habit of intercourse, average number of times per week?

   1st yr. about 2 [times] weekly. Now 1 [per] week.

   per month?

   per year?

20. Was intercourse held during pregnancy? If so, how often?

   Yes. Continued thro' pregnancy about 1 [time per] week until 3/4 of term. Not at end. Less during 2nd pregnancy.

(b) Had you any desire for it during this period?

Yes, desire for it.

21. At other times have you any desire for intercourse? a) **how** often?

Desire for it at other times about 1 [per] wk.

(b) At what time in relation to your menses?

After period is over [week?]. **When tired [even?] acceptable** wants petting & this natural result.

22. Is intercourse agreeable to you or not?

Yes.

Do you always have a venereal orgasm?

1. - When you do,

(a) Effect immediately afterwards?

Just after relaxed - little tired - sleep.

(b) Effect next day?

2. - When you do not,

(a) Effect immediately afterwards?

(b) Effect next day?

23. What do you believe to be the true purpose of intercourse?

(a) Necessity to man?

No. Same as a kiss.

to woman?

No. Same as a kiss.

(b) Pleasure?

No.

BLANK NO. 46   SERIES II, FORM B.

    (c) Reproduction?

        Ultimate.

    (d) What other reasons beside reproduction are sufficient to warrant intercourse?

        A phase of expression of love & could not [be] aware of it without it. A way of showing **emotion.** **Natural, pleasurable, because you love the man.**

24. Have you ever used any means to prevent conception? a) if so, what?

    Cundrum always.

    (b) Effect on your health?

        No effect on health.

25. What, to you, would be an ideal habit?

    1 pr. wk.

Husband is very active physically. Husband always waits until [s] **he is** satisfied & never [seeks intercourse?] when she is too tired.

BLANK NO. 47   SERIES II, FORM C.

Date: Dec. 25, 1913.

   1. Date of your birth?
      Oct. 10, 1853.
      Born what child of your mother?
      1st.
      Of your father?
      1st.

   2. Early life in city or country?
      [Town?] life.

   3. Your height?
      5 ft., 8 in.

   4. Your weight?
      124 lbs.

   5. Complexion?
      Fair. Brown hair, gray eyes.

   6. Temperament?

   7. Where educated (degrees if any)?
      Public School Kansas City. Vassar [College]--no degree.

   8. Occupations before marriage? a) in city or country? b) time spent?
      Life at home.

BLANK NO. 47   SERIES II, FORM C.

   9. Diseases or tendencies in family:

      Long lived very healthy. [?] on both sides. [Hearty?] folk
      very long lived--disease almost unknown.

  10. Your general health before marriage? b) since marriage?
      Paralysis? Brain Fever? Chronic Headache? Nervous Prostration?
      Catarrh? Hernia? Dyspepsia? Habitual Constipation?
      Appendicitis? Pleurisy? Pneumonia? Bronchitis? Consumption?
      Insomnia? Rheumatism? Jaundice? Varicose Veins?

      Excellent health always: good [before marriage], good [since
      marriage]. Catarrh in childhood after vaccination by old house
      to house method. Varicose veins in right leg during last
      pregnancies. Three pregnancies. Pneumonia about my 8th year.

  11. Have you ever had any trouble with the Uterus (womb) or other
      pelvic organs? Before marriage? Since marriage? And what
      was it?

      Congestion of uterus for some time during first 3 years after
      birth of 1st child. Fibroid tumor of several years' growth
      during "change of life." Formation of tumor preceded by two
      or three years excessive menstrual flow, with much attendant
      soreness.

      Are you or were you ever habitually constipated.

      Seldom--never habitually so.

  12. What knowledge of sexual physiology had you before marriage
      and when did you obtain it?

      Indefinite--can hardly remember how acquired.

  13. Date of marriage:

      Oct. 14, 1875.

      No. of years married:

      38

  14. How long after marriage was first intercourse?

BLANK NO. 47							SERIES II, FORM C.

Within 2 days.

16. No. of conceptions?

    8.

17. No. of children?

    8.

    Son - Sept. 20, 1876. Son - Dec. 30, 1879. Daughter - Dec. 11, 1881. Son - May 21, 1883. Daughter - Dec. 24, 1885. Unable to nurse this child who consequently began life with impaired digestion and has never been strong like the rest. Very badly fed by reason of my ignorance. None of the following children were nursed at all--but are all vigorous. The two sons over six feet & well set up, the last daughter an excellent average. One characteristic true of all my children after the second, they have frail teeth not from lack of care or dentistry. Son - Dec. 29, 1887. Son - Oct. 28, 1889. Daughter - Feb. 22, 1891.

    Menstrual history:

    (a) First menstruation at what age?

        Began at 16.

        and when thoroughly established?

        Established about 18. Repressed by change of climate for two years.

    (b) How often did your menstrual periods come? counting from first day to first day?

        28 days.

    (c) Were they regular or not?

        Regular.

    (d) Was the flow scanty, moderate or abundant?

        Scanty.

451

BLANK NO. 47   SERIES II, FORM C.

   (e) How many days did you have much flow? how many days did
       you have a very slight showing of color? (The total
       length of the period includes all the days on which there
       was the slightest showing of color.) Give the total number
       of days:

       One day of slight color, one of decided color, one of
       lessening. If any soreness on the 3rd day.

   (f) Did you have any pain or discomfort--where was it located
       and was it much or little. On what days of the flow (1st,
       2d, 3d, etc.) did it come & how long (in hours) did it
       last?

       On the last day if at all and not until circumstances of
       housework and children prevented proper care. Ignorance,
       largely, as I look back.

   (g) Did you have any leucorrhoea or whites?

       Never.

18. Did conception occur by choice or accident?

    After the second child, born about 3 1/2 years after the first
    one, it was left to chance, and from that time on my health
    was excellent until the menopause began.

19. Habit of intercourse, average no. of times per week?

    Twice (except during menstruation).

    per month?

    per year?

20. Was intercourse held during pregnancy? If so, how often?

    As usual.

    (b) Had you any desire for it during pregnancy?

        Cannot remember but think I probably had more than when
        not pregnant, as there was not the fear of conception
        present which may account for my good health & good
        spirits during the period.

BLANK NO. 47   SERIES III, FORM C.

21. At other times have you any desire for intercourse? a) how often?

   So much affected by chance influences - fatigue, sorrow, anxiety, fear. **Always a response to affection otherwise an offense, simply endured.**

   (b) At what time in relation to your menses?

22. Is intercourse agreeable to you or not?

   (Answered above.)

   Do you always have a venereal orgasm?

   A matter of will, mostly. Seldom beyond absolute control.

   1. - When you do,

   (a) Effect immediately after:

   Under ideal conditions relaxed and sleepy.

   (b) Effect next day:

   And the next day filled with the joy of life--mentally and physically alert.

   2. - When you do not,

   (a) Effect immediately after:

   If I remain indifferent, there is no effect on me. But if not and I remain unsatisfied the result is bad, even disastrous, nerve racking, unbalancing, if such condition continues for any length of time. I have attributed the tumor I referred to to such a condition obtaining for months or even a number of years, from about my 45th to my 50th year.

23. What do you believe to be the true purpose of intercourse?

   (a) Necessity to man?

   Apparently.

   to woman?

BLANK NO. 47   SERIES III, FORM C.

  Probably.

(b) Pleasure?

(c) Reproduction?

(d) What other reasons beside reproduction are sufficient to warrant intercourse?

  Probably the incentive to lead man to carry on the race. Apparently a necessity for the <u>average</u> person. In a limited field of observation, it seems to me that only superior individuals can be independent of sex relation with no evident ill results.

24. Have you ever used any means to prevent conception? a) if so, what? b) effect on your health?

  In the two years following the birth of the first child I used a "Good-year rubber ring" and have thought it contributed to the congestion already spoken of, though there were other causes--the lack of an orgasm.

25. What to you would be an ideal habit?

  Poise and repose, physically and mentally, peace of mind. Response to affection. Once or twice a month in the hey-day of life. Conservation of force after middle life. [My] conclusions [come] **both from experience and observation.**

  Were you athletic in college?

  Mild gymnastics. "Began about 45th yr. to flow excessively for 5 & 6 days at menstrual period. Sometimes spend several days in bed; last day or two sometimes in much pain; always the same pain & soreness in lower front of abdomen no attention (from ignorance) at this time began to suffer from intercourse; unresponsive, would not recover from one experience till time for another. Congestion, pain in the back, unnerved, wretchedly unhappy and morbid--purely physical causes."

  Did you have any trouble at your menopause (change of life)? b) at what age did it occur? Has it affected your desire for intercourse?

  "After tumor developed flow lessened and became normal for

two years more. Very averse to intercourse because of ill
effects, kept my troubles to myself; learned to control
effects to prevent any sensation, thus preventing pain. Much
sorrow and misfortune in family history during these years--loss
of money, first death of oldest son. Husband's health broken.
He never really recovered. He changed utterly in views of life.
Kindest and most chivalrous of men. I often wonder whether I
am responsible--whether I have been below normal and been a
drain instead of a stimulant--whether nature made me for a good
mother, but did not fit me for a good wife.

"Tumor (a large fibroid) absorbed under treatment by Dr.
Wallace A. Briggs of Sacramento. A pill three or four times
a day for a year. Then reported to him; continued the medicine
another year--reported again--found the tumor entirely gone.
Reported a third year, found no sign of the tumor. Do not
know the nature of the medicine--but think it was a sex
stimulant."

"He gave no cause for the existence of the tumor and asked no
questions along the line of this discussion."

BLANK NO. 49

Dyspareunia

Well developed sphincter vaginae. Could stop all circulation in one finger by contraction of this muscle. Gradual stretching of muscle. Later conceived.

BLANK NO. 50   SERIES II, FORM B.

[The editors provided the questions for this blank, incomplete in the original.]

Date: Dec. 15, 1913.

Yourself:

1. Date of birth?

   [Age] 37.

2. Early life in city or country?

3. Height?

   Ht. 5 ft., 3 1/2 in.

4. Weight?

   About 120 lbs.

5. Complexion?

   Blond.

6. Temperament?

7. Where educated, give degrees if any?

   Stanford.

8. Occupations before marriage? a) in city or country? b) time spent in each?

9. Diseases in your family? from father or mother's side? Nervous Disorders? Rheumatism? Consumption? Dyspepsia? Varicose Veins? Heart Disease? Hernia? Habitual Constipation? Catarrh?

   Father weak man.

BLANK NO. 50　　　　　　　　　　　　　　　　SERIES II, FORM B.

10. General health before marriage? b) since marriage? Paralysis? Brain Fever? Chronic Headache? Nervous Prostration? Catarrh? Hernia? Dyspepsia? Habitual Constipation? Inflammation of Bowels? Pleurisy? Bronchitis? Shortness of Breath? Spitting Blood? Consumption? Laryngitis? Tonsillitis? Insomnia? Rheumatism? Pneumonia? Jaundice? Varicose Veins?

Before entering college tho't to be delicate. Not allowed to lift even a [?]. On crutches 1 1/2 yrs. before [entering college?]. Trouble with knee.

(b) Well since [marriage]. Stronger right along. Habitual constipation.

11. Menstruation:

First menstruation at what age?

About 13.

and when thoroughly established?

Present condition as regards menstruation:

(a) How frequent?

Every 35 days.

(b) Is it regular or not?

Reg.

(c) Amount? how many napkins?

Very abundant (excessive).

(d) Duration?

4 (3). [Maximum and minimum days duration?]

(e) Pain or not? at what time as to the flow?

No pain. Does same [activities] as usual.

(f) Is there any leucorrhoea (whites)? character?

Amount?

Constant or occasional?

BLANK NO. 50   SERIES II, FORM B.

   (g) Have you pain either frequently or habitually in the head,
       small of the back? abdomen or limbs?

   (h) Disease or trouble in Uterus (womb) or other pelvic organs?

   (i) Habit of bowels; how often?

       Tend to constipation.

12. What knowledge had you of sexual physiology before marriage?
    b) how did you obtain it?

    No knowledge of sexual physiol. Knew what marital relation was.

13. Number of times married. If more than once additional blanks
    will be furnished you to answer the following questions
    separately in regard to each marriage?

14. Number of years married?

    Married 12 yrs. Marc[h] 26, 1901.

15. Do you habitually sleep with your husband? b) what reasons
    for so doing or not?

16. Number of conceptions?

    4.

17. Number of children? State in connection with each, a) date
    of birth? b) sex? c) whether healthy or not? d) note any
    characteristic and the cause. e) note either immediate or
    after effect on your health of the birth of each of your
    children. f) give time of first menstruation after birth of
    each child.

    [First child]

        (a) Mar. 6, 1902.

        (b) Girl.

        (c) Healthy. Nursed about 3 mo. then to 5th mo. 1 per day.

(e) Effect on health: better after.

(f) Mens. returned about 5th mo (?).

[Second child]

(a) Mar. 5, 1904.

(b) Boy.

(c) Healthy. Nursed same way.

(e) Slightly better after. Could not walk as well for 1 mo.

[Third child]

(a) March 29, 1906.

(b) Girl.

(c) Healthy. Nursed about same.

(f) Prolonged period had to be started.

[Fourth child]

(a) Nov. 30, 1908.

(b) Boy.

(c) Healthy. Nursed until 7 mo. old.

18. Did conception occur by choice or accident?

Accident[al] conceptions, but willing, except [one child was] deliberate.

19. Habit of intercourse, average number of times per week?

About 1 pr. wk.

per month?

per year?

20. Was intercourse held during pregnancy? If so, how often?
    During pregnancy until about 5th month.
    (b) Had you any desire for it during this period?
        No desire.

21. At other times have you any desire for intercourse?
    Sometimes.
    (a) How often?
        About 2 pr month.
    (b) At what time in relation to your menses?
        After periods.

22. Is intercourse agreeable to you or not?
    Do you always have a venereal orgasm?
    Always orgasm.
    1. - When you do,
    (a) Effect immediately afterwards?
        Relaxation & sleep.
    (b) Effect next day?
        Ok next day.
    2. - When you do not,
    (a) Effect immediately afterwards?
    (b) Effect next day?

23. What do you believe to be the true purpose of intercourse?
    (a) Necessity to man?
        Yes.

BLANK NO. 50   SERIES II, FORM B.

        to woman?

        Yes - not so marked.

    (b) Pleasure?

        Yes.

    (c) Reproduction?

        Yes.

    (d) What other reasons beside reproduction are sufficient to warrant intercourse?

        a, b, c.

24. Have you ever used any means to prevent conception? a) if so, what?

    Rubber cap over uterus. Syringe of cold water. **Condrum**.

    (b) Effect on your health?

        No effect.

25. What, to you, would be an ideal habit?

    About twice a month.

In college 4 1/2 yrs. [Was active in] gymnastics and basketball [for] 4 yrs. Steadily stronger in college.

BLANK NO. 51   SERIES II, FORM B.

[The editors provided the questions for this blank, incomplete in the original.]

Date: Dec. 17, 1913.

Yourself:

1. Date of birth?

    Born May 27, 1871. 3rd child of father & mother **(age 29)**.

2. Early life in city or country?

    City.

3. Height?

    5 ft., 6 in.

4. Weight?

    119.

5. Complexion?

    Dark.

6. Temperament?

    Nervous.

7. Where educated, give degrees if any?

    Stanford, A.B., 1894.

8. Occupations before marriage? a) in city or country? b) **time** spent in each?

    Taught High School 1 1/2 yrs in city. Assistant in university. 1/2 yr.

BLANK NO. 51   SERIES II, FORM B.

9. Diseases in your family? from father or mother's side? Nervous
   Disorders? Rheumatism? Consumption? Dyspepsia? Varicose
   Veins? Heart Disease? Hernia? Habitual Constipation? Catarrh?

10. General health before marriage? b) since marriage? Paralysis?
    Brain Fever? Chronic Headache? Nervous Prostration? Catarrh?
    Hernia? Dyspepsia? Habitual Constipation? Inflammation of
    Bowels? Pleurisy? Bronchitis? Shortness of Breath? Spitting
    Blood? Consumption? Laryngitis? Tonsillitis? Insomnia?
    Rheumatism? Pneumonia? Jaundice? Varicose Veins?

    Health before marriage not good. Constipation. Not strong.
    Health better after [marriage].

11. Menstruation:

    First menstruation at what age?

    1st at 15.

    and when thoroughly established?

    Established 2 yrs. later.

    Present condition as regards menstruation:

    (a) How frequent?

        Periods every 28 days.

    (b) Is it regular or not?

        Reg[ular].

    (c) Amount? how many napkins?

        Scanty until college. Profuse after treatment when went
        to college.

    (d) Duration?

        Before college 3. Later 7 days.

    (e) Pain or not? at what time as to the flow?

        (Before children) usually **cramps ["cramps" is crossed out
        in original] and backache** 1st day, trouble in standing
        2nd day.

BLANK NO. 51   SERIES II, FORM B.

(f) Is there any leucorrhoea (whites)? character?

No.

Amount?

Constant or occasional?

(g) Have you pain either frequently or habitually in the head, small of the back? abdomen or limbs?

(h) Disease or trouble in Uterus (womb) or other pelvic organs?

No uterine trouble. Displaced kidneys.

(i) Habit of bowels; how often?

Very constipated always.

12. What knowledge of sexual physiology had you before marriage? b) how did you obtain it?

Everything. Mother gave book - boarding school gossip. Talked over before marriage.

13. Number of times married. If more than once additional blanks will be furnished you to answer the following questions separately in regard to each marriage?

14. Number of years married?

May 13, 1897.

15. 1st intercourse how soon after marriage?

1st night.

16. Number of conceptions?

4 conceptions.

17. Number of children? State in connection with each, a) date of birth? b) sex? c) whether healthy or not? d) note any characteristic and the cause. e) note either immediate or

BLANK NO. 51   SERIES II, FORM B.

after effect on your health of the birth of each of your
children. f) give time of first menstruation after birth of
each child.

[First child]

    (a) Feb. 1899.

    (b) Boy.

    (c) Very delicate until 8 or 9 yrs old. Nursed 7 mo.

    (e) Mother did too much hard work before birth. Father much run down. Rapid birth. Mother's health better after it.

    (f) Return of menses at 8th month.

[Second child]

    (a) Sept. 8, 1901.

    (b) Girl.

    (c) Kept too cold in sanitarium where delivery took place - nervous & constipated. Nursed 6 - 7 mo.

    (f) Periods returned 8th mo. [Illegible phrase.]

[Third child]

    (a) Apr. 1903.

    (b) Boy.

    (c) Very delicate. Too weak Mother nursed 6 mo.

    (f) Periods returned 7th mo.

[Fourth child]

    Pregnant now 3 1/2 mo.

18. Did conception occur by choice or accident?

First two from choice. 3rd accident. 4th chance, [but] willing.

BLANK NO. 51   SERIES II, FORM B.

19. Habit of intercourse, average number of times per week?

   per month?

   About 4 - 5 per month.

   per year?

20. Was intercourse held during pregnancy? If so, how often?

   During pregnancy all through - reg[ular], same, often. Always takes 3 mo. after birth with none at all.

   (b) Had you any desire for it during this period?

   Less during pregnancy. No desire in latter months.

21. At other times have you any desire for intercourse? a) how often?

   Yes. Reaction very slow. Yrs. before it was realized [how?]. For yrs. very disagreeable owing to slow reaction. Then abstained except when wife insisted for husband's sake, never when husband thought it would be acceptable.

   (b) At what time in relation to your menses?

   Most desire night before & after finish.

22. Is intercourse agreeable to you or not?

   Agreeable.

   Do you always have a venereal orgasm?

   Orgasm if time is taken.

   1. - When you do,

   (a) Effect immediately afterwards?

   Congested after [orgasm] unless uses cold douche after.

   (b) Effect next day?

   2. - When you do not?

BLANK NO. 51   SERIES II, FORM B.

When no orgasm - took days to recover.

(a) Effect immediately afterwards?

(b) Effect next day?

23. What do you believe to be the true purpose of intercourse?

(a) Necessity to man?

[Yes]

to woman?

To some women - not to self.

(b) Pleasure?

At times.

(c) Reproduction?

Yes.

(d) What other reasons beside reproduction are sufficient to warrant intercourse?

Not complete sympathy - it is the one thing a woman gives which no one else can give - brings intimacy & closeness.

24. Have you ever used any means to prevent conception? a) if so, what?

Yes. Wife used rubber cap with syringe warm water. 3rd conception in spite of cap & carbolized douche. **Cundrums.** also. Withdrawal.

(b) Effect on your health?

No effect on health.

25. What, to you, would be an ideal habit?

Ideal habit 2 - 3 times a month for complete harmony. No dif[ference] to her physically, although she thinks may have been good for her.

BLANKS

No. 1	Form A	Pages: 4
No. 2	Form B & Supplement(2)	Pages: 9
No. 3	Form A & B	Pages: 4 + 9 = 13
No. 4	Form A	Pages: 4
No. 5	Form A & B	Pages: 4 + 9 = 13
No. 6	Form A & B	Pages: 4 + 9 = 13
No. 8	Form B	Pages: 6
No. 9	Form B	Pages: 9
No. 10	Form B	Pages: 9
No. 11	Form B	Pages: 9
No. 12	Form B	Pages: 9
No. 13	Form B	Pages: 9
No. 14	Form B	Pages: 9
No. 15	Form B	Pages: 9
No. 16	Form B	Pages: 7 (1 & 2 received blank)
No. 17	Form Y	Pages: 2
No. 18	Form B	Pages: 9
No. 19	Form B	Pages: 9
No. 20	Form Y	Pages: 2
No. 21	Form B	Pages: 9
No. 22	Form B	Pages: 9
No. 23	Form B	Pages: 9
No. 24	Form B	Pages: 9
No. 25	Form B	Pages: 9
No. 26	Form B	Pages: 9
No. 27	Form B	Pages: 4 (pp 6-7-8-9)
No. 28	Form B	Pages: 9
No. 29	Form B	Pages: 9
No. 30	Form B	Pages: 9
No. 31	Form B	Pages: 6 (pp 4-9)
No. 32	Form B	Pages: 6 (pp 4-9)
No. 33	Form B	Pages: 9
No. 34	Form B	Pages: 9
No. 35	Form B	Pages: 8 (pp 2-9)
No. 36	Form B	Pages: 9
No. 38	Form W	Pages: 1
No. 40	Form W	Pages: 3
No. 41	Form B	Pages: 6 (pp 4-9)
No. 42	Form W	Pages: 2
No. 43	Form W	Pages: 2
No. 44	Form W	Pages: 3
No. 45	Form W	Pages: 3
No. 46	Form W	Pages: 3
No. 47	Form C	Pages: 8
No. 49	Form W	Pages: 1
No. 50	Form Y	Pages: 3
No. 51	Form W	Pages: 3

47 cases

DATE DUE

Demco, Inc. 38-293